A Classical Response to Relational Theism

A Classical Response to Relational Theism

*A Reformed Evangelical Critique of Thomas Jay Oord's
Evangelical Process Theology*

Brian J. Orr

FOREWORD BY
Paul Helm

☙PICKWICK *Publications* • Eugene, Oregon

A CLASSICAL RESPONSE TO RELATIONAL THEISM
A Reformed Evangelical Critique of Thomas Jay Oord's Evangelical Process Theology

Copyright © 2022 Brian J. Orr. All rights reserved. Except for brief quotations in critical publications or reviews, no part of this book may be reproduced in any manner without prior written permission from the publisher. Write: Permissions, Wipf and Stock Publishers, 199 W. 8th Ave., Suite 3, Eugene, OR 97401.

Pickwick Publications
An Imprint of Wipf and Stock Publishers
199 W. 8th Ave., Suite 3
Eugene, OR 97401

www.wipfandstock.com

PAPERBACK ISBN: 978-1-6667-1062-5
HARDCOVER ISBN: 978-1-6667-1063-2
EBOOK ISBN: 978-1-6667-1064-9

Cataloguing-in-Publication data:

Names: Orr, Brian J., author. | Helm, Paul, foreword.

Title: A classical response to relational theism : a reformed evangelical critique of Thomas Jay Oord's evangelical process theology / by Brian J. Orr ; foreword by Paul Helm.

Description: Eugene, OR: Pickwick Publications, 2022 | Includes bibliographical references and index.

Identifiers: ISBN 978-1-6667-1062-5 (paperback) | ISBN 978-1-6667-1063-2 (hardcover) | ISBN 978-1-6667-1064-9 (ebook)

Subjects: LCSH: Oord, Thomas Jay. | Evangelicalism. | Process theology. | Theology.

Classification: BT98 .O77 2022 (print) | BT98 .O77 (ebook)

01/06/22

Scripture quotations marked CSB have been taken from the Christian Standard Bible®, Copyright © 2017 by Holman Bible Publishers. Used by permission. Christian Standard Bible® and CSB® are federally registered trademarks of Holman Bible Publishers.

Scripture quotations marked NET have been taken from the NET Bible® copyright © 1996, 2019 by Biblical Studies Press, L.L.C. http://netbible.com Scripture quoted by permission. All rights reserved

Scripture quotations marked ESV have been taken from the *ESV® Bible (The Holy Bible, English Standard Version®)*, Copyright © 2001 by Crossway, a publishing ministry of Good News Publishers. Used by permission. All rights reserved.

Scripture quotations marked NIV have been taken from the Holy Bible, New International Version®, NIV®. Copyright © 1973, 1978, 1984, 2011 by Biblica, Inc.™ Used by permission of Zondervan. All rights reserved worldwide. www.zondervan.com The "NIV" and "New International Version" are trademarks registered in the United States Patent and Trademark Office by Biblica, Inc.™

Scripture quotations marked NRSV have been taken from New Revised Standard Version Bible, copyright © 1989 National Council of the Churches of Christ in the United States of America. Used by permission. All rights reserved worldwide.

Contents

Foreword by Paul Helm | ix
Preface | xi
Acknowledgements | xv
Abbreviations | xvii

1: Introduction | 1
2: Oord and Process Philosophy | 30
3: Oord's Divine-Love Theology | 74
4: Scripture and Metaphysics | 110
5: Essential Kenosis—Oord's Relational Account of Divine Providence | 124
6: Conclusion | 183

Bibliography | 187
Index | 203

Foreword

THOMAS OORD IS A leading and productive process and "openness" theologian, centering his theology on divine love, and making this central to his account of a Christian doctrine of providence. Brian J. Orr subjects these themes, divine love and divine providence, to be foundational to Christian theology. His critique of what Professor Oord calls divine "coercion," a somewhat novel idea, is for him unwarranted both in God's providence and in divine love. Oord thinks that it is a critique of classical Christian theism, that it entails a doctrine of divine coercive will and action, and so a loving gospel which entails it is theologically inadequate. But his sole emphasis on love is an inadequate treatment of Scripture, which has Paul affirming the twin pole of God's revelation and action: "Note then the kindness and severity of God; severity towards those that have fallen, but God's kindness to you, provided you continue in his kindness" (Rom 11:22). This principle is at work in Scripture, in both Testaments. Divine providence and God's love cannot be understood without it.

In his critique, Dr. Orr marshals conclusions in several dimensions, exhibiting a number of academic skills. With the exegesis of the scriptural text and with the reasoning of classical theism at the front, Orr draws out the implications of God's perfections, interrogating Oord's contention that a "traditional" God is a God of coercion. If Oord is in turn a 'biblical' theologian, how does he handle and justify, for example, Paul's bipolarity, bearing in mind that the poles are unequal. In an effort to elucidate Oord's process theology, unsurprisingly Dr. Orr shows it lacks correspondence with the oracles of God. He shows clearly enough that Oord not only gives selective attention in his treatment of Scripture, but he is also at odds with the mainstream Christian theological tradition. When measured against the foundational Christian documents, and theological history, the inevitable verdict on Oord's theology of love is clear.

All this Dr. Orr examines in detail and with skill. In his treatment he begins at the beginning, with the development of process theism, and its offspring "openness" theism. This bequeaths to Oord the space to work at a theology of divine indeterministic action, of divine love, and one that is productive of a reciprocal give-and-take relationship between the Creator and his creatures made in his image, a theology of divine, free vulnerability. However, with his earlier assumptions, the satisfactoriness of divine providence is inevitable, and his kenoticism fails in his account of evil.

Paul Helm
Former Professor of the History and Philosophy of Religion
King's College, London

Preface

THE CLASSICAL DOCTRINE OF God expresses that the God of the Bible is triune, *a se*, simple, immutable, impassible, eternal, and the sovereign Lord over his creation, which he created *from himself*. Modern streams of theology continue to promote a doctrine of God that sharply contrasts the classical view—the traditional view of God in Christian theism. Contemporary strands of *Evangelical* theology, guided by a socially oriented philosophy, no longer see the God who *is*; rather, it sees God as the one who is *becoming*. Therefore, a critical response to such a theology is needed. And that is the intention of this study: to critically evaluate a current contemporary theological model representative of a view of God as *becoming*, with attention to shared key Christian doctrines and commitments to scriptural teachings, formulated from a view of God who *is*.

This study explores the method and content in the Evangelical process model of relational theism as advanced in the writings of Thomas Jay Oord. Oord identifies as an open/relational Evangelical theologian from the Wesleyan tradition. Oord's theology is the focus of this study because I think he offers the most consistent model of open/relational theology that advocates the primacy of divine-human relationality in the nature of God. And while Oord offers the most consistent form of open/relational theism, Oord's theology further opposes the classical view of God than articulated in the general stream of open theism. Oord's move is not a short step out of the bounds of the classical view of the Christian tradition; rather it is a giant leap, in that open theism affirms the classical doctrines of God's unilateral sovereignty (though modified to account for libertarian human freewill) and *creatio ex nihilo*. Oord rejects both in his relational model. However, Oord affirms key teachings of the Christian tradition that classical theists affirm as well, which were formulated from a classical view (i.e., classical metaphysics). The Christian doctrines affirmed between Oord's brand of relational/open theology and classical theism, while both are metaphysically opposed to each other, presents a need for an evaluative study.

The specific aim of this study is to evaluate and critique Oord's relational model of divine providence, identifying the internal inconsistencies within Oord's philosophical and theological framework, problems in his methodology, and clearing up misconceptions he and the process tradition have of classical theism, while constructively showing that the general sense of Scripture agrees more with classical theism than process theism, as it pertains to divine power. The flow of the study is as follows.

Chapter 1 introduces the reader to the historical landscape, the relational turn in modern Evangelicalism, in which open theism developed, observing the foundation of process theology, which undergirded its development. Then the doctrinal commonalities and distinctions shared between open theology and process theology are identified, thus forming the backdrop in which Oord emerges. And then Oord's theological and philosophical upbringings are outlined, observing the notable differences between Oord's theology and prevailing views of open and process theologies. And lastly, the aim, scope, and methodology of the study are outlined.

Chapter 2 evaluates the coherency of Oord's process philosophy/metaphysic and his claims based on this construct with other doctrines of the Christian tradition. I argue that Oord's assumption of God's necessary relatedness to his creation conflicts with the orthodox doctrines of the Trinity and divine simplicity, which he affirms. I also identify inconsistencies in his doctrine of creation that disqualify it as a biblical doctrine because it collapses the Creator-creature distinction. While Oord claims his process metaphysic situates love in a more centralized manner than classical theism, it disrupts the coherency and framework of the traditional model of Christian theism (e.g., Creator–creature distinction, essence and attributes of God, and the Trinity) he seeks to retain. And then I will touch on Oord's process notion of divine power, with a brief critique, which I will elaborate on further in chapter 5 in my evaluation of Oord's doctrine of providence.

Chapter 3 evaluates and critiques Oord's divine-love theology. And from my evaluation of Oord's doctrine of love, I conclude that his attempt to formulate a uniform definition of love from Scripture was unsuccessful, in that his methods failed to account for the diverse contexts of love found in the Bible. He admitted on the out-set of his endeavor that the Bible *does not* articulate a monolithic definition of love, but he claimed that one general meaning of love dominates the biblical witness. While he argued for a scriptural definition of love, his methods were flawed because he limited his scope to the biblical texts that supported a philosophically contrived definition of love, rendering his model of love inadequate.

Chapter 4 compares and contrasts the process and classical approach to interpreting metaphysical statements in Scripture. The intention of the chapter purposed to establish an interpretive foundation, in substantiating that the interpretation of the biblical text generally agrees more with a classical metaphysic than that of process theology.

Chapter 5 examines the *apex* of Oord's Evangelical process theology: *Essential Kenosis*, which functions as a relational model of divine providence but also an ontological expression of God. Essential Kenosis affirms involuntary divine self-limitation, which means that God is necessarily self-giving. And Essential Kenosis is Oord's solution to the problem of evil. My evaluation sought to determine the adequacy of Oord's model of divine providence based on questions pertaining to its biblical comprehensiveness as a doctrine of providence. Oord states that God *exclusively* uses compelling power to persuade local, physical bodies to exert direct, physical influence, which I refute through scriptural examples that demonstrate God's power is not restricted to persuasion only, while constructively demonstrating that the general sense of Scripture agrees more with classical theism than process theism, as it pertains to divine power. In conclusion, my findings demonstrated that Oord's relational model was unsuccessful in constructing a robust and supportive account for the complexities and nuances of the doctrinal themes presented in Scripture.

Chapter 6 briefly reflects on the importance of classical theology in the Christian tradition, followed by a restating of the intention of my study, summarizing the key distinctions between Oord's theology and a classical view, delineating an enumerated account of the results determined by this study, and a conclusion statement.

Acknowledgments

FIRST AND FOREMOST, I give honor, praise, and glory to the One and only living God. It is humbling to know that he decided from eternity past to lavish his grace upon me in the revealing of his Son, the Lord Jesus Christ. To Him be the glory—Romans 11:36.

I want to express my deepest gratitude to my loving and faithful wife, who has sacrificed so much over the last ten years as I have followed the Lord's calling in my life to pursue higher education for the purposes of edifying his church. Her love and support over the years in giving up her husband week-after-week to his study room, apart from the grace of God, made my endeavors possible. And to my other favorite lady, my daughter, who, as far as she can remember, has always woken up in the mornings to see me in my "work room," as she calls it, sacrificing her time with me as well. I greatly cherish all of her good-morning visits to my study, accompanied by her hugs, sometimes sharing dreams she had that night or any other thoughts on her mind that morning.

I am thankful to my father for his great enthusiasm in my doctoral studies. I, like every other son, am honored to make him proud of my efforts and accomplishments. My in-laws, Jeff and Roberta Anway, have loved me like their own son, supporting and encouraging me along the way.

I am thankful to my fellow elders, Steve Feinstein and Josh Ritchie, who I serve alongside with at Sovereign Way Christian Church in Hesperia, CA. They and the church have been a source of continued support and enthusiasm. I am looking forward to investing what I have learned and gained through my studies into the ministry.

Academically speaking, I am thankful for Rick Walston, Jason Crowder, Benjamin Arbour (who tragically passed away a month before the awarding of my degree), Stephen Edgar, David Rathel, and John Sanders for their support and influence in my journey. And I am especially thankful to Thomas Oord, who has been very charitable through this process, considering the critical nature of my work.

And last but not least, my doctoral supervisors, Tony Lane and Paul Helm. Your support of my work and critical interaction with my ideas have been instrumental in shaping me into a theologian. Pursuing doctoral work at LST under your supervision was a dream come true.

Abbreviations

BDAG   Walter Bauer et al. *A Greek-English Lexicon of the New Testament and Other Early Christian Literature*. Edited by Frederick William Danker. 3rd ed. Chicago: University of Chicago Press, 2001.

DDS   Doctrine of Divine Simplicity

DL   Thomas Jay Oord. *Defining Love: A Philosophical, Scientific, and Theological Engagement*. Grand Rapids: Brazos, 2010.

ETS   Evangelical Theological Society

GC   Thomas Jay Oord. *God Can't: How to Believe in God and Love after Tragedy, Abuse, and Other Evils*. Nampa, ID: SacraSage, 2019.

IET   Francis Turretin. *Institutes of Elenctic Theology*. Edited by James T. Dennison. Translated by George Musgrave Giger. 3 vols. Phillipsburg, NJ: P&R, 1997.

PR   Alfred North Whitehead. *Process and Reality*. London: Free, 1978

PRRD   Richard A. Muller. *Post-Reformation Reformed Dogmatics: The Rise and Development of Reformed Orthodoxy, ca. 1520 to ca. 1725*. 4 vols. 2nd ed. Grand Rapids: Baker, 2003.

MTP   Thomas Jay Oord. "Matching Theology and Piety: An Evangelical Process Theology of Love." PhD diss., Claremont Graduate University, 1999.

NOL   Thomas Jay Oord. *The Nature of Love: A Theology*. St. Louis: Chalice, 2010.

ST   Thomas Aquinas. *The Summa Theologica of St. Thomas Aquinas.* Translated by Fathers of the English Dominican Province. 5 vols. New York: Christian Classics, 1981.

ULG   Thomas Jay Oord. *The Uncontrolling Love of God: An Open and Relational Account of Providence.* Downers Grove, IL: InterVarsity, 2015.

1: Introduction

A Relational Turn in Contemporary Theology

The Arrival of Open Theism

IN 1994 INTERVARSITY PRESS published *The Openness of God*, which proposed a biblical challenge to the traditional understanding of God.[1] The book's contributors, comprised of theologians and philosophers, aimed to advance a view of God who

> in grace, grants humans significant freedom to cooperate with or work against God's will for their lives, and he enters into dynamic, give-and-take relationships with us. The Christian life involves a genuine interaction between God and human beings.... Sometimes God alone decides how to accomplish these goals. On other occasions, God works with human decisions, adapting his own plans to fit the changing situation. God does not control everything that happens. Rather, he is open to receiving input from his creatures. In loving dialogue, God invites us to participate with him to bring the future into being.[2]

The Openness of God was not just another polemical work to add to the ongoing intramural debate between Calvinists and Arminians.[3] Rather, its key distinctive—God's knowledge of the future is "open"—separated it from an *intramural* status within the debate.[4] The publishing of this work

---

1. Pinnock et al., *Openness of God*. The "traditional" view is classical theism.
2. Pinnock et al., *Openness of God*, 7.
3. Both are grounded in the classical tradition. The debatable aspects are primarily soteriological. See Pinnock, *The Grace of God*; Schreiner and Ware, *Still Sovereign*.
4. On November 21, 2002, at the forty-fourth annual meeting of the Evangelical Theology Society, a special session was called to bring forth charges against Clark Pinnock and John Sanders regarding their views on divine foreknowledge. Roger Nicole, the charter member and past president of ETS, charged Pinnock and Sanders (both ETS members) with violating the inerrancy clause in the ETS doctrinal statement,

was a pivotal turning point in contemporary Evangelical theology,[5] in that a foundational orthodox belief (i.e., Divine foreknowledge) was up for reappraisal within *orthodoxy*.[6]

Open theists believe God's sole purpose is divine-human relationality; therefore, for that relationality to be genuine, man must freely (in the libertarian-freewill sense)[7] choose to love God. Any coercion on God's part violates that purpose. And in that sense, the future is unsettled; it is open to possibilities and not a settled, predetermined outcome.[8] Furthermore, God is freely vulnerable, limiting his sovereign power in order to enter into mutually reciprocal give-and-take relationships with free human creatures, even suffering with them.[9]

Why the relational turn? Clark Pinnock argues that the lack of a relational experience with God is due to the doctrinal "tilt toward divine transcendence over against God's immanence."[10] For the last century, systematic theology drifted away from the practical aspects of biblical religion, failing to address believers' needs and concerns.[11] Open theists argue

---

putting forward a motion to expel them from the ETS. However, at the 2003 ETS annual meeting, members voted for Pinnock to remain but fell twenty-five votes short of the two-thirds needed for expulsion of Sanders (his views of "probabilistic prophecy," which mean that predictions of future events may not be true, was unacceptable by the Executive Committee of ETS). Interestingly, at the annual ETS meeting in 2001, the members voted 253-to-66 in favor of a resolution that denied open theism. See Koop, "Closing the Door"; Neff, "Open to Healing."

5. I say *Evangelical* theology because open/relational theology was already a construct within process theology, which is considered outside the bounds of not only Evangelical theology but *orthodox* Christianity (i.e., liberal theology). See Howell, "Openness and Process Theism," 59. *The Openness of God* was a comprehensive treatment, attempting to erect a relational view of God within Evangelical theology.

6. Open theists redefine omniscience, stating that "God knows the past and present with exhaustive divine foreknowledge and knows the future as partly definite (closed) and partly indefinite (open)." Sanders, *God Who Risks*, 15.

7. I will define this term in chapter 5.

8. For other seminal works on open/relational theism, see Rice, *God's Foreknowledge*; Pinnock, *Most Moved Mover*; Sanders, *God Who Risks*; Boyd, *God of the Possible*.

9. Pinnock, *Most Moved Mover*, 126–31; Oord, *NOL*, 75–84; Fretheim, *The Suffering of God*, 60–78; Pinnock, "Systematic Theology," 117; Vanstone, *Love's Endeavour*, 57–74; Sanders, *God Who Risks*, 161–62; Boyd, *God of the Possible*, 136–37.

10. Pinnock, "Systematic Theology," 105.

11. Davis, "Why Open Theism," 115. Davis argues that the trends of the current cultural environment in America (i.e., suspicion of authority, infatuation with liberty, impatience with mystery, and pragmatism about community) and the spiritual environment (i.e., unmet spiritual needs and ecclesiastical individualism) are what has allowed open theism to flourish. Davis, "Why Open Theism," 122–34.

that classical theism[12] places precedence on the power and transcendence of God, specifically his eternality, immutability, and impassibility,[13] creating insuperable biblical–theological and practical issues in human–divine relationality,[14] thus distorting the personal God Scripture portrays.[15] Open theism's greatest appeal to an Evangelical audience is that it tackles pastoral problems such as the existence of evil and suffering when God is supposed to be omnipotent and the purpose of prayer and how it affects an omniscient God. According to openness advocates, abstract teaching within classical theology has failed to provide rational and psychologically satisfying answers to such issues, relegating these matters to "mystery." Open theism claims that its approach to God is truth-seeking because its methodology is grounded in scriptural fidelity, and it desires to connect the believer in a more intimate communion with God.[16]

The Relational Synopsis

While the dissatisfaction of genuine human-divine relationality in traditional theology has functioned as a catalyst in the relational turn, the metaphysical-philosophical structure is grounded in aberrant views of divine impassibility.[17] Furthermore, a shifting emphasis from divine transcendence toward divine immanence is deeply interwoven into it.[18] Kevin

---

12. The classical model ascribes God as monarchial (but not a *tyrant*), who is the sovereign Lord over his creation, which he created *from himself* (*ex nihilo*). Specifically, the classical God is *a se*, simple, transcendent, omnipotent, omniscient, omnipresent, omnibenevolent, immutable, impassible, and timelessly eternal. He has decreed every event—past, present, and future; thus, nothing happens apart from his sovereign will. And though he has decreed evil to exist, he is not the cause of evil nor does he do evil; rather, he fulfills his purposes through it. For a succinct explanation of classical theism and the various expressions within it (e.g., Calvinist/Arminian), see Feinberg, *No One*, 504.

13. Vanhoozer, *Remythologizing*, 81–124.

14. Davis, "Why Open Theism," 113.

15. Witham, *God Biographers*, 1–2, writes, "The [monarchial] image of God ... most unanimously won the hearts and minds of the God biographers of Western history. ... This is the God who was canonized along with the Bible and early Christianity. But there has always been another idea about God waiting in the wings—a deity somehow limited in power, living in dynamic relationship to the universe."

16. Davis, "Why Open Theism," 118.

17. The classical doctrine of divine impassibility "is the Achilles heel of classical theism, in that if it is modified or rejected, *everything* must be modified or rejected." Rennie, "Divine Passibility," 282.

18. See Grenz and Olson, *20th-Century Theology*.

J. Vanhoozer identifies six key factors contributing to the conception and expansive force of this "new orthodoxy" of divine impassibility, with three of them being most pertinent for the present study: a phenomenology of love, the decline of Christendom and its supernaturalistic world view, and the problem of evil.[19]

A relational construal of the being of God places an emphasis on the necessity for the suffering of God to be experienced ontologically. God has to experience suffering in his being in order for his love of humanity and the pain and suffering it goes through to be genuine.[20] Relational theists have redefined and reapplied the doctrines of Kenosis[21] and perichoresis, in a manner not consistent with that of classical theism. Relational models project "kenosis onto the immanent Trinity and perichoresis onto the Creator/creation relationship, [thus making] God's love for the world a relational affair."[22] Christologically speaking, a relational view puts less emphasis on "its categories of substance and person, [reconceiving] Jesus' divinity in relational terms."[23] The end-result is a relationship of mutual reciprocation, in which creation has the ability to affect the Creator. God can only be passionate, compassionate, empathetic, and 'love' if his experiences are phenomenologically human.[24] Claiming to place a greater emphasis on God's love than classical theology, the traditional open view of God[25] aims to offer a more

---

19. Vanhoozer, *Remythologizing*, 392. The six are: (1) the decline of Christendom and its supernaturalistic world view; (2) the rise of democratic aspirations; (3) the problem of human suffering and evil; (4) the scholarly reappraisal of the Bible (e.g., The Biblical Theological Movement); (5) the centrality of Christology and Jesus' passion; (6) a phenomenology of love (Vanhoozer, *Remythologizing*, 392–93). The first four points he pulled from Goetz, "The Suffering God," 385–89.

20. Vanhoozer, *Remythologizing*, 442. In a footnote, Vanhoozer notes other theologians who fall under the "kenotic-relational rubric." "'Love must by its very nature be a relationship of free mutual give and take,' (Vincent Brümmer, *Model of Love*, p. 161); 'love is the sharing of experience' (Paul Fiddes, *Creative Suffering of God*, p. 16); 'A God who cannot suffer cannot love either' (Moltmann, *Trinity and the Kingdom of God*, p. 38); 'God risked suffering when he decided to love and be loved by the creature. A lover's existence is inescapably affected by the other, especially when the loved one acts in ways that grieve and disappoint' (Pinnock, 'Systematic Theology,' in *The Openness of God*, p. 119)."

21. Kenosis will be explained further in chapter 5.

22. Vanhoozer, *Remythologizing*, 394.

23. Olson, "Postconservative Evangelicals," 480, 482.

24. This phenomenal shift is a result of giving priority to figurative language (i.e., anthropomorphic) over metaphysical language. Helm, *Providence of God*, 51–54.

25. "Traditional open theism" refers to the open theology as articulated in *Openness of God*. "Relational theism" functions synonymously with open theology. However, open theism seems to be the preferable term for those who identify as an Evangelical.

scripturally faithful and intellectually satisfying theology, while remaining consistent with the historic tradition of the Christian faith.

An Open View of Divine Power

One of the pioneers of open theism, the late Clark Pinnock, affirms the classical ascription of divine power, when he states that God "is the power to exist and the power to control all things."[26] And though "no power can stand against him, God wills the existence of creatures with the power of self-determination."[27] The God of open theism, though having "the right to dominate and control,"[28] "voluntarily limits the exercise of his power in relation to [his creatures]."[29] God does not use his power to "overcome his enemies by forcing but loving them."[30]

Open theology prefers to emphasize the almightiness of God, when speaking of the form of God's power. This is a reactionary measure to coercion, the (dubiously) classical view of divine power, which has neglected God's persuasive use of power. Clark Pinnock writes, "Divine sovereignty involves a flexible out-working of God's purposes in history. It refers to his ability, as the only wise God, to manage things, despite resistance to his will."[31] According to John Sanders, God does not micromanage his creation; he macro-manages it, granting humans a role in collaborating with him on the course that human history takes, while "achiev[ing] his overall project of establishing loving relationships with significant others."[32] However, "God does not give up his power but he does promise to adhere to the creational structures he has made."[33] God "simply chooses not always to exercise it to its fullest extent."[34] And while God has "all the power necessary to deliver and care for [his creatures], . . . he has chosen not to override [human] free will."[35] However, "God is endlessly resourceful and wise in working toward the fulfillment of his ultimate goals. God sometimes unilaterally decides

---

26. Pinnock, "Systematic Theology," 112.
27. Pinnock, "Systematic Theology," 113.
28. Pinnock, "Systematic Theology," 113.
29. Pinnock, "Systematic Theology," 112.
30. Pinnock, "Systematic Theology," 114.
31. Pinnock, "Systematic Theology," 116.
32. Sanders, *God Who Risks*, 248.
33. Sanders, *God Who Risks*, 241.
34. Sanders, "Divine Providence," 197.
35. Sanders, "Divine Providence," 197.

how to accomplish these goals."[36] So, in his flexible plan, "God aims for the best in every situation and is even willing to work with options that are less than the best."[37] God does not overpower his creatures; rather he works with them, adjusting his plans due to the imperfect decisions *free, fallen* creatures make.[38] Greg Boyd writes, God could "micromanage everything, if he wanted to, but this would demean his sovereignty, so he chooses to leave some of the future open to possibilities, allowing them to be resolved by the decisions of free agents."[39] But while God gives his creatures freedom, "freedom is always restricted within set parameters by God and other factors . . , which *condition* the scope of human freedom, but they do not eliminate it."[40] God's full demonstration of his sovereignty is not manifested now; rather, it will be displayed in his future glory, his revealing at the end of history.[41]

Another key factor in the relational turn in Evangelical theology can be traced back to a shift in contemporary philosophy, from the "substance" metaphysics of the Fathers, medieval Schoolmen, and early modern Western theology, to a "relational" metaphysic,[42] which open/relational theologians claim better represents the world-picture of today.[43] "With the rise of biological sciences," writes Pinnock, "we now think of the world as a living organism and a community of relationships in process of development."[44] Pinnock, a few sentences later, writes:

> We now understand the world as an interrelated process. Conventional theism relates poorly to this kind of world but trinitarian thinking relates well. Nowadays dynamic relational categories are more fundamental than substantialist categories, and the open view is in a better position to communicate because its worldview is more dynamic.[45]

36. Sanders, "Divine Providence," 197.
37. Pinnock, "Systematic Theology," 116.
38. Pinnock, "Systematic Theology," 116.
39. Boyd, *God of the Possible*, 31.
40. Boyd, *God of the Possible*, 43.
41. Pinnock, "Systematic Theology," 117.
42. Weinandy, *Does God Suffer?*, 1–26.
43. Fiddes, *Creative Suffering*, 37–38, notes the dominant theme of *hierarchy*, from the Fathers to the rational theology of the eighteenth century, in which all created beings occupied a place within, making God remote and static, as the impassible law giver and not the God of the cross. For treatments documenting this transition, see Grenz and Olson, *20th-Century Theology*; Placher, *Domestication of Transcendence*; Vanhoozer, *Remythologizing*, 113–77.
44. Pinnock, *Most Moved Mover*, 120.
45. Pinnock, *Most Moved Mover*, 120.

The relational shift in contemporary philosophy found a niche in the late twentieth-century Trinitarian resurgence, which began to look at God's life in relation to each person of the triune Godhead, as observed in the meta-narrative of salvation history.[46] God's being, writes Pinnock, "is an eternal becoming in the liveliness of God's triune being and in his reaching out to creatures." The story of God, understanding his identity, is now a narrative journey,[47] not metaphysical contemplation. Jesus as God incarnate, not God as Supreme Being, was now the lens through which theologians could formulate a more relational doctrine of God. Contemporary metaphysics placed "relations" as primary above the categories of "being" and "substance," becoming the new, socially oriented paradigm in understanding the intra-Trinitarian relations, i.e., *social* Trinitarianism,[48] which emphasizes God's very being as an inclusive community of fellowship of love.[49]

Pertinent to our discussion ahead, as observed in the language of Pinnock (and open theism in general), is the appropriation of a new philosophy, a philosophy of process in an *Evangelical* thinker. Certain questions need to be answered: What is process philosophy? What is its relation to open theism? And why is there a divide between the two and between process and orthodox Christian theism? These are important questions to address. In the next section, I will provide a brief overview of process philosophy, observing its key distinctions, and then I will bring open and process theology together in dialogue, identifying their commonalities as well as points of departure.

---

46. Vanhoozer, *Remythologizing*, 107. For a sampling of the driving themes in contemporary Trinitarian theology, see Holmes, *Quest for the Trinity*, 1–32.

47. Jenson, *Systematic Theology*, is an example of a *metaphysic of narrative*, when he writes, "the second identity of God is directly the human person of the Gospels.... That Christ has the divine nature means that he is one of the three whose mutuality is the divine life, who live the history that God is.... Christ's human history happens because his divine history happens." Jenson, *Systematic Theology*, 137–38.

48. "Social Trinitarians start from the analogy of persons in relation, insisting that the three divine *hypostases* are fully personal in the modern sense of the term, possessed of distinct centres of consciousness; they attempt to develop an account of the unity possible to three such person. This generally involves a willingness to sacrifice traditional accounts of divine unity (particularly accounts of divine simplicity)." Holmes, *Quest for the Trinity*, 30.

49. Vanhoozer, *Remythologizing*, 114.

Process Philosophical Theology

Alfred North Whitehead—The Father of Process Philosophy

As post-Enlightenment thought generated diverse positions on the doctrine of God, one such phenomenon, a type of panentheism[50] to gain popularity in North America[51] is *process theism*. While pantheism and panentheism can be traced back to previous thinkers in the German theological tradition (Schelling and Hegel),[52] process theism is primarily based on the philosophy of Alfred North Whitehead (1861–1947), who was a mathematician and professor of philosophy at Harvard (1924–37).[53] It was in response to the scientific naturalism that arose in the eighteenth and nineteenth centuries, which dismissed all notions of supernaturalism. Process theology is a form of naturalism. However, unlike materialism, it took religious and moral experience seriously, giving legitimacy to a *genuine* relational experience between God and creation *and* creation and God.[54] Process theism adopts a coexistent, coeternal God-and-world dualism, grounding man and the natural world together with God, who *together* participate in the universe's and God's development.[55] For Whitehead, God is "not *before* all creation, but *with* all creation."[56]

A process philosophy of religion sought "to show how religion and science can be fused 'into one rational scheme of thought.'"[57] Whitehead started with experience, viewed through the lens of science, and asked in what

---

50. Panentheism affirms, supported by Paul's statement in Acts 17:28, that God is both transcendent and immanent, ontologically distinct from the world, yet the world is in God.

51. Cooper, *Panentheism*, 165.

52. See Cooper, *Panentheism*, 90–120. Schelling and Hegel were the first to articulate panentheisms where God is intrinsically involved with his creation, as "he develops in and through the world—nature, history, and the human quest for transcendence." Cooper, *Panentheism*, 90.

53. Key figures in the later development of process theology are Hartshorne, *Man's Vision*; Cobb, *Christian Natural Theology*; Griffin, *Process Christology*.

54. Griffin, "Process Philosophy," 142. Wesleyans and Pentecostals have branched out to process thought looking for notable contributions (also bringing criticism as well) constructive for their theologies. See Oord, "MTP"; Cobb and Pinnock, *Searching for an Adequate God*; Culp, "Is Mutual Transformation Possible?," 132–46; Coleman, "The World at Its Best," 130–52; Zbaraschuk, "Process Theology Resources," 154–67; Truesdale, *God Reconsidered*; Reichard, "Of Miracles and Metaphysics," 274–93.

55. Cooper, *Panentheism*, 165. A dialectical construct as in Hegel's thought resides in process theism.

56. Whitehead, *PR*, 343.

57. Griffin, "Process Philosophy," 131.

manner can such an experience occur.⁵⁸ In order for a person to experience an event, one must go through sequential moments of actual occasions of experience, which occur rapidly beyond one's ability to fully grasp.⁵⁹

For example, a person's eye looking at a green spot. A ray of light coming from the molecules on the green spot enters the eye and activates particular cells to relay information to the occipital lobe, which then translates the data to the subject (the "holder" of the eye) as the color green and then is projected back onto the surface where the green spot is located. Thousands of complex processes have occurred, which create an experience, bringing about a causal effect on the subject. These types of phenomena are happening all of the time, demonstrating the impactful nature the physical world plays in one's experience.⁶⁰ This cause-and-effect-related experience, Whitehead calls the "physical pole." While the experience appears instantaneous, it, and all experiences, are actually located and derived from events in the recent past, which then manifest in "physical feelings" or "physical prehensions."⁶¹ *Prehensions* are the feelings that arise during the passing from past to present, one momentary occasion followed by another. The feelings one has are *always* felt from a past occasion. The causative element and the prehensive elements are asymmetrical; cause comes before effect, not simultaneously, as was the commonsense view of the time. Whitehead applied Newtonian mechanics to express what transpired at the microcosmic level, thus providing a superior understanding to cause-and-effect relations. Such application allowed intelligibility for expressing how past experiences influenced future ones.⁶² Whitehead's ultimate aim was to "frame a coherent, logical, necessary system of general ideas in terms of which every element of our experience can be interpreted."⁶³

Whitehead saw the entire God-world complex as an organism.⁶⁴ And the basic notion of entities experiencing actual occasions leading to actualization through process is primary in Whitehead's philosophy. Rather than speak of "being" or "substance," "process" served as Whitehead's basic metaphysical concept.⁶⁵ And from a process ontology, Whitehead defines "*causality* as the present's appropriation of the past, not the past's determination

---

58. Wright, "The Method of Process," 39.
59. Cobb, *Christian Natural Theology*, 5.
60. Cobb, *Christian Natural Theology*, 6.
61. Cobb, *Christian Natural Theology*, 6.
62. Cobb, *Christian Natural Theology*, 7.
63. Whitehead, *PR*, 3.
64. Cooper, *Panentheism*, 167.
65. Cooper, *Panentheism*, 168.

of the present."[66] The process is the carrying of past actual occasions into future actual occasions that form the experience in present realities. But while the past vanishes,[67] actual occasions acquire "objective immortality" and are carried on into the next experience and actively impress, or serve as efficient causation, in the experient's present experience. This affects the experient's prehension of *that* and the next, successive, actual occasion, which will then "perpetuate one's continuing effect through the universe."[68]

The ultimate aim, referred to as the "subjective aim," is the *telos* of the individual entity. However, this does not presuppose a predetermined outcome, but rather it is a process of becoming that is governed by self-actualizing or self-creative occasions, which even God cannot bring about, becoming the potential data for future occasions in the actual entity's[69] process of becoming. God's aim is to increase the value of his and his creatures' lives, and his life is enriched in the actualization of value in the life of his creatures.[70]

Process theology, while seriously considering the scientific advancements in physics and biology of the nineteenth and twentieth centuries, was not well-received in the Christian community. However, it did have some appeal in the wake of WWII and the Holocaust, in that Whitehead's conception of God as "the fellow-sufferer who understands,"[71] who is unable to direct the flow of humanity away from its desire to commit evil atrocities, brought some comfort. Nevertheless, it still followed a Protestant liberal path in its espousal of a natural theology, functioning as the framework of Christian thought taught in liberal Protestant seminaries.[72] Some early thinkers in the Wesleyan heritage, particularly in the Church of the Nazarene denomination, were attracted to the core tenets of process theology, finding expression in a strand of theology called *personalism*, which affirmed the centrality and the ultimate value of a person and his/

---

66. Cooper, *Panentheism*, 170.

67. This happens after the occasions *concresce*, the uniting of feelings into the emerging event, and achieve "satisfaction," the final phase of concrescence. Truesdale, *God Reconsidered*, Appendixes.

68. Quoting, Suchocki, *God Christ Church*, 258–59, in Truesdale, *God Reconsidered*, Appendixes.

69. *Actual entity* and *experient* are synonymous terms referring to a human creature.

70. Cobb, *Christian Natural Theology*, 95.

71. Whitehead, *PR*, 351. This statement became a "mantra" of sorts within contemporary relational theology.

72. Olson, *The Story of Christian Theology*, 602; Howell, "Openness and Process Theism," 59.

her unique relations among other beings.[73] These educators propagated this form of process thought, which continues to be taught in the Nazarene/Wesleyan tradition today.[74]

Charles Hartshorne's Process Theism

Charles Hartshorne (1897–2000) served as Whitehead's assistant at Harvard and then moved on to hold teaching posts at the University of Chicago, Emory University, and the University of Texas.[75] Hartshorne developed a more thorough process theology than Whitehead (whose concepts were within a "scientific-philosophical cosmology"), elaborating on its doctrine of God, aligning it more with the God of Christian theism.[76] While Hartshorne adopted Whitehead's process ontology, he modified Whitehead's view of God as "organism" or as "single actual occasion" to that of a living person, with a dipolar nature. God's dipolarity truly makes God personal because, unlike the God of classical theism, who is strictly absolute, immutable, and infinite (and ultimately abstract, thus impersonal, according to Hartshorne),[77] dipolarity accounts for the two poles of God's nature, one absolute and the other relative.[78] These "poles" remain a consistent metaphysic in Hartshorne's ontology, where God, for example, can experience the suffering and pain of another human being through "sympathetic participation" via his "concrete" pole (or relative pole), while his "abstract pole" (or absolute pole) remains unaffected, thus experiencing no change in his divine essence.[79] Hartshorne's proposal gives intelligible meaning to the idea of perfection in God because as the "purely absolute cannot be relative [i.e., the claim against the God of classical theism], . . the super-relative can be absolute in one aspect or abstract element of being and can also contain a world of relative things as its concrete parts."[80]

As super-relative, Hartshorne's conception of God "is that of a social being."[81] And as a social being, he has relations with man: reciprocity, sympathy, influence, and the ability to be pleased and displeased in man's

---

73. Oord, "Perfect Theology," 151.
74. Oord, "Perfect Theology," 151.
75. Cooper, *Panentheism*, 177.
76. Cooper, *Panentheism*, 179.
77. Hartshorne, "The Dipolar Conception," 287.
78. Cooper, *Panentheism*, 180.
79. Geisler and Watkins, "Process Theology," 17.
80. Hartshorne, *Reality as Social Process*, 122.
81. Hartshorne, *Reality as Social Process*, 40.

efforts.[82] This notion of God has been contradicted in "technical theology," which has defined God in primarily non-social terms. Absolutely perfect and independent of man, this God is unaffected by humanity, which, for Hartshorne, makes divine love nonsensical.[83] The concept of a perfect being who is completely independent from all of creation yet, Hartshorne writes, "clutter[s] up existence with beings which add nothing to the value that would exist without them . . . destroy[s] the intellectual prestige of the older types of theology."[84] However, Hartshorne's next statement reveals the role of contemporary philosophy in his thinking:

> The *socially oriented philosophy of our period* puts the whole matter upon a new level, free from the difficulties referred to. God is not viewed as a being uniquely able to maintain a society of which it is member, the *only* social being unconditionally able to guarantee the survival, the minimal integrity, of its society, and of itself as member of that society. This is a new definition of omnipotence. It means power adequate to preserve the society no matter what other members may do. It does not mean, power to prevent any and all evil or conflict; for social power, even, in the perfect form, is still social, that is, it is power set to limits to the freedom of others, but not to destroy all freedom; and where there is freedom, however sharply limited, conflict and evil must always be possible. . . . *Thus, the problem of evil (at least in its most acute form) appears as a false problem due to a faulty or non-social definition of omnipotence.*[85]

God as changing and changeless makes him the "all-surpassing one," who "must be a single individual enjoying as his own all the values of all other individuals, and incapable of failing to do so."[86] However, God, as the all-surpassing one, can have experiences where God's expression of that experience surpasses that of a previous experience, thus the divine essence undergoes change *experientially*. In light of his understanding of God as the "all-surpassing one,"[87] Hartshorne redefines the "divine perfection as an

---

82. Hartshorne, *Reality as Social Process*, 40.
83. Hartshorne, *Reality as Social Process*, 40.
84. Hartshorne, *Reality as Social Process*, 40.
85. Hartshorne, *Reality as Social Process*, 40–41. Emphasis added.
86. Hartshorne, *Divine Relativity*, 20.
87. Hartshorne's test of deity is one who is "unsurpassable by any conceivable other individual." Hartshorne, "The Dipolar Conception," 283.

excellence such that rivalry or superiority on the part of other individuals is impossible, but self-superiority is not impossible."[88]

In God, the process of becoming is like that of a creature but on a much grander scale. God encompasses every experience in the universe; every existents' prehensions, concrescence, and multiplicity of relations affect God. As God, "the all-encompassing society of occasions," prehends all of these experiences and relations, his divine state becomes greater (i.e., he surpasses the former state); God becomes actualized. And as a singular entity consisting of a society of occasions, God is therefore unchangeable in his essence but changing in that "the *contents* of the divine society have changed [i.e., the experiences and relations they bring into the society]."[89] And this divine society exists as the "physical or spatial whole of God's body, the Soul of which is God."[90] Therefore, one could say that God evolves as his "body" does,[91] since the members of the divine society grow from past prehensions, with God taking in their prehensions until God and his body reach satisfaction.

Combining "Whitehead's scheme" with "Hartshorne's notion of God," one can then posit that God's everlasting adventure occurs in successive states, which provide his creatures initial aims of a multitude of possibilities for actualization.[92] And, as God self-actualizes, he offers initial aims through efficient causation (i.e., the offering of new possibilities through which an actual occasion may unify the diverse influences of the past in the most optimal manner), thus forming the content of the initial phase of an actuality's becoming.[93]

Before we transition into a process-open dialogue in the next section, Nancy Howell, a process/relational theist, offers a "compressed expression" of process theism, which captures the philosophical aspects of Whitehead and Hartshorne in a succinct theological framework, helpful for the discussion. Howell writes, "process theism emphasizes the relational character of God."[94] His relational character means that he gives creatures freedom to experience relationality with God. God's power in the context of relationships is perfect; "it is relational rather than coercive,"[95] luring creatures, rather

88. Hartshorne, *Divine Relativity*, 20.
89. Oord, "MTP," 106. Emphasis added.
90. Hartshorne, *Omnipotence*, 94.
91. Hartshorne, *Omnipotence*, 94.
92. Oord, "MTP," 106.
93. Oord, "MTP," 106.
94. Howell, "Openness and Process Theism," 62.
95. Howell, "Openness and Process Theism," 62.

than controlling them, to move *with* him toward his divine goals. His power and experience have no bounds, which means God is transcendent and immanent, "embodying the world's experience but not limited to the world."[96] And lastly, God creatively and lovingly influences the world toward fulfilling his vision, by which his experiences and relationships with the world contribute to the entirety of that vision.

Process and Open Theologies in Dialogue

Points of Agreement

Process and open theology share many commonalities. Directly undergirding both is the presupposition that God is relational. For both camps, the classical "traditional" view of God as absolute, monarch, unilaterally—tyrannically—controlling every atom, who is unaffected by his creation as he aims to glorify himself does not resonate with the biblical narrative of a creative, responsive, and loving God. Open and process views hold to a divine-love metaphysic, making God's love the priority in their systematic expressions.[97] The centrality of love in God means his power must flow from his love; therefore, love necessitates choice, which means giving genuine freedom to creatures. Both camps reject divine determinism. God's power, governed by love, means that "God achieves his purposes by influencing or 'luring' creatures toward the best options available to them."[98] In summary, the process and open understanding of love as the "supreme divine attribute, the essential nature of God" entails that God relationally experiences the world in a temporal and contingent way, "which has significance for the inner life of God."[99]

Further points of commonality between open and process camps are: (1) a commitment to human freedom, with God's power in relation to that freedom. God truly responds to creatures because both are free to respond as truly loving relationships require. (2) God's relational and responsive power is "endlessly resourceful" in working out his divine vision, in a social and dynamic way that does not negate his freedom. God's influencing use of power means that he does not bring about events in history only by

---

96. Howell, "Openness and Process Theism," 62.
97. Rice, "Process Theism," 184.
98. Rice, "Process Theism," 184.
99. Rice, "Process Theism," 184.

himself. (3) God depends on the world in some manner, which enhances the nature and character of God.[100]

Points of Departure

Process and open theologies diverge on specific points pertaining to Scripture, metaphysics, Creation, and the Trinity. Nancy Howell sees that the greatest point of departure between process and open theologies is the place of Scripture in doctrinal formulation. While open theology makes its agreement with Scripture, "the most important test" in theological formulation,[101] the process tradition includes "culture as a source of stimulus" in its theological formulation.[102] Scripture in open theology is normative;[103] in process theology, experience is a methodological norm.[104]

Richard Rice notes that the most crucial parting-of-the-ways between open and process theologies is in how each one views God's relationship to the world.[105] In process theology, the nature of God's interdependence on the world is problematic for open theism—and for Christian orthodoxy. Rice, citing Hartshorne, writes, "God is 'the world' understood, the world is 'God' understood."[106] Rice understands this to mean that neither God nor the world are comprehensible apart from each other.[107] God cannot exist apart from the world; his reality depends on the relations and experiences that he has with it. The world does not exist because God freely decided to create; rather, it exists because of a necessity in God. God is an experiencing being; therefore, he must experience something. God's reality then depends on "non-divine objects of experience."[108] For Rice (and the Evangelical tradition), process thought on God and the world "resembles . . . classical paganism."[109]

100. Howell, "Openness and Process Theism," 73.
101. Rice, "Biblical Support," 16.
102. Howell, "Openness and Process Theism," 71. She further demarcates process theology from open theism, stating that she "choos[es] to learn explicitly from philosophy." Studying various philosophies (e.g., Whiteheadian and feminist thought), Howell writes, "open fruitful possibilities for my theology." Howell, "Openness and Process Theism," 72.
103. Griffin, "Process Theology," 10.
104. Wheeler, "Response to Nancy Howell," 83.
105. Rice, "Response to Nancy Howell," 89.
106. Hartshorne, *Natural Theology*, 12, in Rice, "Response to Nancy Howell," 89.
107. Rice, "Response to Nancy Howell," 89.
108. Rice, "Response to Nancy Howell," 90.
109. Rice, "Response to Nancy Howell," 90.

The adaption of Whiteheadian metaphysics in process thought that says, "it is true to say that God creates the World, as that the World creates God,"[110] is not only antithetical to the historic Christian tradition but also to open theology. The cosmic, epic drama, where "God and the world stand over against each other, expressing the final metaphysical truth that appetitive vision and physical enjoyment have equal claim to priority in creation, ... [in which] both are in the grip of the ultimately metaphysical ground, the creative advance into novelty"[111] is quite jolting to traditional Christians. What else *can* have a "grip" on God? Is not *God* the ultimate metaphysical ground?[112] In Whitehead's doctrine of God, God, creativity, and the world are essential to the creative process.[113]

The disparity between the two views regarding God's relation to the world stem from how each understand what best exemplifies love in God. In process thought, love implies the necessity of creation. If God is essentially loving, then some world is necessary.[114] If creation exists because God chose to create, then "God's love for the world does not express God's innermost, fundamental reality. It is merely incidental to God's nature."[115] In open theism, God's free choice to create a contingent world strongly argues *for* divine love. Thus, it shows how important the world is to God, in that he *would* freely decide to create, demonstrating a loving commitment, revealing the deepest aspect of his nature.[116] The dualistic relationship between God and everlasting primordial matter, as process theism maintains, makes creation a necessity instead of a gift.[117]

The unique testimony of the God of the Bible is that he is triune. The Old Testament revelation of *Yahweh*—"I AM" (Exod 3:14), who enters into covenant relations with his people Israel (Exod 34), in the New Testament, reveals himself as "Father, Son, and Spirit," his divine name as disclosed by

---

110. Whitehead, *PR*, 348. Process theology rejects the doctrine of *creatio ex nihilo*.
111. Whitehead, *PR*, 348–49.
112. Lodahl, "Creation out of Nothing?," 223.
113. Cobb, *Christian Natural Theology*, 119.
114. Griffin writes, "the God-world relationship is not arbitrary, not based on a contingent decision, but is natural, being rooted in the very nature of God. This idea entails ... that some other world or—some plurality of finite actualities—always exists." Griffin makes a metaphysical claim, stating these "plurality of actualities are guaranteed by the very nature of God, and in that sense exists as necessarily as does the divine nature itself." Griffin, "Process Theology," 6. So, in some manner finite actualities exist ... *necessarily*.
115. Rice, "Response to Nancy Howell," 92.
116. Rice, "Response to Nancy Howell," 92.
117. Pinnock, *Most Moved Mover*, 145.

Jesus of Nazareth (Matt 28:19). A consistent hermeneutic of the two Testaments forces us to move from YHWH to the baptismal formula because of the unitive pressure of the biblical writers in the telos of the New Testament.[118] The common ascription that YHWH is the Father *only*, the New Testament use of *Kyrios* (= YHWH, the divine name of God in the Old Testament), is now attributed to the Father *and* the Son.[119] Its pairing with Old Testament citations in the New Testament, which the authors explicitly apply to the Son (e.g., John 12:37–42; Acts 2:34–35) particularly in prayer and confessional formulas of worship (Rom 11:33–36; 2 Cor 13:13; Eph 3:14–21), soteriological statements (Acts 2:12; 11:20–21; Rom 10:9–10), and divine attributes (John 1:3, 18; Phil 2:6–11; Col 1:15–17) draws us to the central affirmation that the God of the Bible is three persons, one being.[120] While the metaphysical and ontological framework is not developed in the New Testament, man was made to worship the true God, with no other gods before him (Deut 5:7). And therefore, there is no other God but he who is Father, Son, and Spirit—regardless of metaphysical constructs.

My purpose in outlining the doctrine of the Trinity[121] was to emphasize its *biblically* unique position in the Christian faith, in that it is the quintessential revealing of the personal (and also relational) nature of God. I emphasized this point because process theology considers it a *secondary* and *tertiary* doctrine.[122] Openness philosopher, William Hasker, "baldly" states that the biblical evidence, interpreted and further developed by the early church fathers through Nicaea,[123] identifies and testifies that the Gospels portray a relationship between Jesus and the Father within a trinitarian union.[124] For open theism (and the historic Christian faith), "there are no more significant beliefs."[125] The doctrine of the Trinity is not secondary; it is *primary*. For John Sanders, the triune nature of God grounds God's

---

118. Rowe, "Biblical Pressure," 303.

119. The New Testament writers attribute *Kyrios*-status to the Spirit, in that the unitive pressure of the text, using Rowe's angle, does not allow us to say otherwise. In the New Testament authors' minds, there is no deliberation; the Spirit is of God (cf. 2 Cor 2:10–16).

120. To codify this statement: "There are three divine *hypostases* that are instantiations of the divine nature: Father, Son, and Holy Spirit." Holmes, *Quest for the Trinity*, 146.

121. On the interpretive method of the early church having consolidated "person" language to express the three-in-one mystery. See Bates, *The Birth of the Trinity*, 7.

122. Griffin, "Process Theology," 8–9. In fact, Whitehead did not incorporate the Trinity into his system. Pugliese, *The One*, xv.

123. See Gregory of Nazianzus, *On God and Christ*; Augustine, *The Trinity*.

124. Hasker, "Reply to David Ray Griffin," 50–51.

125. Hasker, "Reply to David Ray Griffin," 50–51.

intention in creation: "to produce significant others who could experience the divine love and reciprocate that love both to God and to other creatures; . . . a community reflective of the triune life."[126]

Process theism sees that apart from creatures, the Father, Son, and Spirit "are empty formulae—power-to-do without any doing."[127] Love for themselves is an "empty answer" to the question of "what is love?" within the *mystery* of three divine persons, co-eternal, co-equal, sharing the same divine essence. Rather, "God-with-creatures is the answer."[128] Whitehead and Hartshorne were not "Trinitarian thinkers."[129] However, they thought of God as social. The process notion of relationality is that "God is *really* related to his creatures."[130] Because process theology starts with man's experience of the real world, grounding relationality in a triune, incomprehensible, and infinite unity does not properly address the human situation—the problem of evil.[131]

Dialogue Concludes

Clark Pinnock expresses the fundamental *impasse* between open and process theologies, which for Pinnock and open theists (and the majority of Evangelicals) leaves process theology outside the bounds of Evangelicalism:

> The decision of the open view to adhere closely to the biblical text creates problems for intelligibility that can be avoided by the more liberal approach of process theology which feels free to engage in more radical reconceptualisations. But it may feel to readers that the open view has the merit of maintaining a biblical tension and not eliminating it.[132]

The divide between the two views is a biblical one. As observed, the liberal strand in process thought is willing to release the tension that the biblical text would place on it. For open theology, the process-dualistic ontology of the God-and-world interrelatedness moves it away from a

---

126. Sanders, *God Who Risks*, 178.
127. Hartshorne, *Omnipotence*, 82.
128. Hartshorne, *Omnipotence*, 82.
129. Bracken et al., "Trinity and World Process," 205.
130. Bracken et al., "Trinity and World Process," 205. Emphasis added. Axiomatic to process thought is God's interrelatedness with his creation in real, mutual, and reciprocal relations rather than *logical* as explicated in Thomistic thought. However, I think process thinkers misunderstand Aquinas. I will cover this later.
131. Kelly, "Trinity and Process," 394.
132. Pinnock, *Most Moved Mover*, 149n86.

biblical theology, grounded in a philosophical schema that cannot adequately support nor be supported by the biblical text. While both share views of a divine-love metaphysic, human freedom, and divine power that is not coercive, for open theists, process theology must be refashioned to align more distinctively with the gospel narrative.[133] So, is there a way for process theology to cross over into Evangelicalism?

An Evangelical Process Theology of Love

In 1999, open and relational theologian Thomas Jay Oord completed his PhD dissertation, proposing an Evangelical Process Theology of Love. In researching the current state of Evangelicalism in North America, he concluded that of all the central doctrines one must affirm in order to be Evangelical, the doctrine of God was not one of them.[134] Below Oord outlines key distinctions of Evangelicalism. While Oord points out that none of the works he surveyed on Evangelicalism dogmatically assert a doctrine of God as a key distinction identified within Evangelicalism, he includes it in his findings because such beliefs about God are accepted within it:[135]

1. The Bible is principally authoritative for matters of faith and practice.

2. A conversion from sin, made possible by Jesus Christ, is necessary for salvation.

3. Christians should be active in the midst of a decadent culture, attempting to evangelize and transform it.

4. Spiritual formation (labeled variously as "discipleship," "Christian morality," "holiness," "growth in Christ," etc.) is indispensable to the Christian life.

5. God is perfect in love, almighty, without beginning or end, one (although trinitarian), personal, free, omniscient, the creator and sustainer, both transcendent and immanent in relation to the world, the ground of hope for the final victory of good over evil, and the proper object of worship.[136]

---

133. Pinnock, *Most Moved Mover*, 148.

134. Oord references nine major works specific to identifying and tracing out Evangelicalism, none of which identified a distinct doctrine of God central within Evangelicalism. Oord, "MTP," 12n23.

135. Oord, "MTP," 28–29.

136. Oord, "MTP," 11–12.

In looking at the Evangelical distinctions above, distinction five, Oord notes that most Evangelical scholars do not include any views pertaining to theology proper in their core features of Evangelicalism.[137] This failure to do so, Oord writes, does not necessitate that such affirmations are unnecessary; rather, it "may be that the theological diversity within Evangelicalism discourages attempts to offer a doctrine that all Evangelicals could agree upon."[138]

What is probably the case, says Oord, is that a shared affirmation among Evangelicals exists; therefore, listing a doctrine of God is unnecessary. However, the doctrine of God Oord proposes, he says, is most likely a version Evangelicals affirm.[139] Oord's dissertation aimed to offer an Evangelical model of theology that, for him at least, relieves God of his burden of responsibility for evil, which a process metaphysic provides, while retaining biblical familiarity.

In Oord's theological system, he offers a vision of God who, while being the mightiest in power, does not have sovereign, unilateral power.[140] Rather, God is uncontrollingly loving and does not have the *capacity* to coerce anyone or anything.[141] An uncontrollingly loving God has given every created thing (animate or inanimate) free agency. And God, as Spirit, since he does not have a localized, divine body, cannot exert direct, bodily impact on another bodied creature or object. God can only persuade or compel another person to act. Oord's most novel contribution to Christian theology is that he offers a solution to the problem of evil: God does not have the power to control anyone, therefore he is unable to stop evil, thus he is not accountable for the existence of evil. He may want to stop evil, but he does not have the power to unilaterally do so. Evil persists when people do not respond to God's loving call to act against evil; therefore, people are responsible for evil.

Oord's theological views have gained notoriety. In 2015, he published, *The Uncontrolling Love of God: An Open and Relational Account of Providence*, with InterVarsity Press, receiving IVP's 2016 Reader's Choice Award. And in January 2019, Oord released a new book, *God Can't: How to Believe in God and Love after Tragedy, Abuse, and Other Evils*, from

---

137. Oord, "MTP," 28n85.
138. Oord, "MTP," 28n85.
139. Oord, "MTP," 28n85.

140. In process philosophy, power is viewed somewhat like a commodity. It is impossible for one person or being to have "literally *all* the power." Griffin, "Process Philosophy," 135.

141. Oord sees that Arminian and open theologies are inconsistent on this point. If God has the capacity/ability to use his power unilaterally to stop or prevent evil, yet he does not, then God is not all-good or all-loving as the Bible portrays.

SacraSage Press, which debuted on Amazon US, with the first week's sales making it number one in nine categories.[142] In 2017, Oord had numerous speaking engagements in the US, but he also had many at various universities in Europe: Manchester, Oxford University, Amsterdam, Dordrecht, University of Leeds, University of St. Andrews, University of Edinburgh, and others.[143] So, while he has gained popularity in the US, his theological views have gained popularity abroad.

Why Thomas Jay Oord?

Oord's theology is what I determine to be the most progressive form of open theism. He sees the severe misstep with the prevailing model of open theism in its failure to follow through on its "claim that God's preeminent attribute is love."[144] Oord has moved beyond the "traditional" open theologies of Rice, Sanders, Pinnock, Boyd, and Hasker because he recognized that in their adoption of a modified version of divine sovereignty, God's ability to use his power as he sees fit impinges on the axiom of libertarian free will, which is not what a truly loving God *can* do. And, most importantly, there are evils in the world that God could have stopped but chose not to (according to open and classical theologies), which makes God culpable for evil. Therefore, Oord has opted to "drop" a core doctrine of Christian theism, divine sovereignty, to solve the problem of evil. The *loci* of Oord's theology is love. In fact, he has been referred to as a "love theologian."[145] Oord's prolific works produced from an interdisciplinary approach and study of love have given him a niche within Academia but also in the pews.

Furthermore, whether one is an active, Bible-believing Christian or an atheist, the problem of evil is a *problem*. If the God of classical theism (and open theism) is all-good, all-loving, and all-powerful, yet there is evil that makes the world worse than it would otherwise be,[146] and God does not prevent or stop it, then it must mean that God does not exist. But Oord does not frame the syllogism to cancel out the existence of God, as others have done. Rather, he re-frames it to conclude that because God

142. These categories are: Good & Evil Philosophy, Christian Counseling, Christian Ministry to Sick & Bereaved, Psychology & Christianity, Adult Christian Ministry, Science and Religion, Christian Church Leadership, Spirituality & Health, and Religious Counseling.

143. His speaking schedule for 2019 almost mirrored 2017.

144. Oord, *ULG*, 133.

145. Vanhoozer, "Love without Measure?", 509.

146. This is Oord's definition of genuine evil, which he adapted from process theology pioneer David Ray Griffin. Oord, "Divine Power," 5.

is all-loving and all-good, God *cannot* stop or prevent evil. Oord, self-confessedly, has taken the route few would travel, in that he is willing to reformulate classical doctrines of Christian theism to espouse a God who is as loving as he believes the Bible depicts.

Parting Ways from Open Theism

The problem of evil is where Oord parts ways from traditional open theism, which is also why I say Oord is the most consistent open theist. While he believes open theism "functions as an impressive framework for an adequate theology of love,"[147] the versions espoused by Pinnock and Sanders are inadequate in accounting for the problem of evil. They fail to take open theism's ruling and controlling axiom of God's love to its logical conclusion, making it the central and logically prior attribute of God to all other attributes.[148] In the open theologies of Sanders and Pinnock, Oord observes that God's sovereignty is still logically prior in their doctrine of God. "God's foremost and governing attribute [of love] does not come first."[149] Oord's reason for making it the priority is because God's nature must first and foremost be love and not power or sovereignty otherwise God cannot be trusted.[150]

In Oord's critique of Pinnock, he concludes that his theology is inconsistent in that though he says God has made creatures genuinely free agents, God can and does use coercive power.[151] Pinnock writes, "Open theists believe that God is not bound to persuasion alone. . . . [God] can decide that certain things will happen in the future because he plans to do them."[152] For Oord, "Divine power involves God's persuasion and exercise of indirect bodily impact without unilateral determination."[153] God providentially guides the flow of history. From an open view, though he has given freedom to creatures to make choices, he chooses to exercise his coercive power in order to bring about certain events in the world to ensure his plan of redemption comes to fruition.[154]

Oord objects to this type of unilateral involvement because of how he defines love—and ascribes to God: "To love is to act intentionally, in

---

147. Oord, *NOL*, 113.
148. Oord, *ULG*, 163.
149. Oord, *ULG*, 144.
150. Oord, *ULG*, 164.
151. Oord, *NOL*, 96–98. See Pinnock, *Most Moved Mover*, 147.
152. Pinnock, *Most Moved Mover*, 146–47.
153. Oord, "MTP," 8.
154. Pinnock, *Most Moved Mover*, 147.

sympathetic/empathetic response to God and others, to promote overall well-being." And in that definitive framework, love does not command, compel, or override human freedom; otherwise, it is not genuine, true love.[155] "Pinnock's version ... does not provide a satisfactory answer to why a loving God capable of controlling others through coercion fails to prevent genuine evil."[156] If God has the capacity to be coercive, then he has the capacity to prevent genuine evil in the world.[157]

In his critique of Sanders's view of providence, though Sanders sees that "[p]ersonhood, relationality, and community—not power, independence and control—become the center for understanding the nature of God,"[158] Oord's primary objection is that God, according to Sanders's model, permits evil for the good of creation, which does not comport with a God of love.[159] Quoting Sanders, he writes, "God chooses not to renege on the conditions he established[160] [the freedom he has given human beings to act good or evil].... God does not give up his power, but he does promise to adhere to the creational structures he made."[161] To Oord, a God who permits genuine evil does not sound like Sanders's God, who is "fundamentally opposed to sin, evil, and suffering."[162] "This God," Oord writes, "sounds more like a project manager and less like the personal Lover who cares for each creature."[163]

Herein lies Oord's fundamental objection with the current model of open theism (including that of classical theism): "The God who could prevent any genuine evil unilaterally is responsible for *allowing* genuine evil. The one who could stop genuine evil by restraining the perpetrator of evil is morally responsible—or better, culpable—for permitting the painful consequences."[164] Therefore, Oord finds Sanders's (and Pinnock's) model of open theism unsatisfying because it fails to answer the problem of evil, in light of a God who is perfectly loving. "The heart of the problem is this: Sanders's version of open and relational theology does not make love

---

155. Pinnock, *Most Moved Mover*, 97.
156. Pinnock, *Most Moved Mover*, 113.
157. Pinnock, *Most Moved Mover*, 97.
158. Sanders, *God Who Risks*, 177.
159. Oord, *ULG*, 140.
160. Quoting Sanders, *God Who Risks*, 233, in Oord, *ULG*, 140.
161. Quoting Sanders, *God Who Risks*, 241, in Oord, *ULG*, 140.
162. Quoting Sanders, *God Who Risks*, 116, in Oord, *ULG*, 141.
163. Oord, *ULG*, 141.
164. Oord, *ULG*, 142–43.

God's foremost and governing attribute. Love does not come first."[165] In fact, "divine love is sacrificed."[166]

Aim of Work and Original Contribution

As mentioned earlier, traditional open theism makes Scripture the dividing line between it and process theology. And open theists claim that their views are more faithful to the Scriptures than classical theism (though open theism has more in common with process theology than classical theism). But Oord believes his Evangelical process model advances open and relational theism in a more consistent manner with the teachings of the Bible than traditional open theology or classical theology. He proposes a divine-love relational doctrine of providence, which, he claims, holds to the traditional elements of Evangelical Christianity, while offering a view of God that adheres more consistently to a metaphysic of love, than open and classical theology.

However, thus the purpose of my evaluative critique, I believe Oord's Evangelical process model is still guilty of Pinnock's charge: it does not look to Scripture, it looks to Whitehead.[167] Pinnock emphasizes, in contrast to process thought, that open theists are "orthodox Christians who hold to the Trinity, the ontological otherness of God and divine activity in history, including miracles."[168] But Pinnock sees that process theology imposes a philosophy—a substitute metaphysic—on the Bible that cannot consistently articulate these orthodox views. And I agree with Pinnock about process thought *and* in regard to Oord's proposed hybrid Evangelical-process model.

Oord's open and relational model does not sufficiently account for nor maintain the integrity of key doctrines in orthodox Christianity. It attempts to hold onto central doctrines of the Christian faith but with a substitute metaphysic. And herein lies the aim of my thesis: to evaluate a system of doctrine that epitomizes a framework of a proposed model of Christian theism that substitutes classical metaphysics[169] with another, *while* attempting to retain foundational doctrines that the now *cast out* philosophy aided to develop. In other words, Oord argues that process

---

165. Oord, *ULG*, 144.
166. Oord, "MTP," 255.
167. Pinnock, *Most Moved Mover*, 142.
168. Pinnock, *Most Moved Mover*, 142.

169. For works that address the same concerns with open theism, see Helm, *Providence of God*; Ware, *God's Lesser* Glory; Frame, *No Other God*; Piper et al., *Beyond the Bounds*.

philosophy can consistently uphold and better account for the orthodox doctrines of Christian theism (i.e., the nature and character of God, divine providence, and divine-human relationality) than the classical metaphysic they were constructed with. My claim, simply put, is that Oord's Evangelical process theology cannot. His model is unsuccessful because process philosophy governs his theological decision making, functioning as the "handler" *of* instead of a "handmaiden" *to* his theology.

My review and critique of his theology also aims to clear up misconceptions he and the process tradition have of classical theism. Oord's relational model is insufficient as a biblical model due to its inability to harmonize with the various complexities and themes found in Scripture (e.g., various aspects of love; the divine-sovereignty and human-responsibility tension; God's divine activity in his creation; the specificity in redemption), which a robust biblical doctrine of providence requires.

The aim of my work, thus my original contribution to knowledge in the academic field of systematic theology, is to advance a sustained, critical evaluation of Oord's Evangelical process theological model, identifying its internal inconsistencies, thus determining it as an inadequate option for Christian theism. To date, no other theses/dissertations of this scope have been advanced.[170]

Current Research on Oord

While there are no other theses to date offering a critical review of Oord's relational model of divine providence,[171] some people have interacted with Oord's works and aspects of his views in academic literature. Evangelical scholars have engaged in critical dialogue with Oord regarding his views on divine impassibility,[172] the problem of evil,[173] miracles,[174] doctrine of

---

170. As of June 4, 2020.

171. Kallhovd, "Developing a Rigorous Theology," evaluated Oord's theology of love determining it was not philosophically rigorous.

172. Oord identifies as a strong passibilist. See the interaction and critique in Matz and Thornhill, *Divine Impassibility*, 129–65.

173. Oord claims to have solved the evil problem in his essential kenosis model. See the interaction and critique in Meister and Dew, *God and the Problem of Evil*. See also Sanders, "Essential Kenosis," 174–87.

174. Sanders, "Essential Kenosis."

creation,[175] divine providence,[176] the love of God,[177] his reading of Barth on God's love,[178] and eschatology.[179] The content of the dialogue found in these writings will be expounded throughout the study. But the key point of disparity, serving as the impetus to the various critiques, is the place of process philosophy in Oord's theological construction. To put it bluntly: Oord's critics' objections stem from his claim of being an Evangelical while at the same time advocating views and concepts that conflict with teachings "that are central to the Christian vision of things."[180]

Presuppositions

All theologians have presuppositions. And as a theologian, I am committed to a classical model of Christian theism, in the Reformed Evangelical tradition, holding to the Bible as the authoritative, inspired, inerrant, and infallible Word of God. Key aspects of the faith that I proclaim and hold to, as a Reformed classical theist, are: the doctrine of *creatio ex nihilo*; the doctrines of grace (i.e., Calvinism); God is simple; God is timelessly eternal; God is immutable; God is impassible; God's knowledge is complete and perfect (divine exhaustive foreknowledge), meaning he has decreed what will come to pass, according to the purpose of his will (Eph 1:11). Furthermore, within a classical framework, I hold to a theological metaphysic formulated in the Nicene/Chalcedonian era (notably in the Augustinian–Thomist tradition), which has functioned as the "grammar" in articulating the Christian doctrine of God (i.e., essence and attributes of God, the Trinity, hypostatic union, and the Holy Spirit)[181] up through the Reformed and Post-Reformation era.[182]

---

175. Rice, "Creatio Ex Nihilo," 110–23.

176. Hess, Review of *Uncontrolling Love of God*, 473–79; Highfield, Review of *Uncontrolling Love of God*.

177. Vanhoozer, "Love without Measure?"

178. Gockel and Holloway, "God's Essential Will," 184–99.

179. McLaughlin, "Unreasonable Hope," 259–74.

180. Rice, "Creatio Ex Nihilo," 118. It appears that the underlying objection from those critical of his theology is that he does not hold to a doctrine of God that is unquestionably orthodox to Christianity, one that affirms God's distinctness from creation, his ability to exercise sovereign power over his creation, and *creatio ex nihilo*.

181. Hanson, *Search for the Christian Doctrine of God*, documents the early church's development of a metaphysical grammar to precisely articulate an orthodox biblical doctrine of God.

182. As delineated in Volume 3, "The Divine Essence and Attributes," in Muller, *PRRD*.

I think it would be helpful for the sake of clarity of this study to get Oord's understanding of what comprises classical theology, since he does *not* identify as a classical theist, which will allow the reader to see the theological differences between him and me that define classical theism, which he rejects. Classical theology, according to Oord, understands that "God is in all respects timeless; either controls all things or could do so; and has exhaustive foreknowledge." And he also writes, this often includes views like: "God's actions are totally unlike creaturely actions; God voluntarily chooses to love (or not); and God created the universe *ex nihilo*."[183] Oord's understanding of the basic distinctions of classical theology is accurate. However, some classical theologians differ in their views of God and time[184] and divine foreknowledge.[185] With that said, making matters simple, I affirm the general distinctions Oord attributes to classical theism.

While classical theism uses a metaphysical grammar to express divine truth, a chasm exists between God and man because it is impossible for the finite to comprehend the infinite. But God, as an act of grace, comes down to us because we cannot ascend up to him. In fact, even in God's coming down to reach sinners, so that we could behold his glory in the face of Jesus Christ (2 Cor 4:6), that act, in and of itself, is ineffable—the God of the universe taking on flesh (John 1:14). God's coming down is an act of *accommodation* to his creatures' finitude, so that we can comprehend him.[186]

John Calvin is a *go-to* source regarding the theory of divine accommodation, when he writes:

> The Anthropomorphites, also, who imagined a corporeal God from the fact that Scripture often ascribes to him a mouth, ears, eyes, hands, and feet, are easily refuted. For who even of slight intelligence does not understand that, as nurses commonly do with infants, God is wont in measure to 'lisp' in speaking to us? Thus such forms of speaking do not so much express clearly what God is like as accommodate the knowledge of him to

---

183. Oord, personal email to author, January 30, 2019.

184. For example, God is everlastingly temporal; relatively timeless; atemporal without creation but temporal with creation. See Ganssle, "God and Time."

185. Various views are: simple foreknowledge (i.e., God has a simple knowledge of the future, as in he can see what will happen); exhaustive divine foreknowledge (i.e., God decrees what will come to pass, which immutably comes to pass); middle knowledge (i.e., God decides what to do based on counterfactual knowledge, which is the knowledge of what a creature would choose given various states of affairs).

186. Sunshine, "Accommodation," 238–65; Muller, *PRRD*, 2:300–302.

our slight capacity. To do this he must descend far beneath his loftiness.[187]

And Calvin, commenting on 1 Peter 1:20–21, writes:

> It is hence evident that we cannot believe in God except through Christ, in whom God in a manner makes himself little, that he might accommodate himself to our comprehension; and it is Christ alone who can tranquillize consciences, so that we may dare to come in confidence to God.[188]

While the revelation of Jesus Christ is the ultimate form of God accommodating himself to humanity, God's primary form of accommodation is that of Holy Scripture through which the hearing of faith comes (Rom 10:17; Gal 3:5). God communicates to us in a simple language that we all can understand, using figurative and metaphorical language and literary genres to reach his audience.[189] Staying within the confines of these literary structures, along with a theological metaphysic, safeguards the interpreter from straying off into complete anthropomorphism, taking it to the extreme "to express the inexpressible"[190] or the other direction of univocal incomprehensibility.

And within these literary strictures, the Rule of Faith principle of letting Scripture interpret Scripture, giving priority to the biblical texts that speak to the nature and character of God, and then interpreting the more obscure passages in light of the clearer, dominant ones situates the interpreter in a framework of unity, consistency, and clarity in his understanding of Scripture and the God it reveals.

Methodology

It is not my intention to screen Oord's theology through my own theological presuppositions. The biblical text is the standard. And Oord claims that his theology is chiefly derived from the text. However, I will assess his system's internal consistency by evaluating it against his own standard (Scripture) but also against itself, particularly Oord's methodology and his conclusions. Furthermore, while Oord's understanding of classical theism is generally accurate, his assertions and judgements regarding classical theology will be evaluated as well.

187. Calvin, *Institutes*, 1.13.1.
188. Calvin, *Catholic Epistles*, 54.
189. Sunshine, "Accommodation," 254.
190. Helm, *Providence of God*, 52.

Oord's Evangelical and Wesleyan heritage has a classical footprint, which Oord understands, in that key doctrines of the Christian faith he affirms (i.e., Creator–creature distinction, essence and attributes of God, Trinity, the natures of Christ, the deity of the Spirit) were historically formulated through a classical, theological metaphysic. Oord's challenge in constructing a viable Christian theology with an alternative metaphysic is whether or not it can sufficiently hold up *or improve upon* the *same* traditional framework classical theism originally established. However, classical theology is not the standard of biblical truth. But what is telling is that Oord's model attempts to retain the same doctrinal expressions (as noted above) that were formulated by classical exegesis and metaphysics, which places classical metaphysics as an anchor point, supporting a consistent and long-standing expression of biblical truth.

2: Oord and Process Philosophy

An Introduction to Thomas Jay Oord

THOMAS JAY OORD, BORN November 10, 1965, is a theologian and philosopher, a twelve-time Faculty Award winning professor, who teaches at institutions around the globe, and is an ordained elder in the Church of the Nazarene. He earned a Master of Divinity degree at Nazarene Theological Seminary in Kansas City, Missouri and went on to earn a Master of Arts in Religion and a Ph.D. at Claremont Graduate University in Southern California. He has a particular interest in research on love and relational theology, as well as science and religion, and is involved in consulting and administration for various academic institutions, scholarly projects, and research teams.[1]

Oord grew up in a Christian home on a small farm in Othello, Washington. In his high-school years he lived as a committed Christian. He leaned toward evangelism, so he joined Campus Crusade for Christ and engaged in street evangelism and door-to-door witnessing. He was passionate and well-studied in his faith, which made him the "more informed" one in conversation. But, toward the end of his college career, while preparing for the ministry, he took a philosophy course that explored arguments against theism. The strength of these arguments convinced Oord to doubt his belief in God. Thus, he turned to atheism.[2]

On his way back to Christianity, of the many arguments, experiences, and evidences pointing to the plausibility of God's existence, the arguments he found most convincing were those related to love. "God's love for creation and God's call to love in response," says Oord, "make most sense out of reality."[3] His discovery "that the themes of love are at the heart of the Bible" brought about his deep conviction, trust, and love for

---

1. Oord, "Bio/Contact."
2. Oord, personal email to author, February 14, 2018.
3. Oord, *NOL*, xi.

God.[4] For Oord, "love reigns supreme for how I understand what it means to trust God and live a Christian life. Love is the core of my faith in God."[5] While the Scriptures and the Christian tradition established his faith in God, he believed arguments drawn from these sources could not hold up in the "realm of public discourse."[6]

Upon entering seminary, he took a course in process thought, which provided a clearer understanding of process theism. His introduction to process philosophy was the book, *A Natural Theology for Our Time*, by Charles Hartshorne. Some parts of process theism he found attractive and others not so much, but it was the idea that "God cannot coerce" that led him to a rethinking of God's power.[7] He wanted to understand how a loving God could exist yet not prevent evil in the world.

Oord attended Claremont Graduate School of Religion because of its strong process tradition. His understanding of process thought intensified, reshaping his thinking, leading him to formulate an open, relational theology. Oord's open/relational theism gleans the positive elements of process thought as well as the central ideas of the Bible and the Christian faith. To understand love, Scripture has served as Oord's chief source for understanding Christ and the loving God revealed in him. His Christian heritage, the Wesleyan/Holiness tradition, greatly supported him on his quest to understand a love that surpasses all understanding (Eph 3:19).

In 1999, Oord completed his PhD dissertation, titled, "Matching Theology and Piety: An Evangelical Process Theology of Love."[8] In his thesis, Oord advances an alternative theology making an "explicit use of process thought," which establishes relationality at the metaphysical level, to "offer a more adequate basis for formulating the love themes central to the Bible."[9] Oord believes that classical metaphysics, which emphasizes "substance," "essence," and unilateral power of formal theologies, has resulted in misconceptions about God, particularly divine causation and the expressions and forms of love, the doctrine of creation, and the problem of evil.

While open theism addresses such issues, Oord sees its views of divine power and God's essential "unrelatedness to a world" as problematic.[10] Oord believes process philosophy better addresses such issues, from which God

---

4. Oord, *NOL*, xi.
5. Oord, *NOL*, xi.
6. Oord, personal email to author, February 14, 2018.
7. Oord, personal email to author, February 14, 2018.
8. Oord, "MTP."
9. Oord, "MTP," ix–x.
10. Oord, "MTP," xii.

as the "perfect omni-Lover"[11] expresses his perfect love to all, demonstrating that his relations with creatures and the world are necessary—in fact *essential*. His claim is that an Evangelical process theology of love centralizes love's "diversity, richness, and distinctiveness."[12]

It is Oord's contention that "a formal Evangelical theology that draws upon the philosophy of process thought can offer a more adequate basis for the centrality of love"[13] than Christian theologies that draw upon "Neoplatonic philosophy or any of the other philosophies informing conventional Christian theism."[14] While Scripture and Christian tradition provided the foundation for Oord's faith, he believes natural theology (from where process originates)[15] provides stronger arguments for the faith in the realm of public discourse. And for Oord, the lure of process theology resides in its claim that God cannot unilaterally determine or control (coerce) anyone or any state of affairs. In fact, this claim is central to all aspects of process philosophical theology.[16]

Notions of Oord's Process Philosophy

While Oord says the version of process philosophical theology he adopts is drawn primarily from Whitehead and Hartshorne, he has some reservations about Whitehead's doctrine of God that leads him to prefer Hartshorne's and Cobb's model, which more appropriately regards God as a living person. Inconsistencies Oord observes in Whitehead's conception of God are as follows: (1) Whitehead classifies God as a single, ever-growing, actual entity. However, a single, actual entity, according to Whitehead, can only exert influence on other entities "*after* an actuality has reached satisfaction, not *during* its becoming." (2) If God is eternally becoming, having no end to his process, then he cannot interact with temporal actualities and thus cannot affect the world. (3) Whitehead shies

---

11. Oord, "MTP," xiii.
12. Oord, "MTP," xiii.
13. Oord, "MTP," 77.
14. Oord, personal email to author, June 6, 2018.
15. Cobb observes that a natural *Christian* theology seeks to replicate the synthesized theologies that have come before us in the stream of the Christian tradition, such as "Augustine's work with Neoplatonic philosophy and Aquinas's adaptation of Aristotle and Augustine's Neoplatonism." Cobb, *Christian Natural Theology*, 173. Natural theology does have a necessary place in Christian theism, in that the doctrines of divine simplicity, immutability, impassibility, and eternality are known through Natural theology. See Haines, "Natural Theology and Protestant Orthodoxy," 53–85.
16. Oord, "Evangelical Theologies," 260.

away from speaking of God as a temporal being. However, because his God is one whose natures are "ever-becoming," he is then outside of time, and thus would be a non-temporal entity who cannot experience a *process of becoming*.[17] Whitehead classifies God as "non-temporal actual entity ... the supreme God of rationalized religion."[18]

Oord's version, having its foundation in the process construct offered by Whitehead and Hartshorne, is also "heavily influenced" by the modern advocates of process thought, John B. Cobb Jr. and David Ray Griffin.[19] The basic notions of Oord's process philosophical theology are: (1) actual existence is a process of becoming rather than a fixed state of being, where the actual existent exists first as subject then as object. God experiences a process of becoming as well. (2) All actual existents (also referred to as actual entities, actual occasions, and occasions of experience) are all interrelated. God as the omnipresent being is related to *all*, thus he is essentially related to the world—they are interdependent. (3) Individuals perceive other individuals, most often in a non-sensory way. God prehends all, and all prehend him. (4) All existents are essentially free, exercising some level of self-determination. God exercises the greatest level of self-determination but cannot exert unilateral determination on another existent; rather, he uses persuasion. (5) God is everlasting, though changing and unchanging, influencing the world while being influenced by the world as well.[20] And ultimately immanence envelopes transcendence, in that God and creation are considered fully dependent on one another.[21] While God's dipolar nature is unlike human nature, he is not an exception to the metaphysical principles of process thought.

Succinctly stated, the qualities of process theology attractive to Oord are: God is relational, prayer changes things, God made us free, God is not responsible for evil, community and individuality matter, contemporary issues must be engaged, and love reigns supreme.

However, some weaknesses of process thought Oord recognizes are: (1) Scripture is not always considered the principal authority. (2) Process theologians have not done well in laying out what the role and authority of the church should be. (3) Those of the process persuasion are mostly associated and engaged with social ethics from the liberal side of the political spectrum. (4) Process theology lacks robust and coherent doctrines of

---

17. Oord, "MTP," 85n1.
18. Whitehead and Auxier, *Religion in the Making*, 90.
19. Oord, "MTP," 79.
20. Oord, "MTP," 80.
21. Cobb, *Christian Natural Theology*, 103.

Christ and the Trinity.[22] Oord's acknowledgment of these weakness is commendable, in that these are key friction points in process theology that need development, especially if the tradition desires to align itself with Evangelical (and orthodox) Christianity.

Examination of Oord's Basic Notions of Process Philosophy

Of the five notions of Oord's process thought, I will limit my examination to points two and four because they are most pertinent to the discussion.[23] Point two pertains to the Creator-creature distinction, which is a *sine qua non* of orthodox Christianity. Point four pertains to the nature of divine and human freedom, which accounts for the dynamic of the relationship between the Creator and the creature. A great deal of literature is dedicated to the divine sovereignty and human responsibility debate,[24] and space does not permit me to recast the entire discussion here. My focus will center on Oord's proposal of divine power that is restricted to persuading and compelling. After my examination of notions two and four, I will then examine Oord's doctrine of creation, with my critique of notions two, four, and creation to follow.

Oord's claim is that process thought, though not perfect, is the best philosophical resource "more consonant with the broad biblical witness"[25] than classical theism. Oord asserts that his "arguments, hypotheses, and theories rest primarily . . . on the witness of Scripture."[26] Oord claims that philosophy, in its proper role, "is a helper,"[27] or, as more commonly known, the "handmaiden" to theology. Therefore, the biblical witness, not pre-conceived philosophical judgments, should ground his theological conclusions.

Relations and the Essentially Related God

Oord writes, "Process philosophical theology acknowledges the essential relatedness of all existence."[28] The process of an existent's becoming actual

---

22. Oord, "A Perfect Theology Never Existed," 153–57.

23. Oord writes, "The notion that God is *essentially* related to others separates process philosophical theology from classical theism." Oord, "MTP," 88.

24. To name a few: Basinger and Basinger, *Predestination & Free Will*; Beilby and Eddy, *Divine Foreknowledge*; Carson, *Divine Sovereignty*.

25. Oord, "A Perfect Theology Never Existed," 152.

26. Oord, *NOL*, xii.

27. Oord, "A Perfect Theology Never Existed," 153.

28. Oord, "MTP," 86–87.

is through the influence of a multiplicity of relations.[29] And because of the interrelatedness actual entities have with past experiences (internal relations) and the relations an actual entity will have with those to follow (external relations), Whitehead concludes that there is "an essential relatedness of all things." Hartshorne, likewise, determines there is a "social nature of reality,"[30] making interdependence primary and essential to *being* because "all actual existents are essentially in community."[31]

In process thought, the interrelatedness of all things closes the gap between the temporal realm and God's eternal nature.[32] Process theologians prefer a sempiternal or everlasting view of God, rather than the classical eternal view. An eternal God cannot have relations because his "mode of being . . . is possessed in a simple and indivisible unity."[33] A process doctrine of interrelatedness brings God into relation with his creation, which an eternal God is bereft of having. And this essential relatedness between God and individuals "separates process philosophical theology from classical theism."[34]

The relations God has with the world are necessary to God's nature and to that of the world,[35] thus implying that a "realm of finite actualities . . . has always existed" because of God's everlasting being.[36] And therefore, an essential relatedness between the temporal creation and the eternal Creator means that God *and* some world have always existed. "[I]t is a property of the divine essence that God relates to all existing creatures, all of the time."[37] For Oord, a God who has always been loving *a* world *necessarily* can be trusted more than a God whose love is *free* in the sense that God could have *not* created the universe and God could have chosen *not* to love his creation, thus making God arbitrary.[38] Therefore, because of God's essential relatedness to *a* world, God then did not create *ex nihilo*;

---

29. Oord, "MTP," 87.
30. Oord quoting Hartshorne, "Whitehead's Idea of God," 527, in Oord, "MTP," 88.
31. Oord, "MTP," 88.
32. Whitehead, *Adventures*, 168.
33. Tomkinson, "Divine Sempiternity," 184.
34. Oord, "MTP," 88.
35. Whitehead's metaphysic requires an inhering union between God and the world. Whitehead, *Adventures*, 168.
36. Oord, "MTP," 89.
37. Oord, "Types of Wesleyan Philosophy," 162.
38. Oord, *NOL*, 113.

rather, God brought about an ordered creation from a primordial chaos and continues to recreate from creation.[39]

This understanding forms the process doctrine of *panentheism*, which means all things are *in* God. Panentheism is not to be expressed conversely, that God is in all things; rather, God and the world function like a mind and a body. Oord's analogy is significant to the discussion: "Just as the mind naturally interacts with the brain and other members of the body without being ontologically different, so God naturally interacts with the world *without being ontologically different*."[40] And as the mind controls and has dominant influence over the body, God, likewise, controls and influences the world.[41]

At this point, Oord indicates the common ground process panentheism[42] has with classical theism, in affirming God's distinction from his creation, to the effect that the world–finite relations do not *fully* govern God. However, these relations are essential; therefore, panentheism does not agree with classical theism's espousal that God *chose* to be in relation with a world. The God depicted in process panentheism is *essentially* immanent because he is necessarily influenced *by* all and is *essentially* transcendent because he necessarily influences all.[43]

Creatures and God as Essentially Free

Process philosophy asserts that all existents "from an electron to God"[44] are essentially free, exercising some level of self-determination. For Oord, freedom is "the notion that one's free choice originates in oneself and is not dependent upon conditions that make it the case that one cannot do otherwise."[45] God exercises the greatest level of self-determination but cannot exert unilateral determination on another existent; rather, he uses persuasion. And because the power of self-determination is a necessary

---

39. Oord, "MTP," 89.

40. Oord, "MTP," 90. Emphasis added.

41. Oord, "MTP," 90. However, Oord ensures to clarify that this by no means implies *complete* control over the body parts (i.e., the creatures), thus God is not responsible for the evil that creatures commit.

42. Oord coined the term "theocosmocentrism" to define his panentheism, which, he says rightly places God first, while placing creation at the center of his concern. Oord, *NOL*, 147.

43. Oord, "MTP," 91.

44. Oord, "MTP," 97.

45. Oord, "MTP," 225.

component for all actualities, not even God can exert unilateral determinative power—coercion—on any other existent. In fact, "[d]ivine coercion is not merely a moral inability but a metaphysical inability."[46] Such a view ensures creatures are responsible for their actions. And though God and others influence other individuals, "our loving God is unable to interrupt the creature's free choice to act in an evil way."[47]

Oord's notion of omnipotence distinguishes itself from the free-will conception of power, in that free-will theists (e.g., open theists) believe that God has the ability to "act alone" because relegating God's power only to that of persuasion makes God providentially too passive.[48] The problem for Oord is that such a view conflicts with God's loving nature. If God has such power, then his failure to intercede in the face of evil leaves us to assume that horrors like the Holocaust, rape, murder, and genocide are not genuinely evil. However, if such events are truly evil, then it seems that God does not care—"God isn't love."[49] However, because he is uncontrollingly loving, his nature compels him to love, thus he cannot override or hinder any of his creatures, and he is unable to prevent evil, thus bearing no culpability for the evil acts humans do.[50]

Oord notes that other process thinkers (such as Daniel Day Williams and Charles Hartshorne) "recognize the use of force may be the most loving option available in a given situation." However, Oord asks, "Must force be equated with the ability to coerce or determine unilaterally the actions of others?"[51] Oord's concept of divine omnipotence attributes to God the power of persuasion, as an indirect means of physical force without unilateral determination. Oord believes his proposal takes into account "the main thrust of the Biblical record and our own experiences"[52] and also provides a theology that better combines God's love and power than found in traditional open theism.[53] In defining his terms, Oord equates coercion with unilateral determination, which is "the ability of one individual to control *entirely* an action of another." Persuasive power is one that "attracts or lures another to make a specific choice among options." And compelling power "is the power exerted upon another whereby one option is a [sic] far more

46. Oord, "MTP," 97. Oord does not cite any biblical texts to support this claim.
47. Oord, "MTP," 99.
48. Citing Pinnock, "Systematic Theology," 116, in Oord, "Divine Power," 4.
49. Oord, "Divine Power," 4.
50. Oord, "Process Wesleyan Theodicy," 201.
51. Oord, "Divine Power," 6.
52. Oord, "Divine Power," 7.
53. Oord, NOL, 127.

attractive when compared to other options."⁵⁴ While compelling power is more observable among persons, Oord operates under the assumption that "God exerts compelling power."⁵⁵

Oord, however, does not believe God's compulsive influence is *physical*; rather, it is indirectly applied through local, physical bodies. The physicality of the Spirit of God operates in a manner that gives him the ability to persuade or compel a localized body to exert physical force on another physical body. For scriptural support, Oord refers to such examples as the laying on of healing hands in James 5:14, feeding the hungry (Matt 25:37), giving a holy kiss (1 Thess 5:26), expelling one from the church (1 Cor 5:1–5), and the use of the sword (Matt 10:34).

Interestingly, Oord makes the caveat that this does not require one to believe that God commanded Israel to commit genocide; Israel misinterpreted God's call, as many do so today. "God's call, however, is always a perfectly loving call for the best given circumstance."⁵⁶ As with most discussions regarding evil in the world, Hitler comes into the picture. Oord "asserts that murdering Hitler would have been one of the most loving acts in all of history."⁵⁷ However, because God cannot unilaterally determine any event, the influence he exerted on local, physical bodies, in the end, was not compelling enough to guarantee God's intended outcome.⁵⁸ The thwarted attempts to murder Hitler, Oord notes, does not negate God's perfect loving activity; God's desired outcome can only be realized if local, physical agents respond to God's call.⁵⁹

Oord addresses the possible objection that God's use of indirect physical force cannot be ascribed to him because he relies on others to carry it out. In recognizing the validity of the objection, Oord provides an illustration of a soccer player referring to his foot falling asleep, as if it did so on its own. However, to support his point that such indirect physical force *can* be attributed to God, Oord gives an illustration of the soccer player scoring a goal. While the leg and foot kicked the ball into the goal, the player does not say "his foot kicked a goal"; rather, *he* kicked it.⁶⁰ The leg and foot responded to the mind's aim of scoring the goal.

54. Oord, "Divine Power," 8.
55. Oord, "Divine Power," 9.
56. Oord, "Divine Power," 11.
57. Oord, "Divine Power," 11.
58. Oord refers to Bonhoeffer's botched assassination attempt.
59. Oord, "Divine Power," 12.
60. Oord, "Divine Power," 12.

The examples above, Oord says, support Whitehead's "panexperientalist hypothesis that muscles, tissues, cells, etc. have a degree of self-determination such that the mind does not exert complete (unilateral) control over them."[61] Sometimes we can control our limbs; sometimes they have a "mind" of their own. The God-world/mind-body is an integral part of process thought; as the mind has dominant influence over the body parts, God has the dominant influence over the cosmic body parts.

Oord notes that it is crucial to understand that the soccer player's foot may never wake up because his other body parts may not respond to his attempts to get them to exert physical force upon his sleeping foot. Though it is more likely that they will, Oord says so it is to those whom God calls; most will respond, but others may fail to respond to his call for them to act, just as the Israelites "thwarted God's intentions for well-being by their disobedience."[62] He cannot exert causal force to intervene over his creatures' free choices, though evil as they might be, which is why God is not culpable for evil.

With that said, Oord asks, how can one still affirm God as omnipotent? The term needs to be redefined in light of what Oord claims is impossible for God to do: exercise unilateral determinative power. The kind of power God *does* possess is "the greatest we can reasonably believe God to possess given what has been observed in history, including events recorded in the Bible."[63] A more biblical ascription to use when referring to God's power would be the word *almighty*. As Oord sees it, God as "mightier *than all* others, . . . [is] the only One who exerts might *upon all* that exists, . . . [and is] the ultimate source of might *for all* others."[64] And for Oord, this concept of divine power coupled with God's love better "coincides with the broad Biblical witness."[65] Oord notes, however, that this does not mean that passages supportive for omnipotence cannot be found in Scripture.[66] Oord's model attempts to offer a balanced account of divine love and power that both Evangelicals and process theists would be obliged to adopt, without giving up each one's primary theological and philosophical commitments.

---

61. Oord, "Divine Power," 13.
62. Oord, "Divine Power," 14.
63. Oord, "Divine Power," 15.
64. Oord, *ULG*, 189.
65. Oord, "Divine Power," 16.
66. For example, Matthew 19:26.

Oord's Process Account of Creation: Creatio ex Creatione a Natura Amoris

It is apparent that Oord's doctrine of creation has a dominant role in his process philosophical theology. While other process theologians have proffered alternative doctrines of creation in place of *ex nihilo*,[67] Oord believes his doctrine of creation, unlike the alternatives, resolves the problem of evil and satisfies openness theologians in that his model does not make God overly dependent upon creation as open theists observe in process philosophy. Oord's aim is to create a version of process theism that coheres with Evangelicalism.[68] And because the current models of open theism are considered Evangelical, if Oord's model successfully removes the objections openness theologians raise, then his model should be a viable option for open theists, thus Evangelicalism, to accept.[69] Lastly, and most importantly for Oord's cause, he claims that his alternative doctrine of creation establishes God's essential and everlasting love for creation. For Oord, affirming *creatio ex nihilo* "provides no grounds to trust that God will continually love us. If God's nature does not include love for creation, we cannot be confident that God will love creation in the future or has always loved it in the past."[70]

Oord's theodical convictions motivated him to abandon *creatio ex nihilo* because a God who unilaterally creates something from nothing can unilaterally prevent evil from occurring.[71] However, Oord has biblical and historical objections and arguments against *creatio ex nihilo*, but space does not allow me to expound them here. My intention in this chapter is only to address the philosophical aspects of his alternative doctrine of creation.

In place of *creatio ex nihilo*, Oord proposes a doctrine of "*creatio ex creatione a natura amoris*"—God creates from creation out of love for his creation.[72] Because of his self-giving love, God is always creating and relating to his creation. God's omnipresence in his creation negates the phenomenon of miracles, as traditionally understood. His presence in the world and his continual creating and sustaining of it constitute his supernatural activity, not a *miraculous* one.[73]

---

67. Such as, *creatio ex profundis* (meaning, chaos) put forth by Keller, *The Face of the Deep*, and *creatio ex chaosmos* put forth by Griffin, *Reenchantment*, noted in Oord, "An Open Theology Doctrine of Creation," 28–52.

68. Oord, "MTP," 307.

69. Oord, "MTP," ix.

70. Oord, "God Always Creates," 119.

71. Oord, *NOL*, 133.

72. Oord, *NOL*, 134.

73. Oord, *NOL*, 147.

Inherent in Oord's process thought is God's essential and necessary relatedness to his creation. Now, while this concept is true of orthodox Christianity, process thought assumes that God's relatedness to his creation is an ontological necessity. And therefore, God and *a* world have always existed. Such an assumption is purposed to bridge the gap (as Oord believes exists in classical theology) between God and his creatures. The idea of God's independence from his creation, where God *chooses* to love his creation or not love it, creates great tension in a religion with the illocutionary revelation that "God is love" (1 John 4:8).[74] However, it seems that such an assumption leads to the conclusion that since God is eternal, yet he is necessarily related to his creation, then creation is also eternal. In other words, and more precisely, if creation contributes necessarily to who God is, then creation is a necessary "part" of God's being, thus making creation necessary for God's existence. God, then, has no necessary existence *apart* from creation.

Oord recognizes the problem with such an assertion. While the normative meaning of "ontological dependence" denotes that God is necessarily dependent on creation to exist, Oord addresses the concern by redefining "ontological dependence" to "mean the content of God's experience depends at least partly upon God's loving relations with creatures."[75] When Oord says *necessary*, he means that "the relation *must* be so. This relation is involuntary, and it pertains to a thing or being's essence."[76] Oord concludes, "God necessarily exists *and* necessarily relates to creatures. There's no logical contradiction in this view. It means that relating, creating, and giving existence are part of God's essence."[77] And such an understanding of a necessary relationship God has with his creation makes it part of his very being; therefore, God's love for the world expresses an essential element of God's nature, which is love. Other theologies cannot affirm as such because God's love for the world is arbitrary.

From a process perspective, ordered creation comes from a prior chaos (which is still some sort of composite creation). Oord adopts the big-bang origin of the universe, advocating a theistic model of evolution, where God is "cooperative [and] noncoercive."[78] The big-bang was brought about by God's creative actions prior to the existence of this universe.[79] Oord believes

---

74. Unless otherwise noted, all Scripture references will be taken from *The Christian Standard Bible*.

75. Oord, "God Always Creates," 114.

76. Oord, *NOL*, 107.

77. Oord, "God Always Creates," 114. Emphasis added.

78. Oord, "Open Theology Doctrine," 36.

79. Oord, "Open Theology Doctrine," 52.

that God creates through evolution,[80] adopting a *cyclic theory*,[81] which suggests that the universe emerged from the chaos of a previous universe (Gen 1:2), and God reshapes it into a new creation. While Oord does not believe any world or creature exists eternally, God creates everlastingly, which is the basic idea of *creatio ex creatione a natura amoris*: "God has always been creating out of creation because God's nature is love."[82] And "God creates something new from that which God previously created emphasizes that God *acts first* [in line with his doctrine of prevenient grace] in each creative moment."[83] Oord affirms, however, that "[n]o single world or creature exists eternally. In fact, no creature, world, or universe exists eternally. . . . God is the only One who eternally and necessarily exists."[84] Oord's proposed alternative, he claims, is more biblically supported and maintains God's independence from the created world.

Oord's doctrine of creation proposes a framework establishing God's essential relatedness to all of creation. God loves *necessarily*, i.e., he cannot choose to not love. Metaphysically speaking, according to Oord, God does not have the capacity, desire, or ability to *not* love his creation.

Critical Evaluation of Oord's Process Philosophy

The intention in this response is to provide a critical evaluation of Oord's philosophical conclusions (specifically points two and four observed above starting on 33) to demonstrate that Oord's process axioms govern his theological decision making. With that said, it was observed in the beginning of this chapter that a metaphysical presupposition primary to Oord's process philosophical account of divine power is that God cannot unilaterally determine or control anyone or any state of affairs. I believe Oord's *a priori* assumption is his necessary framework for constructing his theological conclusions.

First, I will address notion two, observing the inconsistencies in Oord's philosophy, in that it conflicts with the doctrines of divine simplicity, the Trinity, and creation. Second, and of greater importance, it will be demonstrated that Oord's philosophy is insufficient as a substitute to support the orthodox doctrines of the Trinity and divine simplicity as Oord affirms, which

---

80. Oord, *ULG*, 37.

81. Interestingly, this is how the early Greeks interpreted history. Pelikan, *The Christian Tradition*, 37.

82. Oord, "God Always Creates," 117.

83. Oord, "God Always Creates," 118. Emphasis added.

84. Oord, "God Always Creates," 115.

are established on a classical foundation.⁸⁵ And third, I will challenge Oord's assumptions regarding the nature of divine power, specifically addressing his misappropriation of the term, as he defines it, to classical theism, and then through an examination of specific biblical texts, I will demonstrate that God's power is not restricted *only* to that which Oord defines.

Relations and the Essentially Related God—Evaluation and Critique

INCONSISTENCY IN DIVINE SIMPLICITY

Earlier, we observed Oord's interesting analogy describing how God and the world function from a panentheistic perspective—but with problematic implications. He stated that God and the world interact similarly to how the brain and the body interact, "*without being ontologically different.*"⁸⁶ In an email, I addressed my concern to him regarding his statement, seeking more clarity. In his response, he stated that "God and creation are different. They are not identical. God is a divine being, and creatures are creaturely beings."⁸⁷ Oord intended to show the analogous relationship between God and creatures. As God "acts," so also creatures "act," which is why he asserts that both are subject to the same metaphysical parameters. Oord writes,

> In the mind-body analogy, I'm speculating that the mind is an entity numerically distinct from the brain and other bodily entities. But the mind shares the same basic ontological categories. Analogously, God is like the mind/soul of the universe. God is numerically distinct, and yet God shares some of the same ontological aspects.⁸⁸

While Oord's response clarified some things, his position is still problematic. One issue is that his analogy misappropriates ontological categories. A man's mind and body are of the same ontological category (composed of existence and essence); God and the world are not (God's existence and

---

85. While some may not consider the doctrine of divine simplicity as a vital aspect of Christian orthodoxy, recent explications on simplicity convincingly argue that divine simplicity is, in fact, vital in upholding the doctrine of the Trinity. See Goad, "Simplicity," 97–118; Ortlund, "Divine Simplicity," 436–53. For a strong defense of the classical position from an analytical philosophical approach, see Dolezal, *God without Parts*. And for a defense from an exegetico-dogmatic approach, see Duby, "Divine Simplicity." See also Sanlon, *Simply God*, 57–81.

86. Oord, "MTP," 90. Emphasis added.

87. Oord, personal email to author, June 9, 2018.

88. Oord, "MTP," 90. Oord's response purposed to address theologians who state God is nothing like his creation (i.e., negative theology).

essence are identical, while the world is composite). And while Oord states that "no specific actuality other than God is necessary,"[89] his doctrine of creation, as will be observed later, deems that creation, likewise, is a necessary actuality. Furthermore, God does not belong in a *genus*,[90] otherwise there is something outside of God that measures or catalogues him; or, worse yet, God and creatures could be conflated, ontologically speaking.

The process notion that "God is *essentially* related to others"[91] still muddles the issue. In stating that God has an essential relation to others (i.e., *a necessary* aspect of God's nature), it seems that the world and God require a *necessary* union in order for both to exist. And if God is eternal (or timeless), then it would follow that *a* creation exists eternally. And that is the connection process philosophy assumes. Whitehead's attempt to address the problem Plato left behind, the one and the many and the gap between the transient and eternal, is the solution that "the World [requires] its union with God, and God [requires] his union with the World."[92] In this vein of thought, a process philosophy asserts that a *necessary* dependence exists between God and the world.[93]

However, it presents this dilemma: If God has *always* been creating from some previous creation, thus no part of his creation ever ceases to exist in some form, then how is creation not eternal as God is eternal? And second, if God is eternally, experientially in process, then it follows that God needs a creation to be experientially in process with for eternity. A few additional problems remain.

First, God *still* relies on something outside of himself to make God who he is. Positing that God *necessarily* exists, means that it is in God's essence to exist. Oord agrees, stating, "We should not say that to exist, God depends on the world. As *a se*, to use the Latin expression, God is self-existent. . . . God exists necessarily."[94] And in positing that God *necessarily* relates, it means that it is in God's essence to relate. And if "relating, creating, and giving existence

---

89. Oord, "MTP," 109.

90. Aquinas writes, "God is not related to creatures as though belonging to a different *genus*, but transcending every *genus*, and as the principle of all *genera*." Aquinas, *ST*, 1.3.3.

91. Oord, "MTP," 88. Recall that Oord said *this* is what separates process thought from classical theism.

92. Whitehead, *Adventures*, 168.

93. While I am inclined to assert the dependence is ontological, Oord does not make that judgement. However, the conflict remains in holding to a view that a non-eternal creation has always existed with an eternal, uncreated being. If the relation is not ontological, then what else could it be?

94. Oord, *NOL*, 108.

are part of God's essence," and God's essence requires existence and there never was a time when God's essence did not exist, then relating, creating, and giving existence have always had to exist. So, while Oord demonstrates consistency—according to his model—in his affirmation that God has always been creating with *something*, because such actions are part of his essence, which does not change, and thus necessarily makes God who he is, the logical outcome is *inconsistent*, in that "something's" existence becomes necessary to complete the essence of God.[95] Therefore, I see it as an inescapable conclusion that if God *is* existence[96] and is eternal, then creation, likewise, must also be existence and eternal. Creation is not divine, yet it somehow contributes to who God is; thus, God is made up of "parts," or "substances," which negates the doctrine of divine simplicity that Oord affirms,[97] revealing inconsistency in his doctrine of divine simplicity.

Secondly, Oord says "*the* unchanging pole of God is *the* divine essence. Attributes often ascribed to divinity in classical philosophical theologies (e.g., necessity, impassibility, infallibility, eternality, and immutability) apply to it."[98] The emphasized words seem to conclude that the unchanging pole of God is *the* divinity of God—it is what makes him divine. But then Oord refers to the changing aspect of God (i.e., suffering, rejoicing, sympathy, and contingency), which Oord says is not *the* divine essence of God. Is it something *ad extra*, an accidental property, to the being of God? If the unchanging pole of God is his divine essence, that which makes him God, then what essence is the changing pole of God?[99] On the one hand, God is

---

95. Some have argued that if God creates from an internal necessity, then pan/panentheism is unavoidable. Justin J. Daeley provides a response that invalidates that argument. He demonstrates that (1) because God is existentially prior to creation, he cannot depend on creation, (as a parent is not dependent on its child), and (2) because existence and essence are the same in God and since God's existence is prior to the created order, then God's essence cannot depend on the created order's existence. Daeley, "Creatio Ex Nihilo," 291–313.

96. Aquinas, *ST*, 1.4.2.

97. Oord said, "Yes, I think God's nature is simple, in the sense of it being without parts/substances." Oord, personal email to author, March 14, 2018. And "I affirm divine simplicity, in so far as this means God has no parts." Oord, personal email to author, March 15, 2018.

98. Oord, "MTP," 103–4.

99. In Acts 14, where Paul and Barnabas are mistaken for gods in Lystra, the first few clauses of verse 15, in the Greek, says, "*Andres, ti tauta poieite? kai hēmeis homoiopatheis esmen hymin anthrōpoi*." Luke uses *homoiopatheis*, which BDAG, 706, defines "as to experiencing similarity in feelings or circumstances, *with the same nature*." The NET highlight the proper distinction: "We too are men, with human natures just like you!" According to Luke, quoting Paul and Barnabas, experiencing feelings is proper to the human nature, not the divine nature.

immutable and impassible, but on the other hand, he suffers, and he experiences change. What purpose does it serve in a process construct to retain the classical attributes and posit a di-polar understanding of God? Why not eliminate them altogether, since what ultimately governs process ontology, making God real and known to his creation, is the *changing* aspect of God—his *becoming*? I believe Oord (and the process tradition) adopts the classical heritage for the purposes of retaining an orthodox footprint of traditional Christian theism; however, it is evident that his process metaphysic governs his philosophical determinations.

If Oord is to be consistent in maintaining a distinction between divine being and creaturely being, which classical and process metaphysics both affirm, either the finite realm has to have an actual beginning and God is complete in his essence, *apart* from creation, or creation is ontologically part of God's essence and thus eternal with God. The latter option voids the doctrine of divine simplicity, as Oord defines, making God a composite being, with "parts" *not* of God that he is dependent on to make God who he is.

Sustaining Simplicity

In the critique above that identified inconsistency in Oord's theology with the doctrine of divine simplicity, (DDS hereafter) as he affirms, many in contemporary Evangelicalism see simplicity as inconsistent with a biblical doctrine of God. Therefore, offering some argumentation that the DDS is an essential part of theology proper is warranted, particularly as it relates to this study.

While the DDS has been the "governing concept" and "normative assumption" in the classical doctrine of God since the time of the church fathers,[100] it has become widely rejected in contemporary theology,[101] with some arguing that it should be left "in the arid wastelands of scholastic philosophy."[102] Challenges against simplicity are many: it is too abstract, reticent of a personal, thus unknowable God; it makes God a

---

100. Muller, *PRRD*, 3:38–39. Cf. Stead, *Philosophy in Christian Antiquity*, 130–31; Ayres and Barnes, "God," 378–87; Osborn, *Emergence of Christian Theology*, 112; Ayres, *Nicaea and Its Legacy*, 278–81; Prestige, *God in Patristic Thought*, 229–30; Gregory of Nazianzus, *Orations*, 28.7; Augustine, *On the Trinity*, 7.1.2; Gregory of Nyssa, *Cont. Eun.* 13.

101. Richards, "Divine Simplicity," 157. Cf. Plantinga, *Does God Have a Nature?*; Nash, *Concept of God*, 95; Feinberg, *No One*, 330–35; Davies, "Modern Defence," 549–64; Mullins, "Simply Impossible," 181–203; Ortlund, "Divine Simplicity," 436–53.

102. Holmes, "'Too Plain to Say," 137. I am merely quoting Holmes's reflection on what others have expressed toward him.

property and identical to all his properties; we lose our ability to predicate diversity of attributes in God; it obscures the incarnation, negates God's freedom, cannot sustain the doctrine of the Trinity, and is unbiblical.[103] However, challenges aside, it will be argued that simplicity "is a formal feature of divinity."[104] It is not an attribute of God; it is his "ontological constitution."[105] To cast away simplicity is to cast away his divinity and so the worshipfulness of God. Hence, my aim will be to demonstrate simplicity as an integral aspect of the doctrine of God, showing that it can be reconciled with his attributes in a cogent and sustained manner.

A Classical Definition of Simplicity

Though there are other versions of the doctrine,[106] the unitive principle of the DDS negatively predicates that God is not composed of parts.[107] Contemporary defender, James Dolezal, provides a distinctly *classical* definition of DDS:

> The principal claim of divine simplicity is that God is not composed of parts. Whatever is composed of parts depends upon its parts in order to be as it is. A part is anything in a subject that is less than the whole and without which the subject would be really different than it is. Moreover, the parts in an integrated whole require a composer distinct from themselves to unify them, an extrinsic source of unity. If God should be composed of parts—of components that were prior to Him in being—He would be doubly dependent: first, on the parts, and second, on the composer of parts. But God is absolute being, alone the

---

103. Ortlund, "Divine Simplicity," 436–37.
104. Burrell, *Knowing the Unknowable God*, 3.3.2.
105. Burrell, *Knowing the Unknowable God*, 3.3.2.
106. Augustine, Aquinas, Anselm, and St. John of Damascus all had variations in their doctrines of simplicity, with Anselm and St. John distinct from Augustine and Aquinas. Ortlund, "Divine Simplicity," 438. The variations of the DDS can be lumped into two camps, with the "stronger version" affirming that God is identical with his essence and attributes and the "weaker version" affirming that God instantiates his attributes rather than being the same as his attributes. For example, the early church fathers affirmed what would be considered *weak* because their main use of simplicity was to exegetically substantiate the triunity and unity of God, not extending its use any further. See Ayres, *Nicaea and Its Legacy*, 281, 287.
107. We can find the expression that God does not have a body/parts in: *Westminster Confession of Faith*, 2.1; Reeves, *1689 Baptist Confession*, 2.1; *The Thirty-Nine Articles*, 1.1. However, the confessional forms represented a greater and more extensive understanding of simplicity than a mere denial of body parts.

sufficient reason for Himself and all other things, and so cannot in any respect derive His being from another. Because God cannot depend on what is not God in order to be God, theologians traditionally insist that *all that is in God is God*.[108]

One of the key differences between process and classical theism is how each understand divine relationality. Many modern theologians and philosophers consider God as a person or individual, having "a consciousness or mind with beliefs and thoughts."[109] However, earlier generations would not have spoken of God in such terms. Augustine, Anselm, and Aquinas assert God does not belong to a class of any sort, so he cannot be a person or individual.[110] What they mean, as Brian Davies explains, is "that God belongs to no class at all and that he defies the conceptual equipment by means of which we identify things and single them out as members of a world."[111]

When we look at the development of the DDS, the early church fathers affirmed simplicity in a distinctly exegetical manner[112] to substantiate and defend monotheism, Trinitarianism, and the divine operations.[113] Later theologians ambitiously expanded simplicity[114] in order to differentiate—immutable from mutable—Creator from creation,[115] which incipiently moved the development closer to a classical view.

It is important to observe that the common link uniting the objectors of the DDS is the assumption of a univocal rather than analogical relationship between God and creation (of which Oord falls subject to as well). Basically, it is an inconsistent understanding and application of ontological distinctions.[116]

---

108. Dolezal, *God without Parts*, 40–41. Emphasis added.

109. Davies, "Modern Defence," 551.

110. Davies, "Modern Defence," 551.

111. Davies, "Modern Defence," 551.

112. For example, they did not strictly read terms such as *light*, *power*, and *glory* as metaphor; rather, such terms biblically demonstrated the unity of God. Ayres, *Nicaea and Its Legacy*, 279.

113. Ayres observes, "One of the most important principles shared by pro-Nicenes is that whenever one of the divine persons acts, all are present, acting inseparably." *Nicaea and Its Legacy*, 280.

114. Distinctively apart from the earlier tradition of thought, St. John of Damascus, writing in the seventh century, observes, "We, therefore, both know and confess that God is without beginning, without end, eternal and everlasting, uncreated, unchangeable, invariable, simple, uncompound, incorporeal, invisible, impalpable, uncircumscribed, infinite, incognisable, indefinable, incomprehensible, good, just, maker of all things created, almighty, all-ruling, all-surveying, of all overseer, sovereign, judge; and that God is One, that is to say, one essence." Damascus, *Orthodox Faith*, 1.2.

115. As observed above. Damascus, *Orthodox Faith*, 1.2.

116. As Dolezal notes, "the outstanding common denominator" is a "strong commitment to ontological univocism." Dolezal, *God without Parts*, 29.

While we speak about God by what we know of creatures, the blurring of the lines between the two produces a tendency toward *literal* predication about the uncreated in created terms—*strong* anthropomorphism. Furthermore, another mistake contemporary critics make is the assumption that simplicity is intended to speak positively about God. Following the stream of articulation in Augustine, Anselm, and Aquinas, Brian Davies observes that one should have noticed the obvious fact that the DDS "is a piece of negative or apophatic theology and not a purported description of God."[117] It is intended to tell us what we should *not* say about God.[118]

Oord's few words about the DDS demonstrate that he is misguided on what simplicity actually is. He writes, "Most reject traditional ways of thinking about God's timelessness, simplicity, impassibility and immutability. These attributes interrelate, at least loosely, and rejecting one often means rejecting the others."[119] His error is to refer to simplicity as an attribute among other attributes. However, simplicity is not an attribute of God; it is the absolute divinity of God,[120] from which we *can* qualitatively and assuredly predicate a *divine* attribute of God. God is simple because he is transcendent. Transcendence necessitates simplicity (and vice-versa) because God is completely present and immanent to all of creation, a consequent of his spirituality. If he were composite (i.e., made up of parts), then he could not be transcendent, as pure deity is and so not the Creator of the universe. God is immutable because he is simple; God is holy because he is simple; God is eternal because he is simple; God is omniscient because he is simple. And with these misguided operable assumptions in contemporary theology, the critics appeal to incoherency seems to have merit.

Simplicity and Impassibility/Immutability

Saying that God is impassible, as John Webster articulates, means he is "inexhaustibly alive, stable and entire in himself and so beyond the reach of any agent or act of contestation or depredation."[121] A more standard definition of impassibility states it "is that divine attribute whereby God is said

---

117. Davies, "Modern Defence," 555.

118. Emery, "Immutability of the God of Love," 63, writes, "when one affirms that God is immutable, this necessarily means that one *denies* of God that which we experience of realities of our world."

119. Oord, *ULG*, 124.

120. Emery, *The Trinity*, 92, writes, "To say God is simple is therefore to affirm the *divinity* of God."

121. Webster, *God without Measure*, 120.

not to experience inner emotional changes of state, whether enacted freely from within or effected by his relationship to an interaction with human beings and the created order."[122] And lastly, confessionally stated, impassibility means God is "without passions."[123]

Looking to Webster again, God's immutability means he is "already infinitely sufficient and complete and therefore beyond alteration or acquisition."[124] More so than simplicity, impassibility and immutability have come under fire in contemporary theological/philosophical discussions.[125] Contemporary objectors to the classical doctrines claim that it has a cryogenic effect on God. To them, immutability and impassibility mean God is immobile, unaffected, and unaffecting.[126] However, that is a modern notion foreign to the historic Christian tradition. G. L. Prestige, in his classic work, *God in Patristic Thought*, a compilation and synthesis of what the Greek fathers understood and taught about the nature of God, notes that "it is clear that impassibility means not that God is inactive or uninterested, not that He surveys existence from Epicurean impassivity from the shelter of a metaphysical insulation, but that His will is determined from within instead of being swayed from without."[127] A few pages later he concludes, reemphasizing the point that at no time in the early church did the doctrine of impassibility indicate or express God having a

---

122. Weinandy, "Impassibility of God," 357.

123. Reeves, *1689 Baptist Confession*, 2.1; *The Thirty-Nine Articles*; *The Westminster Confession of Faith*; *Savoy Declaration*.

124. Webster, *God without Measure*, 120.

125. One of the fiercest critics of immutability, Barth, *CD* 1/1:493, opining about immutable equating it to immobile, writes, "if the 'immutable' as such is in fact to be God, this is undoubtedly the most dangerous assumption conceivable not only for the doctrine of God in particular but for every statement about God." However, classical theism never taught that immutable meant immobile. Rather, as John Webster's definition stated, actually the opposite is true; God is infinitely sufficient, which means, God is unmoved because "he is identical with his life and actuality and therefore cannot be determined to any further actuality of life than he already has." Dolezal, *God without Parts*, 86–87.

126. Pinnock, *Most Moved Mover*, 85–88; Sanders, *God Who Risks*, 163–64; Goetz, "The Suffering God," 385–89. Modern treatments on impassibility/immutability are vast, so I will list a few important works, with the others listed in the bibliography. Muller, "Incarnation," 22–40; Ware, "An Evangelical Reformulation," 431–46; Bauckham, "'Only the Suffering,'" 6–12; Fretheim, *Suffering of God*; Sarot, "Suffering of Christ," 113–19; Heschel, *Prophets*; Fiddes, *Creative Suffering of God*; Weinandy, *Does God Suffer?*; Gavrilyuk, *Suffering of the Impassible God*; Baines et al., *Confessing the Impassible God*.

127. Prestige, *God in Patristic Thought*, 7. Prestige does reference some Latin writers, but the Greek fathers are the main focus of this work.

lack of interest for his creation or care and concern for the world. "[S]uch theory," he writes, "is manifestly absurd."[128]

Why does contemporary theism continue "to beat, not a dead, but a nonexistent horse"?[129] As pointed out in the introduction of this study, contemporary philosophy has undergone a paradigm shift. As Pinnock and Hartshorne so openly admitted, the philosophy of our day is *socially oriented*.[130] In an article on the DDS, philosopher Nicholas Wolterstorff observes the ontological differences in which the medieval forbearers and the contemporary milieu operate.[131] He notes that the ontological style of the medievals was a *constituent* type, whereas moderns function within a *relational* type. The disparity comes down to understanding the entailment of a thing's essence. For the medievals, Wolterstorff writes, "*having an essence* was having an essence as one of its constituents, for us [relational ontology], having an *essence* is having an essence as one of its properties: exemplifying it."[132] Succinctly put: for medievals, essence is what something *is*; for moderns, essence is what something *has*. The relational type assumes that a denial of a particular quality (i.e., *apathaeia*; *passions*) impinges on divine-human relationality. But *passions*, in the context of God's essence and attributes, is conducive to sin, which God cannot do.[133]

The scope of my study does not allow room to elaborate further on a historical development of ontology. However, the notable differences among ontological starting points is important to acknowledge if we are to identify the key issues and disagreements (which I have made clear throughout the study). The aim of this section is to reconcile simplicity and impassibility/immutability. Both are tethered together and established by simplicity. So, what I state about one has the same implications for the other. The claim is

---

128. Prestige, *God in Patristic Thought*, 11. In response to the charge of Hellenization in dogmatic construction (i.e., negative ascriptions of God), Jaroslav Pelikan states that "the chief place to look for hellenization is in the speculations and heresies *against which* the dogma of the creeds and councils was directed." Pelikan, *The Christian Tradition*, 1:55; emphasis added. Citing Irenaeus (*Haer.* 4.4.2; 4.6.6), Theodore of Mopsuestia (*Hom.catech.* 4.6), Apollinaris (*Fid.sec.pt.* 2), and Cyril of Alexandria (*Chr. un.* [SC 97:312–14]), Pelikan notes, "the early Christian picture of God was controlled by the self-evident axiom, accepted by all, of the absoluteness and the impassibility of the divine nature." Pelikan, *The Christian Tradition*, 229.

129. Muller, *PRRD*, 3:310. Muller was echoing Prestige, regarding the claim that impassibility was "the uncritical importation of a Stoic concept."

130. See chapter 1 of this study.

131. Wolterstorff, "Divine Simplicity," 91–113.

132. Wolterstorff, "Divine Simplicity," 101.

133. Muller, *PRRD*, 3:310.

that only a purely simple being can be immutable and impassible.[134] They are inextricably connected to simplicity because everything composite (i.e., *made up of parts* as are all created beings/entities) is divisible, thus mutable. And *passions* are not intrinsic to God *as he is*; therefore, *passions* are in the class of parts because their proper mode is in the framework of experience, which is how creatures gain knew knowledge. God is perfect in knowledge and cannot acquire new [parts of] knowledge, thus God does not undergo experience in a creaturely sense. Oord's adherence to "strong" passibility is inconsistent with the DDS. But how does the classical view of simplicity anchor immutability/impassibility?

Biblical Basis for Impassibility and Immutability

Scripture testifies to the constancy of God, in that heaven and earth will pass away, but he will remain; his years have no end (Ps 102:25–27). God reveals himself to Moses in Exodus 3:14 as, "I AM," not "I become," because he *is*. God reveals himself as the Creator and Lord over all his creation, having existed from before he brought creation into existence (Gen 1:1; Isa 6:5; Ps 47:3; 97:5). He is the living God, active in time and history as Israel's Lord and Master (Deut 10:14–18). Whatever he plans *will* take place, because he will do all that he has willed (Isa 46:10–11). Following God's demonstration of his mighty power in destroying Pharaoh and the Egyptians, Moses' doxology to the Lord reveals the incomparability of God to other gods, when he writes, "Lord, who is like you among the gods? Who is like you, glorious in holiness, revered with praises, performing wonders?" (Exod 15:11). There is no other God like him, who is transcendent *over* and immanent *with* his creation.

Unlike creatures, God does not lie; he does not repent; he does what he says he will do (Num 15:28; 1 Sam 15:29). God is incorruptible and has immortality (Rom 1:23; 1 Tim 1:17; 6:16; Heb 1:11–12). A God who is composite is corruptible. And because "God is Spirit" (John 4:24), he is not composite, thus not corruptible. Since God cannot be changed into something better because he is the most perfect being, "nothing remains except that he must be changed into something worse, and thus be corrupted."[135] Malachi directly states it: "For I the Lord do not change" (3:6). God is the first and the last, who remains who he is (Isa 41:4; 43:10; 46:4; 48:12).

The classic story of Jonah, remembered by many for his time spent in the belly of a large fish, is actually a profound narrative *because of* God's

---

134. Pannenberg, *Basic Questions*, 2:165.
135. Mastricht, *Theoretical-Practical*, 2:147.

immutability. In the closing of the story, Jonah explains that he did not preach because he knew that the Lord would *not* change his mind from being gracious to the Assyrians. He writes, "That's *why* I fled toward Tarshish in the first place. *I knew that you are a gracious and compassionate God*, slow to anger, abounding in faithful love, and one who relents from sending disaster" (Jonah 4:2; emphasis added). He fled because he knew God was going to act true to his character; God is immutable in his ways, demonstrating his gracious will to those who deserve judgment. And then Jonah repents because he is not like God (4:3). In God, unlike Jonah, "there is no variation or shadow due to change" (Jas 1:17 ESV).

Divine aseity teaches us that God is complete, wholly sufficient in himself, in that he has life in himself (John 5:26), because "from eternity to eternity" he is God (Ps 90:2). And he gives and sustains all life (Acts 17:25; Heb 1:3), "never becomes faint or weary" (Isa 40:28), and all that a creature possesses comes from God (Rom 11:35–36; cf. Isa 42:5). And he is beyond the reach of our actions, in that they cannot *affect* God.

In his argument with Job, Elihu says, "If you sin, how does it affect God? If you multiply your transgressions, what does it do to him? If you are righteous, what do you give him, or what does he receive from your hand?" (Job 35:6–7; cf. 41:11). What Job's actions affect (as well as every creature's actions) are other human beings: "Your wickedness affects a person like yourself, and your righteousness, a son of man" (v. 8). And because God is never changing in his character, with justice and grace being pleasing to him, he is "glad to prosper and multiply [his people], but "also be glad to cause [them] to perish and destroy [them]" (Deut 28:63).

It Is Not about Scripture

While Scripture supports the doctrines of immutability and impassibility, the verses cited do not explicitly deny a mutable or passibilist reading. In fact, objectors (even the Calvinist type) to the classical view of immutability have argued that such passages indicate ethical immutability.[136] And many Evangelical Calvinists dismiss or have modified the classical view of impassibility/immutability, allowing room for change in God.[137] The key

---

136. Brown, "Schelling and Dorner," 237–49; Ware, "A Modified Calvinist," 92.

137. Wayne Grudem, up until 2020, rejected divine impassibility (see Grudem, *Systematic Theology* [1st ed.], 166). He revised his position, affirming the doctrine in the sense that God is "incapable of suffering harm" and that God's being cannot experience change from "anything outside of himself." Grudem, *Systematic Theology* (2nd ed.), 196. Ware writes, "God is changeable in relationship with his creation. . . . In this relational mutability, God . . . does interact with his people in the experiences of their

difference as noted through my critique of Oord stems from different metaphysical starting points. Professed classical theologians that have made allowance for a mutability in God's nature do so under the provision that one retains a strong doctrine of divine sovereignty to safeguard such mutability. What they are saying is that God is sovereign *over* his mutability, but he is still immutable from being acted upon. But in doing so, this is exactly what the open/relational theologies were prescribing, so why the objection? The disparity cannot be resolved on a purely scriptural level.

Theological Priority

The position taken in this study is that an ethical immutability requires God's ontological immutability as its foundation.[138] A three-fold implication of immutability is that God is changeless in his essence, his attributes, and in his decree.[139] And these implications are grounded directly in the biblical text: "God is not a man that he should lie" (Num 23:19; cf. 1 Sam 15:29; Hos 11:9). The attributes of immutability and impassibility in classical theology are actually denials of what modern objectors claim (i.e., static, frozen, immobile). To borrow language from Thomas Weinandy, immutability/impassibility implies a dynamism in God, in that his goodness, love, and perfection are dynamic, having *no* fluctuation or change within himself so that he could be *less* or *more* loving, good, and perfect. And God's dynamic, impassible nature does not, nor did it ever, negate passion in God; rather, it affirmed and secured God's unchangeable perfect passions,[140] to which he could never become more passionate because he is perfectly and maximally passionate in his love, compassion, mercy, and righteous anger.[141]

Immutability is necessarily connected to simplicity, in that simplicity implies divinity, which is the perfection of the actuality of God. Following Aquinas, God as *pure act* means there is no potentiality in God. A potentiality in God would be an un-actualized state of existence. However, God as First Cause, who is the necessary being and cause of all, must be in complete

---

lives as these unfold in time." *God's Lesser Glory*, 73. John Frame asserts that God "is not merely an agent in time; he really is in time, changing as others change." *Doctrine of God*, 571. Feinberg supports relational mutability, which, he says, "bears some affinities to the process and open views of divine immutability," in that God's attitude change "is a relational change in virtue of God's unchanging moral rules and governance." *No One*, 275–76.

138. Dolezal, "Still Impassible," 129.
139. Muller, "Incarnation," 26.
140. I think *affections* is a more helpful word choice to avoid confusion.
141. Weinandy, *Does God Suffer?*, 110–11.

dynamic actuality of all perfections as the one who gives being and sustains all beings. Going back to the definition of simplicity, God cannot have parts that make up who he is because a part is less than a whole thus not perfect, and imperfect parts cannot make up a perfect whole, which God is. And if God is made up of parts, then something exists ontologically outside or posterior to God that gave him being. Therefore, God simply is who he is from himself. God's deity is simple and unchanging because a change (*mutation*) in God would change his *simple* essence and being, making God no longer the perfect, simple God that he is, negating what makes him divine. A change in God is the acquiring of something new, "the introducing of something he was previously lacking, and this would shatter the plentitude and perfection of his being that pertains to him."[142]

As mentioned above, merely citing biblical references to support impassibility/immutability does not provide a strong-hold case to substantiate these doctrines, nor do they offer a positive case *against* a passible/mutable reading. So, then what is our adjudicator? Answer: one's logical and theological priority in rightly dividing the Word of truth (2 Tim 2:15). Richard Muller asserts that the manner of consistency hinges upon where one prioritizes one set of statements over another.[143] From a classical view, this means that the interpreter stands in the hermeneutical position that gives precedence to scriptural statements of omniscience, God's will, and goodness over passages of ignorance, indecision, and change.[144]

For example, when reading a text like Malachi 3:6–7, a go-to text for God's declaration of immutability, a proper exegetical approach will observe this divine declaration in the context of covenant. Israel is cutting themselves off from communion with God, but they will be allowed back into covenant relation by means of obedience. Muller notes,

> The text does not refer to a God whose presence is in fact everywhere somehow becoming absent and then subsequently returning. The "absence of God" is one of the ways in which Scripture refers to human alienation, without any hint of a doctrine that God changes location. Nor does the text refer to an ethical change in God: God's "return" or repentance is predicated upon his changelessness.[145]

---

142. Emery, "The Immutability," 61.

143. Muller, "Incarnation," 31. Muller's response is directed at Clark Pinnock who claims classical theism has erred in that it interprets change or repentance passages as figurative. But Numbers 23:19 makes a *literal* affirmation that God does not repent.

144. Helm, *Providence of God*, 51.

145. Muller, "Incarnation," 31. Also, Dolezal, "Still Impassible," 130.

Muller, following the rule of theological priority, situates God's ethical immutability and the will of God *in* the immutability of the divine being. Doing so guarantees the "continuity of purpose" in the divine will.[146]

The interpreter would be hard pressed to consistently maintain the attributes of God if he were to give theological priority to the anthropomorphic style observed in Scripture. For example, when we read texts like Genesis 3:9, where Adam is hiding from God, and God calls out to Adam, "Where are you?", if we conclude that God did not really know where Adam was then God is not omnipresent (nor omniscient). Did God need to "go down" to see what was going on in Sodom (Gen 18:21; cf. 11:5, 7; Exod 3:8; 33:5; Mic 1:3)? When God passed before Moses, revealing his "back," does that mean God was in a different location and then passed by Moses, exposing his back? And does God have a back? God's omnipresence means he is everywhere-present-all-at-once. If we give precedence to the anthropomorphic reading of such passages, we will end up with a theology that denies the very attributes of God that Scripture reveals (i.e., omnipresence, omniscience, aseity, etc.).

The question that arises, then, is what do we do with the incarnation? Was that not a change in God? The church fathers dealt with this issue, observing the distinction between *change* and *assume*.[147] Mastricht captures this understanding with precision, stating that the Second Person of the Trinity can be called incarnate, "not by being acted upon but only by acting, that is, by assuming a human nature."[148] Contemporary theism's objection to the classical attributes is a *doctrinal* problem, not a scriptural one. As I already noted in my exposition of open and process/relational theology, the challenge to a classical point of view is metaphysical. Process and openness theologians, as Muller identifies, "select a different ontology and interpret the texts accordingly."[149] And the ontology of choice, where theological priority begins, is *becoming*.[150] David Burrell notes "Aquinas' pregnant analogy," showing the ontological *fork in the road*: "as *time* measures *becoming*, so *eternity* measures *to-be* (*esse*) (Ia, 10, 4, 3)."[151]

---

146. Muller, "Incarnation," 32.

147. Augustine, *Trinity*, 3.14–15; Aquinas, *ST*, 3.5.1; Calvin, *Institutes*, 2.8.1; Turretin, *IET*, 3.1.28, 3.7.7. For the development of this understanding in Chalcedonian Christology, see Riches, *Ecce Homo*, 91–106.

148. Mastricht, *Theoretical-Practical*, 2:158.

149. Muller, "Incarnation," 34. Muller notes that the competing ontology takes a "traditional view of Scripture and the post-Kantian view of Scripture as interpreted in the manner of Hegel." Muller, "Incarnation," 38.

150. See chapter 1; *becoming* is the ontological foundation of process philosophy.

151. Burrell, "Distinguishing God," 80. Emphasis added. Interestingly, the other

A Concluding Pastoral Observation

An important aspect of the discussion that is often overlooked is that the simplicity of God, which establishes the impassible and immutable being of God, is *why* he could become passible in assuming flesh, the person of Jesus Christ. If Christ were mutable and passible, he might have let the cup pass from him because God's will, his decree of manifesting his glory to the world and bringing human beings into a fellowship of love and bliss, may not have primacy above his own immediate, human desire of self-preservation. He might have failed like the first Adam. God's immutable and impassible nature guaranteed that the Savior would fulfill the Father's work of redemption. The impassible becomes passible to impassibly fulfill what the passible could not.

Simplicity and the Trinity

The challenge in reconciling the DDS with the Trinity is due to the kind of reasoning behind it: $1+1+1=1$.[152] Modern Trinitarianism has pulled away from the DDS, focusing more on the divine persons constituting the One God instead of the traditional One God consisting of three persons.[153] But simplicity actually enables us to argue for God's triunity, maintaining distinction of relation yet in a non-composite sense. Relations within the Godhead are real proper relations, not accidents. Simplicity negates a *composition* in God, not true *distinctions* within God; thus, the divine relations subsist in themselves. And as the subsistent relations are the subsistent persons themselves, with the

---

ontological "pregnant" dichotomy in his statement is that a *becoming* ontology functions within a temporal view of God, which is the dominant view in the process/open/relational camp.

152. Aquinas corrects the logic of the equation, stating, "In the divine Trinity is to be understood both number and the persons numbered. So, when we say, *Trinity in Unity*, we do not place number in the unity of the essence, as if we meant three times one; but we place the Persons numbered in the unity of nature; as the *supposita* of a nature are said to exist in that nature. On the other hand, we say *Unity of Trinity*; meaning that the nature is in its *supposita*." Aquinas, *ST*, 1.31.1.

153. See discussion on the social Trinitarian concepts of Rahner, Moltmann, and Pannenberg, in Letham, *The Holy Trinity*, 312–21. Letham, interestingly, observes the ontology of *becoming* latent in Moltmann's and Pannenberg's social Trinitarian constructs. Thompson, *Modern Trinitarian Perspectives*; Volf, "Being as God Is"; Coakley, "'Persons.'" Oord, however, does not agree with a social-Trinitarian model. See Oord, "Can God Be Essentially Loving?", 353–61.

Father as the paternal, the Son as the filiation, and the Spirit as the procession, the persons are then said to be non-composite.[154]

The perfection of each person of the Godhead guarantees that they are uncompounded, thus remaining simple. The relations subsist in the undivided being of God, thus they relate as *supposita*, the self-subsistent nature in the undivided being of God. If the persons possessed being as a distinct entity, there would be three beings, thus three gods, making God composite. It is important to differentiate *being* from *relations*[155] in a taxonomic sense, in that "the divine being does not itself relate because the relations subsist in the undivided being."[156] God is simple, so we cannot think of each person as a *proper part* of God or the relations as accidents in God as they are in composite beings. They are each fully divine and "each person expresses not a part of God's nature, but the fullness of the *ousia* [being]."[157] And therefore, the divine "relations subsist in virtue of their identity with God's essence."[158] The persons are numerically distinct but conjoined in unity of essence, in which the Godhead,[159] then, "indicates the communicability of the sole, infinite, individual, and singular divine essence to these three without division."[160]

The DDS maintains a strict monotheism, even implying it, removing any hint of tritheism or Sabellianism in the Godhead. Categorical errors arise when one strains anthropomorphism into a literalistic fashion when speaking of the divine persons. The Scripture is full of anthropomorphic language because God is incomprehensible, beyond our understanding. While we can use anthropomorphic language to speak of God, because we

---

154. Dolezal, "Trinity," 79–98. Creatures are composite. Compositeness expresses one's ontological constitution as a creature.

155. The tendency in modern ontology is to equate relations with individuals, who are singular *beings*. And therefore, the individual—the person—"possesses its proper being in a complete manner, in himself and through himself, and exercises on his own the act of existing." Emery, *The Trinity*, 103. In speaking of composite creatures, such language and understanding of the notion of *being* and *relations* makes sense, but God is being itself, with no other *beings* of God apart from himself. Humans have individuation as composite beings. To offer an analogy (though a weak one), if God is the billiard table, humans are billiard balls.

156. Levering, *Scripture and Metaphysics*, 218–19.

157. Holmes, "Too Plain to Say," 149.

158. Dolezal, "God's Personal Relations," 89.

159. Goad, "Simplicity," 103, observes from the assumption of simplicity in patristic defenders of the Trinity and the deity of Christ, is that the DDS is "the only means by which one can affirm eternal generation without division in God or attributing subordination to the Son." This avoids the anthropomorphic tendency of seeing the Son's generation as a material generation.

160. Muller, *PRRD*, 3:283.

dialogue about him from what we know of creatures, apophatic statements (as simplicity entails) provide a *divine grammar* to speak truth about God and his triunity without pulling the Godhead apart.

Simple Activity in Triunity

When we speak of God's activity in the world, we are speaking of God's operation (*energeia*). The Father, through the Word, in the Spirit—the community of action by the three persons, in *act*—is seen as a sole operation of the being of God.[161] This one motion of the will—*act*—of God, the triunity of the persons as being in subsistent relations, is fully in act, thus fully relational.[162] It is precisely because God *is*—"to-be" (*ipsum esse*; and is where Aquinas develops the notion of *pure act*), that he is fully relational because his simplicity entails all three persons are everywhere present, *not partite*, completely and maximally intimate to his creation. Therefore, in God's act of salvation, the subsisting relations of the triune God draw human beings in to participate in communion with the fully-in-act simple God. The simpleness of God, his divine spirituality, can fully relate with creatures who are *not* fully relational because as composite, individuated *supposita*, they must relate to another through mediating actions, having to actualize physically (hugging/kissing/talking), bringing about change of their "inert relational potential" and *becoming* related to each other. The persons of the triune God do not nor cannot do that because they are pure relations fully in act.[163]

Critics challenge the coherency of the DDS with the triunity of God because the distinctions between the Father, Son, and Spirit are not *real* because there is no composition.[164] That term *real* is *the* roadblock for non-classical theists. Comprehending the negation of "real relations" from within a *relational* ontology makes no sense, thus the reason why critics think the DDS needs to be put out to pasture. I do sympathize with them. To briefly explain, the proper understanding of Aquinas's meaning of *real relationship* intended to make a distinction between God and creation—its dependence on him. God does not depend on creation; creation depends on

---

161. Emery, *The Trinity*, 92–93.

162. Weinandy, *Does God Suffer?*, 127.

163. Weinandy, *Does God Suffer?*, 128.

164. To be *composite* is to be composed of substance and accidents. Accidents add something to a substance, which means the substance is prior to accidents, which entails potentiality and actuality in the substance. God is uncaused, perfect, absolute, and nothing can be added to his being. Aquinas, *ST*, 1.3.6.

him; therefore, it has a *real relation* to him.[165] Only God's relations within his divine being—as Aquinas was referring to—are real—the *ad intra* relations in God depend on each other, thus they are *real*. God cannot have a "real" relation with creatures in that sense. Humans can only *participate* in the Spirit, not *coinhere* in the Spirit as subsisting relations. It is important to remember that simplicity also entails that God *is* his relations.[166] With that said, God's relations with his creation are *true*, full, and maximal, more so than human-human relations could ever be.

The complex nature of the discussion throughout the previous paragraphs is mentally contortive. However, discussion about the Trinity and maintaining monotheism and the attributes of God as found in Scripture pushes the envelope of theological discourse to a level of precision that, though challenging to grasp and articulate, is needed to maintain the coherency and constancy of the biblical data of the Christian doctrine of God.

I think Oord would find agreement with the above presentation on simplicity and the Trinity, particularly in articulating the manner of divine-human relations. Oord's point of departure, however, comes by the manner of God's freedom to choose whom he wants to bring into communion. The operation of divine grace is the distinct act of God bringing creatures into fellowship with himself. Oord does not see this distinction; rather, God is essentially related to all of creation and necessarily loves and relates to all of it, even rocks. I agree with Oord that God is essentially related to his creation (as simple being, fully present to every aspect of his creation), but Scripture portrays a distinct love that Christ has for his bride, the church (Eph 5:25–27; Rev 19:7–9; 21:2, 9–11). And that is where philosophy must come back to buttress theology, in Holy Scripture, where God has revealed himself as Creator (Rev 4:11), as "I AM" (Exod 3:14; John 8:58), and as the triune God (John 1:1; 2 Cor 13:14).

"Real" Relations: Clearing up the Classical Paradox

At this point, a brief critique of Hartshorne is appropriate because it bears weight on Oord's view as well and addresses the relational paradox Hartshorne and the process tradition observe in the classical view (which

---

165. Goad, "Simplicity," 110. Aquinas writes, "We should say that the relations we predicate of God temporally are only conceptually, not really, in him, since *there is a real relation where something really depends on something else*, whether absolutely or in a respect." Aquinas, *Power of God*, 7.9. Emphasis added.

166. Emery, *Trinitarian Thought*, 94, writes, "In God, relation is not something which *inheres*: it *is* what God is."

I touched on briefly in the previous section). Hartshorne's dipolar conception of God intended to fill the void the classical tradition created in its espousal, to use Hartshorne's words, of God who is in a "tyrant-subject relationship"[167] with the world; a God who is absolute, impersonal, and disconnected from his creation.[168] The eternality of God's being, particularly divine knowledge, renders successive relations incoherent. Therefore, according to Hartshorne, a God whose knowledge is absolute cannot exhibit relations—i.e., knowing and loving—with contingent creatures; therefore, if God is to have genuine relations with contingent creatures, then the relations themselves must be contingent. His solution of God having an abstract and concrete nature removes the paradoxes inimical to the Christian faith, as found in the classical view.[169] With that said, Hartshorne's God is temporal because part of God's nature is contingent on finite creatures. Oord follows suit with Hartshorne as noted above.

However, Merold Westphal refutes Hartshorne's assumptions of classical theism, particularly that of Aquinas. Westphal points out that Aquinas, in his *Summa Theologiae*, "makes use of the distinction between God as concrete and God as abstract, though not in [Hartshorne's] language."[170] Thomas notes that relations are *real*, in the sense that they are equally distributive and receptive (i.e., symmetrical relations, human-to-human), or they are *logical*, in that relations are asymmetrical because of the improper order of beings involved in the relations. For example, human love relations toward a canine would be an improper relation from a human point of view, thus logical, not *real*, because humans do not relate to a dog in true, *real* canine-to-canine relations.

Westphal points out only a careless reading of Aquinas would assume that he meant "real" compared to that which is "unreal" or "imaginary." Logical relations are *not* real in the sense that they do not exist in reality; rather, they are established in the mind. Some relations are purely of reason, as in the extreme between being and non-being. Other relations exist due to the "habitude [i.e., tendency or way of behaving] existing between two things according to some reality that belongs to both" (i.e., father and

---

167. Hartshorne, *Divine Relativity*, 44.

168. Hartshorne, *Divine Relativity*, 15.

169. The paradox, as Hartshorne sees it, is if God's essence can be absolute, thus unknowable, then "how can we know God as causally related to the world . . . if he has no relative being. If God is purely absolute, then the being which he enjoys simply in himself is his *only* being, and if this cannot be known, then it seems we can know or think *nothing* of God, either as he is in himself or not as he is in himself." Hartshorne, *Divine Relativity*, 15.

170. Westphal, "Temporality," 561.

son).[171] Some relations, Thomas writes, may exist in reality whereas some may exist in idea only. Relations in reality exist where there is a proper order of things;[172] relations in idea exist in an improper order.[173] For Thomas, God is related to his creatures; however, due to the improper ordering of the two (Creator-creature distinction), the relation is a reality only in the creature; in God, it is a relation of idea.[174] Thomas writes,

> Since therefore God is outside the whole order of creation, and all creatures are ordered to Him, and not conversely, it is manifest that creatures are really related to God Himself; whereas in God there is no real relation to creatures, but a relation only in idea, in as much as creatures are referred to Him. Thus, there is nothing to prevent these names [*Lord* and *Creator*] which import relation to the creature from being predicated of God temporally, not by reason of any change in Him, but by reason of the change of the creature; as a column is on the right of an animal, without change in itself, but by change in the animal.[175]

The mixed relation maintains the distinction between the independent and the dependent, expressing that God's presence, as the source of created being, is more intimate to his creatures than that which exists between creatures. Creatures are related to each other through a cause-and-effect relationship, in which the relation exists only in the medium of motion it produces (i.e., creatures are temporal, thus have motion, going from potency to act),[176] whereas God as the cause of *esse* in creatures, who is *Actus Purus*, is thus present to them by his very essence.

God, in bringing a creature into existence, creates a relation closer than a "mutually real relation"[177] that exists within creature-to-creature relationships. In God's act of creating, the creature becomes related to God

---

171. Aquinas, *ST*, 1.13.7.

172. By *order* Aquinas means ontological order.

173. And it is an improper order between God and man because "there is no common motion between them." Dodds, *Unchanging God*, 167.

174. Dodds, *Unchanging God*, 168, quoting, Shanely, *The Thomist Tradition*, 59, writes, "When God acts so as to bring creatures into relationship with him, all of the 'happening' is located in creation rather than in God." See Aquinas, *ST*, 1.45.3.

175. Aquinas, *ST*, 1.13.7. In the analogy using the column, Thomas is speaking of an animal's relation to a column, showing the improper order between the two. We cannot say *on the right* to a column unless we denote that the animal stands to the right of the column. The relation then is not in the column; rather, it is in the animal *to the right* of the column.

176. Duby, "Divine Action," 372.

177. Weinandy, *Does God Change?*, 92.

via his essence. Aquinas writes, "God is said to be in all things by essence, not indeed by the essence of the things themselves, as if He were of their essence; but by His own essence; because His substance is present to all things as the cause of their being."[178] Weinandy makes a salient point, when he notes the shortcomings of a pantheistic view of God because as such, only a "spark" of him, *not his entire being*, is present to the creature.[179]

The distinctions between the Creator and his creatures allows for God to be *a se*, distinct from his creation, while at the same time "for the utter intimacy of his presence to each creature as the source of its very to-be (*esse*)."[180] While Aquinas' language seems paradoxical, in that God is somehow unrelated but related to his creation, Westphal asks that "we must be prepared to forgive Thomas for living in the thirteenth century." He could have used language more "lucid" to us moderns, but, even then, he was able to defend his own language against such claims, as those made by Hartshorne.[181] It is challenging for modern readers to appropriate the language of *real* and *logical* from Aquinas's context.[182]

It seems we have competing philosophical themes, both of which are difficult to square up with Scripture. One view, however, preserves the immutability in God, *as depicted in Scripture* (Exod 3:14; Mal 3:6; Heb 6:8), in that because God's relation is logical to creatures, nothing can obfuscate it (cf. Acts 17:25). However, from a process construct, the contingent nature of the relations Hartshorne and Oord impose on God does not ensure God's relations to his creatures are as pure, intimate, and constant, due to the ontological order of the relation itself. Creature-to-creature relations are mutually subject to change; a Creator-to-creature relation, from the Creator's side (the logical of the mixed relation), is not, for he is "the Father of lights, who does not change like shifting shadows" (Jas 1:17b).

Creatures relate to each other through some mediating act; God relates to his creatures as he is, and therefore, creatures are *really* related to him,

---

178. Aquinas, *ST*, 1.8.3.

179. Weinandy, *Does God Change?*, 93.

180. Dodds, *Unchanging God*, 168–69.

181. Westphal, "Temporality," 564.

182. Hartshorne, in response to Westphal, clarifies that he did not take Aquinas's denial of relations between God and things to mean they were "imaginary." Hartshorne counters, insisting the problem still exists. Granting with respect to God, that in his knowing, the "thing known which is really related, while for the knowing the relation is in idea only." But "[i]f the 'in idea' pertains to God's idea," then, Hartshorne claims, "my point has been granted, the relation is really in God. If it means, in our idea, then we are back at my interpretation of Aquinas's sufficiently clear text, namely that the world is really related to God, not God to the world." Hartshorne, "The Dipolar Conception of Deity," 278.

but not the inverse.[183] From this metaphysic, one can state God is related to man by relationship of reason and with the elect through grace, mediated and communicated by the three divine persons of the Trinity, which is also by reason.[184] So, while God is directly present to all of creation as its Cause, by grace, the elect share in a unique communion with him, by which God brings a creature into relation with himself, mediated through the incarnation and the eternal Spirit. In this relationship, each believer does not "share" God with another believer; rather, the simpleness of the triune God entails his relating to a creature *as God* is, the complete fullness of himself present in and with the creature. The fullness of his infinite, eternal being means he cannot be divided nor does he need to move from one believer to another to relate; rather, he is everywhere and completely present and thus fully dynamic in his relation to his creatures. And that is why Aquinas speaks of God's logical relatedness to his creatures—because of his immediate and *complete* presence in his creatures. Creatures are not infinite in being and fullness; they are temporal creatures, "ordered to God as their beginning, continuation, and end,"[185] and therefore asymmetrical in relation to God.[186] If God had a *real* relation to the world, such a relation would put creatures and God on the same causal level. The only *real* relation(s) in God is that of the intra-Trinitarian processions that necessarily make God who he is, which God mediates by an act of divine grace to the elect. Because of the differences between Uncreated and created being, creatures cannot have direct, logical (i.e., ontologically constitutive) relations with God.[187] But God, who is the cause of goodness and love, "infuses and creates goodness" in his creatures,[188] thereby making the relation in his creatures a *real* relationship (*in the creature*) by which they can now participate in the divine mystical union, through the indwelt Spirit of God in the believer.

The Trinity: The "Hurdle" for Process Consistency

The ontological Trinity resolves the philosophical problem of how God can be a personal being without the need to relate with another contingent being. In process thought, as Oord acknowledges, a developed doctrine

---

183. Muller, "Incarnation," 28, writes, "God, as unmoved Mover, is the eternal one who not only *does* but also *must* relate to all things."
184. Kelly, "God," 202.
185. Vanhoozer, "Love without Measure?," 521.
186. Muller, "Real Relations," 674–78.
187. Webster, *God without Measure*, 121.
188. Aquinas, *ST*, 1.20.2.

of the Trinity is lacking.[189] And this goes for Oord's writings as well;[190] he merely affirms the triunity of God. I contend that he does so because the classical doctrine of the Trinity, as it stands, poses a major obstacle for his position: it renders creation unnecessary, even arbitrary. However, because of its distinctiveness to Christian theism, as a cardinal truth of the faith, I am of the opinion that process theists have refrained from any serious engagement or attempt to explicate the Trinity from a process perspective. I think this is the greatest obstacle for process theism, in that if it fully embraces the orthodox model of the Trinity (as open theists do), it is unable to avoid divine aseity in the strictest sense, with *creatio ex nihilo* as a logical outcome. The doctrine of the Trinity has aided Christian apologists in the affirmation of God as personal because it demonstrates, philosophically, how God can have personhood and be relational, while at the same time remaining independent and self-existent (i.e., God's aseity). But if Oord sides with this view to establish relationality in God, then it has devastating implications for his position.[191]

With that said, another problem emerges in Oord's commitment to God having an everlasting relationality with creation: it negates the necessity for God to be triune. God could be considered a relational being, apart from the Son and the Spirit because since God has always been creating and relating to a world, those relations, which Oord argues are *necessary* to God's nature, have always existed with God. The corollary of such a position is that one is philosophically justified in believing that the monadic God of Judaism, Islam, and the Jehovah's Witnesses is a personal being.[192] But as orthodox Christianity has affirmed, if the triune God has perfect relations within the triune God-head—which means because of the perfect relations shared between the Father, the Son, and the Spirit—then creation's existence is unnecessary to contribute to who God is, contrary to Oord. Scripture testifies to the existence of creation as an act of God's will (i.e., a decision to bring it into existence): "Our Lord and God, you are worthy to receive glory

---

189. Oord, "A Perfect Theology," 153–57.

190. In Oord, *ULG*, the words Trinity/triune/Trinitarian are found ten times, with eight instances occurring as part of a title in a cited reference, one time in the index, and once used to affirm that God's power does not allow him to be other than triune.

191. In *NOL*, Oord discusses the Trinity more often; however, the context of discussion is in the form of argumentation, in that Oord is trying to make the case that God's necessary, inner Trinitarian love is not relegated only to *that* relationship; rather, it is necessary to his creation as well.

192. Philosophically, the Trinity resolves the dilemma in speaking of the existence of love apart from persons required to appropriately exhibit love.

and honor and power, because you have created all things, and *by your will* they exist and were created" (Rev 4:11; emphasis added).

Another concern regarding Oord's view of an everlasting view of God and creation (i.e., what he calls God's *time-fullness*) is that orthodox Christianity, when discussing the begetting of the Son (generation of the Son from the Father), has articulated it in terms of an eternal act. Because we are temporal beings, naturally understanding acts carried out in time, we likewise understand cause and effect relationships along the same course. As it pertains to the begetting of the Son, if we maintained a temporal construct of the act of begetting, then the generation of the Son from the Father would be *sequential*, which would mean "there was a time when the Son was not"—truly an untenable position.[193]

Creatio ex Creatione a Natura Amoris

According to Oord's doctrine of creation, *Creatio ex Creatione a Natura Amoris*, he says that God has been creating "creatures from an everlasting chain consisting of creatures and universes,"[194] yet, he also states that "God *initially* created and continually creates in love from what [he] had previously created."[195] Process thought affirms that God created from a primordial chaos. How can it be said that God created *from* something prior in an everlasting and endless chain of creating? Did God's creative act have a beginning, or is it, as Oord says, an "*endless* chain that God consecutively makes"?[196] An endless chain is exactly *that*—endless—in either direction. Oord believes that God is "time-full"[197] and that "[t]emporal succession occurs" within the Trinity and in God's relations with creation.[198] In Oord's affirmation of a temporal succession, when he says that "each created thing, world, or universe itself had a starting point,"[199] his logic is correct. But, to say "God's creative process had no absolute beginning" is illogical because a process, by definition, has an origin, from which a series of actions then follow to achieve a particular

---

193. Helm, "Eternal Creation," 324, notes that divine causation does not necessarily imply an act of creation in time; rather, an act of creation *with* time. Gregory of Nazianzus explains that in saying the Son is eternally begotten of the Father, we are to understand the Son's generation from the Father as *from* him and not *after* him. Gregory of Nazianzus, *Oration*, 29.3.

194. Oord, "Creation in Love," 115.

195. Oord, *NOL*, 134. Emphasis added.

196. Oord, "Creation in Love," 115. Emphasis added.

197. Oord, *NOL*, 78.

198. Oord, *NOL*, 141.

199. Oord, "Creation in Love," 115.

end.[200] Furthermore, it is also illogical to say a process is beginningless,[201] if Oord believes God's existence is time full.

Oord writes, "Just as God has always existed and is without beginning, God has also been creating out of what God *previously* created. And God's creating is endless; it had no absolute beginning."[202] Logically speaking, if God has a beginningless existence and his "act" of creating is likewise beginningless, then God could not have created something out of something he *previously* created because nothing can come before or previously in an endless or beginningless series. Oord would have validated his argument if he did not state that God *initially* created and then continued to create.

Another puzzling statement from Oord: "There has been no first moment of God's creating, because there has never been a first moment in God's everlasting life."[203] If God has always been "creating new creatures from those [he] created previously"[204] (which is a process, is it not?), but there is no beginning and is endless, then I do not see how matter is ontologically distinct from God. Oord says his doctrine of creation "denies that God happened upon 'stuff' that predates or preexists God."[205] But then a few sentences later, he says, "There was never a time when God was not creating, and there was no absolute first creation."[206] If Oord posits a distinction between God and matter, with God as unoriginated and matter originate, then we have to conclude that God exists prior *to* matter. If not, and matter is eternal, then I think the only other alternative would be to conclude that matter would have to come from God, in exactly the same way as the Son emanates or generates from the Father, which is unacceptable.

In chapter 2 of this study, Oord, quoting Griffin, states that because God does not have a physical body, he cannot manipulate agents with bodies. But this assumption raises the question as to how God is able to create? If he does not create *ex nihilo*, but rather, he creates out of something he previously created, then what does God actually *do* in the creating process? Oord does not elaborate on how God creates; however, he believes that God created through evolution.[207] Evolutionary theory teaches that all human

200. Oord, "Creation in Love," 118.

201. Kallhovd, "Theology of Love," 69–70. The term *sempiternal* would be appropriate to categorize Oord and the process view of timelessness.

202. Oord, "Creation in Love," 117. Emphasis added. Oord admits this concept "presents a mental challenge . . . that's difficult to fathom!"

203. Oord, "Creation in Love," 118.

204. Oord, "Creation in Love," 115.

205. Oord, "Creation in Love," 117.

206. Oord, "Creation in Love," 117.

207. Oord, *ULG*, 52–56.

life began from one common ancestor, a simple life-form, that gradually developed to a more complex life-form; hence, it is a process, with an actual beginning. So, the question is, if God has been relating with his creation from eternity, how can "relating" occur with non-human organisms, which lack personhood and do not have the capacity to relate? After all, as Oord says, "Love requires relations."[208] Granted, a process view holds that entities have the capacity to relate in some fashion. However, love is a moral attribute. Non-personal entities do not have moral obligations, just as we observe in the animal kingdom. Oord does not make the proper distinction needed in his doctrine of creation that separates morally responsible creatures who should respond to God's loving call, who are also accountable to God in failing to respond, and the non-personal organisms who are not morally obligated to respond to God's loving call.

Within the triune Godhead, God's loving nature existed before creation, thus in his perfect being, God's loving nature manifests perfectly between all three persons and is therefore complete. We can argue this case based on the perfections of God; love is expressed perfectly between the members of the Trinity. So, why necessitate that God must create other creatures to love? Oord's definition of love, entails, "self-giving, others-empowering love," but why assume, as Elijah Hess points out, that the "others" necessarily implies material creatures?[209] The traditional view of the doctrine of creation has understood that God creates voluntarily. Oord says that God is not free to not love, but he is free to choose how he expresses love.[210]

Following his logic, God's *choosing* or *power* in love has primacy within his nature of love. We cannot think of love apart from God's will and power. Unacted love is meaningless. The exercising of love must flow from an agent that has the will and power to do so. Therefore, if God has the power to choose *how* he expresses love, as Oord affirms, then it follows that God could choose to have made creation as an expression of how he loves within the relations of the Trinity. As such, a doctrine of *ex nihilo* is entirely appropriate to affirm of God who is necessarily loving. A robust doctrine of the Trinity expresses that perfect, loving relations exist among the persons; therefore, God is not necessitated to love outside of it.

God's necessary love among the persons is extended *by choice* to creatures God decided to create for himself, for his own glory, those who are the Father's love-gift to the Son. We see this love-gift theme in the Gospel of John, where, within the Father-Son relationship exists an explicit love

---

208. Oord, "Evolutionary Theory," 294.
209. Hess, Review of *Uncontrolling Love of God*, 476.
210. Oord, *ULG*, 162.

terminology.[211] In John 3:35, John, with the purpose of validating that Jesus is the One from above—from God, records Jesus saying, "the Father loves the Son and has given all things in his hands." And this "act of giving (δίδωμι) is the dominant medium of the Father expressing love for His Son."[212]

In tracing this out in John's Gospel, we see that the "Father gives the Son 'life in himself' (5:27a), 'authority to judge' (5:27b; cf. 5:22), 'work' (5:36), 'sheep' (10:29); 'authority over all people' (17:2); 'those ... out of the world' (17:6; cf. 17:24), 'words' (17:8), 'the name' (17:11–12); 'glory' (17:22, 24; cf. 13:31–32), and 'the cup' (18:11)."[213] And the specific gift the Father gives to the Son, is that of a people, a believing people (*ho pisteuōn*; cf. John 6:35), who will come to him (John 6:37). Thaddeus Williams observes: "There is a chronology intrinsic to John's logic: Jesus' gifts of love are not such because they first came to the Son, but they come to the Son because they are first the Father's gifts of love to the Son."[214]

John 17 provides the summation of this expression of love between Father and Son, whereby the Father and the Son *choose* to share the love they have between them with a people God created. Jesus says, "I have revealed your name to the people you gave me from the world" (John 17:6), fulfilling the Father's will for the Son that "[he] should lose none of those he has given [him]" (John 6:37 cf. Isa 43:4–7). And Matthew, capturing Jesus' desire in revealing and sharing this unique *knowing*, records him saying: "No one knows the Son except the Father, and no one knows the Father except the Son and anyone to whom the Son desires to reveal him" (11:27). Between the Father and the Son exists a love-union, which we see in John 17:6 as that of knowing the Father's name that he has given to his Son, due to his obedience (cf. Phil 2:9). And it was the Son's prerogative, his choosing, to share his Father's name with a people God had chosen for himself (Acts 15:14, 17).

Oord says God has always been creating; evolutionary theory has a point of origin; melding these positions together creates an incoherent synthesis. Evolution proposes that life had a starting point where nothing existed, no life, then life "sprang" into existence from non-life. Whereas Oord believes that God and *a* living creation have always existed. On a scriptural and pastoral note, Oord's evolutionary account has consistency issues. In his doctrine of creation, he does not take into his billions-of-years model the New Testament depiction of the immediate arrival of the new heavens

---

211. John 3:35; 5:20; 10:17; 14:31; 15:9–10; 17:23–26.
212. Williams, *Love*, 139.
213. Williams, *Love*, 139.
214. Williams, *Love*, 139–40.

and new earth after the Day of the Lord (Rev 21:1–2).[215] Furthermore, the greater concern for the saints who eagerly wait for the redemption of their bodies is: *how* can God, who lacks unilateral power, bring it to fruition? If God cannot unilaterally exert sovereign power, which would include bringing judgment upon the godless, then it seems that bodily redemption is hopeless, since that must happen first.

The implication of Oord's sovereignless-God is that the godless must willingly embrace their own rebellion as immoral and willingly subject themselves to God's judgment. What hope does that provide, in light of Romans 8:7–8, which says those of the flesh are hostile to God and do not submit to his law; in fact, Paul says they are "unable to do so"? Revelation 9:13–21 paints a very bleak picture for such hope, in that after the sixth trumpet of judgment that brings death to a third of the human race, by plague, it is not persuasive enough to cause the rest of the godless people "to stop worshiping demons and idols of gold, silver, stone, and wood . . . [and did] not repent of their murders, their sorceries, their sexual immorality, or their thefts" (9:20–21). Therefore, to adopt such a model as Oord proposes creates a serious pastoral concern. Oord's philosophical framework has consistency issues. And the contradictory nature of his conclusions reveals a commitment to a process metaphysic that denies unilateral, determinative power in God.

Creatures and God as Essentially Free—Evaluation and Critique

In other models of free-will theism, God limits himself and "*could* withdraw or override creaturely powers."[216] According to Oord, in *essential* free-will theism, no room is given, nor is there the "metaphysical"[217] possibility for God to do such actions. God cannot "unilaterally determine others because all actual individuals are essentially free."[218] The greatest contention process theists have with classical theology's view of God is in its affirmation that God is perfect in goodness and has the power to unilaterally overturn human freedom, but he does not do so to prevent horrendous evils.[219] Process

---

215. As Waltke and Yu, *An Old Testament Theology*, 180, point out.

216. Oord, "Process Wesleyan Theodicy," 199. As in traditional open theism (see Sanders, *God Who Risks*, 238–42) and forms of classical free-will theism (see Basinger, *Freewill Theism*, 32–36).

217. Oord, "Process Wesleyan Theodicy," 200.

218. Oord, "Process Wesleyan Theodicy," 200.

219. For Oord, "[I]t is difficult if not impossible to wholeheartedly worship the God who *could* have prevented these [sic] evil." Oord, *NOL*, 143.

theists assert that if such a being existed, we should see displays of divine coercive power more often.[220]

Misconception of Coercion

Oord believes his process concept of God is superior to that of classical theism. In fact, a God of love who is controlling "is fictional."[221] However, classical free-will theist David Basinger makes the claim that there is no good reason to affirm that a process model of God is superior to the classical view of God.[222] Basinger argues that the process concept of "coercion" is misleading in that one does not have to define unilateral coercion, in the process sense, as an act of entirely controlling another, so that he is devoid of all determinative power.[223] Basinger offers a few examples of unilateral control over another while at the same time the one being controlled is not devoid of the power to determine one's self: (1) A parent unilaterally controls his/her child's behavior, as in stopping a fight or having him go to bed. The child still retains some measure of self-determination, either the power to resist physically or the desire to act contrary to his parents' wishes or even plot revenge. (2) A society that commissions a police force to protect the community is not asking for it to remove a felon's self-determinative power; rather, it is being asked to unilaterally control his behavior in a manner that denies him the ability to carry out his criminal tendencies.[224]

Basinger concludes that if God can control others without coercing them (in the process sense of the word), then the process theist's (thus Oord) argument is irrelevant. And in explicating "coercion," Basinger puts process theism in the defensive position, in that one can ask if God (of process theology) can unilaterally stop individuals from evil actions, given the examples of unilateral activity that do not destroy the self-determinative power of the creature, why does he not do so? Basinger's point must be noted.

While Oord defines coercion in the sense of one *completely* controlling another,[225] Oord (and process thinkers alike) has mistakenly imposed this understanding of coercion onto the classical view of God. The Westminster Confession of Faith states that God's decree from eternity comes to

---

220. Process theist Lewis Ford writes, "[I]f God has the power to actualize the good unambiguously, then his goodness requires that he do so." Ford, *Lure of God*, 23.

221. Oord, *ULG*, 181.

222. Basinger, "Divine Persuasion," 332.

223. Griffin, *God*, 266.

224. Basinger, "Divine Persuasion," 336.

225. Oord, *NOL*, 127.

pass; however, by no means "is violence offered to the will of creatures."[226] In other words, the Confession is affirming that God does not violate a creature's will in the sense of taking away its self-determinative ability. In line with the confessional view above, the view taken in this study favors a *compatibilist* understanding of freedom. According to this view, "genuine free human action is compatible with causal conditions that decisively incline the will without constraining it."[227]

God does not act like a puppeteer, who takes over his creatures' minds, forcing them to act against their wills. While God's will is behind man's will, man always *freely* chooses what he most wants to do. Interestingly, Oord's assertion that God compels creatures is more "Calvinistic" than Calvin is. Pertaining to man's choosing to sin, Calvin writes, "man, as he was corrupted by the Fall, sinned willingly, not unwillingly or by compulsion; by the most eager inclination of his heart, not by forced compulsion; by the prompting of his own lust, not by compulsion from without."[228] If man is compelled to sin from an outside force, then he is no longer culpable for his inherent sinful nature.

Oord's solution addresses Basinger's argument by saying because God is not a localized physical body, he lacks the capacity to unilaterally coerce in this manner. And as a Spirit, God *exclusively* exerts compelling power, in which he applies indirect force through persuading local, physical bodies to act. With that said, Oord's solution still does not satisfy Basinger's objection.

Oord offers the illustration of God's mind influencing other minds, only through persuasion. But Basinger provides an example of psychological manipulation in the positive sense, where a child desires to be a sports star and the parent, knowing such desires, convinces him to take up a particular regiment of sleep to get the rest he needs so that the child can attain his aspirations. Because of the child's desire to achieve his goal, he understands that he needs to obey his parents and follow the regiment. In this situation, the child is not constrained to act against his will; however, the parent has brought it about for his child to act according to his demand. And the same can be said of advertisers and social media, using manipulative tactics to get society to change its behaviors. Basinger's examples demonstrate that localized, physical beings have the capacity to coerce without using physical force or entirely controlling another agent. And if the process God is unable to coerce creatures in the same manner that conforms to his desires and will, as the classical God can, then Basinger's criticism holds.

---

226. *Westminster Confession of Faith*, 3.1.
227. Feinberg, *No One*, 637.
228. Calvin, *Institutes*, 2.3.5.

I will expound further on the subject of coercion in chapter 5 as it pertains to Oord's doctrine of providence, which will evaluate Oord's view of divine power situated in the biblical text. My intention will be to demonstrate that, as it pertains to divine power, Scripture finds wider agreement with a classical reading of the Bible than a process approach.

Conclusion

In Oord's acceptance of the DDS, as he understands it, my critique of his position demonstrates an inconsistency within his own process philosophical framework, particularly in his insistence of the interrelatedness of God to the world and the world to God. Though Oord has attempted to offer a view of God that is not overly dependent on creation as traditional process philosophy advocates, Oord's view falls short of his intentions and needs to be revaluated and reformulated if he hopes to offer an alternative doctrine of God that is compatible with Evangelicalism.

Positively speaking, I addressed the issue of how the DDS can be reconciled with the *proper articulation* of the classical doctrines of impassibility, immutability, and the triunity of God further establishing consistency in a classical view of God. And lastly, the orthodox doctrine of the Trinity, *the* quintessential doctrine of the Christian faith, poses the greatest obstacle for Oord's process metaphysic. The implications that come with affirming the orthodox view of the Trinity are disastrous for a process view of God.

The primary concern with process philosophy is that it proposes a view of divine relationality between God and his creation that blurs the line of the Creator-creature distinction—an ontological necessity in orthodox Christian theism. Oord's attempt to promote a process philosophical construct that delineates that distinction proved unsuccessful. And lastly, siding with Basinger, there is no good reason to affirm that a process model of God is superior to the classical view of God because a God who can only persuade yet never be able to unilaterally coerce (as defined here) cannot guarantee any outcome according to his good and perfect will. From a process view, then, creatures are more capable than God in using non-physical power to bring about a particular state of affairs.

In the next chapter, I will evaluate Oord's divine-love theology, which Oord constructs based on what he believes is the general definition of love in the Bible. Others have approached this topic, returning with an understanding that love in Scripture his very nuanced and complex, concluding that to delineate a strict definition does not allow *love* to be faithful to Scripture.

3: Oord's Divine-Love Theology

The Primacy of Love

WHILE OORD'S DISSERTATION DEVELOPS and contributes to his theology of love, his book, *The Nature of Love: A Theology*, captures the more important elements.[1] So, I will start my evaluation there, incorporating his other pertinent writings. With Oord being referred to as a love theologian, this chapter is obviously going to be important in my evaluation. For Oord's model of Evangelical process theology to hold up to his claim of scriptural consistency, his definition of love needs to be *thoroughly* derived from the biblical text.

In *The Nature of Love*, Oord establishes the grounds for proper theological inquiry and formulation—*the primacy of love*. In studying love in the Scriptures, Oord observes that before Christ came and revealed "God's nature most clearly," the biblical authors thought love to be "*the,* primary attribute of God."[2] Canonically speaking, the Bible as a whole expresses this truth. And its primacy in the Christian faith distinguishes it from all other religions.[3] Oord writes, "If love is the center of the biblical witness and the core of Christian experience, it should be the primary criterion for theology. Love should be the orienting concern and continual focus for speaking systematically about theology. We should discard ideas or theories that undermine love."[4] Oord's statement reveals that *love* is axiomatic in how he reads and interprets Scripture and thinks theologically. Because he understands that God's divine action in the world is not coercive (but rather—through prevenient grace—he empowers and inspires creatures to be agents of love and transformation in the world), causal activity can be gauged using a measurement of love: "God's activity is most clearly expressed when an event

---

1. Oord, personal email to author, December 2, 2017.
2. Oord, *NOL*, 2.
3. Oord, *NOL*, 2.
4. Oord, *NOL*, 2.

profoundly promotes overall well-being. [And] the presence or absence of creaturely love indicates the degree to which God is active."[5]

While open theism elevates God's love as the defining and guiding characteristic of all that he does, Oord's problem with the current model is that it does not follow through with its definition completely. While it *theoretically* makes it primary, it does not do so *metaphysically*. For Oord, love "functions underneath [his] full consciousness at the worldview level and defines what is considered axiomatic, valuable, and criteriological."[6]

In establishing love as the primary criterion, Oord observes how theologians Millard Erickson, Paul Tillich, and Karl Barth overreach in choosing their theological themes.

Millard Erickson chooses God's magnificence, focusing on God's greatness, power, and knowledge, thus downplaying love to one attribute among others. Erickson's theology is inconsistent with God's love because in adopting a view of sovereignty and predestination, the "power God exerts makes creaturely freedom and salvation meaningless."[7] Oord assumes a libertarian view of freedom,[8] another key element in his understanding of love, particularly in *how* God loves creatures. He sees Tillich's view of God as the "ground for all being" as flawed because it makes God impersonal, un-responsive, and static. Oord rejects Barth's theology, saying it is flawed because he does not include God's love for the world; "God doesn't necessarily love us."[9]

Following his assessment, Oord outlines why formal theology[10] is not founded on love. Some Christians cannot reconcile reason and love. When the logic of love (i.e., "love that is placed at the center of theology")[11] causes some to arrive at conclusions that oppose conventional theology, "some theologians suffer a loss of nerve."[12] It is here, Oord says,

---

5. Oord, "Love as a Methodological," 96.

6. Yong, "Divine Omniscience," 243. In this article, Yong surveys open theism and classical theism, identifying the key axioms that guide and govern each system's view of God, the God-world relationship, and interpretation of Scripture. While Yong points out how both sides construct a doctrine of God as viewed through the lens of a particular dominating metaphor, for Oord, love is beyond metaphor; it is *metaphysical*.

7. Oord, *NOL*, 6.

8. This will be defined in chapter 5.

9. Oord, *NOL*, 7.

10. Oord uses the term "formal theology" often, which refers to one's foundational construct of Christian theism.

11. Oord, *NOL*, 9.

12. Oord, *NOL*, 10.

mystery functions like a blank check on which one writes whatever dogma desired. Mystery can be the escape hatch allowing one to wiggle out of the uncomfortable choices a theology of love requires. Appeal to mystery in these ways seems at worst disingenuous and at best an implicit recognition that more work has to be done.[13]

The appeal to mystery is a common denominator shared by classical theists. For open/relational theists, the idea that God can have a *hidden* or *mysterious* will is an objectionable assertion. However, Oord concedes that mystery will always have a place in theology, and while "the logic of love does not appeal to the illogical, it cannot overcome all mystery."[14]

Lastly, Oord sees a lack of consistency in the biblical language of love. Even though such texts as 1 John 4:9, "God's love was revealed among us in this way: God sent his one and only Son into the world so that we might live through him," show God's loving act toward the world, according to Oord, the Bible does not offer a clear "internally consistent" definition of love.[15] Oord rightly recognizes that all actions associated with the word *love* do not mean the action was properly loving.[16] And he shies away from a compilation approach, cataloguing the various forms of love found in Scripture because "it fails to acknowledge that we already intuit something about which actions are loving and which are not."[17]

The Holy Spirit, Oord writes, is what empowers, inspires, conditions, and even adjudicates (within), a Christian's intuition. Such an informative means needs to be considered in how one formulates a definition of love.[18] Love in society has diverse meanings, therefore, writes Oord, "reclaiming the centrality of love in theology requires redefining love carefully and from a biblically oriented perspective."[19] Because of the diverse meanings of love, Oord etches out two "mutually enriching paths" toward delineating one meaning of love in the Bible: (1) to examine the Bible to determine if one meaning of love dominates; (2) define love clearly; a good definition of love corresponds with the meaning of love dominant in the biblical witness and "relates well with our best understanding of human nature and existence in general."[20] Thus,

13. Oord, *NOL*, 10.
14. Oord, *NOL*, 10.
15. Oord, *NOL*, 12.
16. E.g., 1 John 3:18.
17. Oord, *NOL*, 17.
18. Oord, *NOL*, 17.
19. Oord, *NOL*, 9.
20. Oord, *NOL*, 13.

the aim of his work is to deduce a general meaning of love in Scripture that "will play the central role in defining love well and regarding love as the core of Christian theology."[21] With that said, it is important to identify the *kind* of love that forms the foundation of Oord's theology.

The Primacy of Love—Critical Evaluation

Oord contends, along with the biblical authors, that love is the primary, metaphysical attribute of God,[22] thus it should be the primary criterion for theology. No doubt, 1 John 4:8, "God is love," is axiomatic to Oord's theology.[23] However, as observed in the biographical introduction, Oord believes a particular definition of love functions as primary in God, and it should be our theological and philosophical starting point in constructing a theology. His starting point does not merit critique at the moment; rather, it generates questions and concerns for working out later, which may reveal flaws in his methods, proving to be problematic in formulating a doctrine of God consistent with Christian orthodoxy. Does Oord's commitment to love's primacy (metaphysically speaking) disrupt his theological methodology and his doctrine of God? An unbiblical definition of love as the starting point will prove disastrous in a theology that makes love—according to such a definition—the primary attribute in God.

In his book, *The Difficult Doctrine of the Love of God*, D. A. Carson observes that the contemporary culture's sentimentalized view of God's love has greatly impacted the church, resulting in its "inability to think through the fundamental questions that alone enable us to maintain a doctrine of

---

21. Oord, *NOL*, 13.

22. Oord, *NOL*, 2.

23. John Peckham, importantly, remarks that while many take this passage to mean God's very essence is love, such assertions run into problems when faced with other passages, such as "God is light" (1 John 1:5) or "God is a consuming fire" (Deut 4:24). Peckham, *Love of God*, 252. Colin Kruse writes, "When the author says that 'God is love,' he is not making an ontological statement describing what God is in his essence; rather, he is, as the following verses (4:9–10) reveal, speaking about the loving nature of God revealed in saving action on behalf of humankind." Kruse, *Letters of John*, 157. And Calvin, also, clarifies that the apostle is not speaking "of the essence of God, but only shews what he is found to be by us." Calvin, *Catholic Epistles*, 239. And Daniel L. Akin observes a tendency of abstraction in process thought to equate God is love as love is God. Akin, *1, 2, 3 John*, 178. Augustine, however, seems to approve of the "flip" in his homily on 1 John, when he writes, "'And again, by what hast thou come to know this? 'Love is God.' . . . Love could not be more exceedingly commended to then that it should be called God." Augustine, *Hom.*, 8.14.

God in biblical proportion and balance."[24] Furthermore, we must call into question the very definition of divine "love" pitted against the divine "will." For example, evil's existence proves that the universe does not primarily seek to "promote well-being" for humanity.[25] The Old Testament expresses that God "loves righteousness and justice" (Ps 33:5; cf. 11:7), and he shows his love to those who keep his commandments (Exod 20:6), with covenant faithfulness as a condition for Israel to be recipients of God's love. But we also see passages setting God's love over his wrath (Exod 34:6; Ps 103:8).[26] Such complexities, as noted above, indicate that a biblical doctrine of love is not a one-note motif; rather, it is a thematic nexus.

Love, as the logical starting point before God's other attributes, creates a dilemma for relational theists in that Scripture makes God's Son, not humanity, the primary object of the Father's love (John 17:22, 24, 26. cf. Matt 3:27). With Christ as the primary object of God's love, his motives are grounded primarily in his love for the Son.[27] Regarding John 17:24, Carson observes that Jesus wants his followers to see "the glory he enjoyed before his mission because of the Father's love for him. The ultimate hope of Jesus' followers thus turns on the love of the Father for the Son." And commenting on 17:26, he writes, "The crucial point is that this text does not simply make these followers the objects of God's love (as in v. 23), but promises that they will be transformed, as God is continually made known to them, that God's own love for his Son will become their love."[28] While God makes his elect the object of his love, thus bringing them into a union the Father and Son share, the love that the Father has for the Son serves as the divine-love paradigm God lavishes onto believers, which is done through Jesus who "has made God's name known, . . . so that God's love for [him] may be in them as he is in them."[29] And Wesleyan scholar, Joseph Dongell, writes, "love characterizes the perfect unity between the Father and the Son."[30]

In fact, many Bible passages situate God *himself* as the primary object of love, or rather, the chief end of God (e.g., Isa 43:6–7; 48:9; Jer 13:11; Ps 106:7–8).[31] Also, metaphysically placing the attribute of love first, as Oord

---

24. Carson, *Difficult Doctrine*, 15.
25. To be observed later, "to promote well-being" is a formative element in his definition of love.
26. Carson, *Difficult Doctrine*, 20.
27. Carson, *John*, 569.
28. Carson, *John*, 569.
29. Köstenberger, *John*, 500.
30. Dongell, *John*, 208.
31. Cf. Ezek 20:14; 36:22–23, 32; John 17:1; 2 Thess 1:9–10. The ministry of John Piper is shaped by such a view. See Piper, *God's Passion*.

does, gives love a transcendent status over God. Based on Paul's sequence of salvation in Romans 8:28–30, the placement of God's foreknowledge (i.e., his divine will), suggests it holds the logical and ontological priority in God, over love.[32] But how can we rank God's attributes, giving one primacy above the rest? Is God's love sovereign *over* God? Or, more appropriately, "is it *God himself* who is love?"[33]

While Christian tradition has maintained a unity in God and an equality of his attributes, Oord concludes that the theologies of Millard Erickson, Paul Tillich, and Karl Barth are inadequate because "love does not function as the orienting concern."[34] As noted, Oord has developed his own definition of love, serving as the general, unified theme of love in Christian theology, which he argues is God's attribute of love. Oord's orienting of love to a place of primacy is *metaphysical;* "God's . . . love is a necessary, eternal, and logically primary aspect of the divine nature."[35] To make a metaphysical claim elevates one attribute above the rest in God's being,[36] thus a violation of the law of irreducible complexity at the divine level. Therefore, it is more appropriate to make a religious claim regarding the primacy of love in God's character, in that he demonstrates love (in the *agape* sense) in reaching down to his creation, taking on flesh, and dying on a cross.[37]

Oord concludes that conventional theologians do not place love at the "center of reflection of God"[38] because love has diverse meanings, and the Bible is not consistent in defining it. Those who cannot reconcile love and reason appeal to mystery because logical love opposes their theology and/or philosophy. And Oord says we should follow the apostle Paul's command in Colossians 2:8 to avoid being held "captive through philosophy."

However, Oord leaves out the rest of the passage. Paul actually says not to be taken "captive through philosophy . . . *based on human tradition*" (emphasis added). Interestingly, following his remark about philosophy, he comments in a footnote that process philosophy is the "best current available . . . system or *tradition* for situating a robust theology of Christian love . . . as proposed by Alfred North Whitehead and Charles Hartshorne."[39] His

32. Peckham, *Love of God*, 271–72.
33. Grudem, *Systematic Theology* (1st ed.), 178.
34. Oord, *NOL*, 5.
35. Oord, *ULG*, 165.
36. Herman Bavinck reminds us that "love is not the essence of God in the sense that it is the center and core of God's being and the other attributes are its modes, for all the attributes are equally God's being." Bavinck, *Reformed Dogmatics*, 2:215–16.
37. Brown, "Love," 71.
38. Oord, *NOL*, 7.
39. Oord, *NOL*, 12n46.

statement, again, raises a concern regarding the kind/type of Christian love he advocates, as well as a commitment to philosophy over exegesis.

Oord's view of mystery as some form of escape hatch shows that he has not taken all the nuances of the "difficult doctrine of love" into consideration. John C. Peckham asks, "How does one adequately address such an integral, complex, and pivotal theological concept?"[40] An appeal to mystery is not disingenuous; rather, to acknowledge that at some point the sidewalk ends demonstrates humility and a healthy fear of the Lord.[41] Thomas Weinandy's statement regarding theological inquiry is a helpful reminder:

> Many theologians today having embraced the Enlightenment presuppositions and the scientific method that is fostered, approach theological issues as if they were scientific problems to be solved rather than mysteries to be discerned and clarified. However, the true goal of theological inquiry is not the resolution of theological problems, but the discernment of what the mystery of the faith is. *Because God, who can never be fully comprehended, lies at the heart of all theological enquiry, theology by its nature is not a problem solving enterprise, but rather a mystery discerning enterprise.*[42]

Contemporary relational theism is an abrogation of the classical understanding of God's love in terms of divine sovereignty—his unilateral activity to will and do good.[43] As Kevin Vanhoozer observes, "The problem is not *that* God loves, but rather *what* God's love is."[44] Geoffrey Grogan's biblical-theological study of God's love yielded nineteen distinctions expressed in Scripture.[45] He ended his investigation with an exegetical study of 1 John, concluding that while love is the central attribute in God, "love's very definition depends on its relation to other qualities."[46] Don Carson observes *some* of the different ways the Bible speaks of God's love, showing it is multi-faceted. Five distinctions he observes are: (1) *The peculiar love between the Father and the Son* (John 3:35; 5:20). (2) *God's providential love over his creation* (Gen 1; Matt 6). (3) *God's salvific posture toward fallen humanity* (John 3:16; 15:19; 1 John 2:2). (4) *God's efficacious and selective love of his elect* (Deut 7:7–8; 10:45; Mal 1:2–3; Eph 5:25). (5) *God's love as sometimes provisional*

---

40. Peckham, *Love of God*, 15.
41. That is essentially Paul's conclusion in Romans 11:33–36.
42. Weinandy, *Does God Suffer?*, 32. Emphasis added.
43. Vanhoozer, "Introduction," 7.
44. Vanhoozer, "Introduction," 7.
45. Grogan, "Biblical Theology," 51–64.
46. Grogan, "Biblical Theology," 66.

and conditional (based on obedience) toward his elect (Exod 20:6; Ps 103:8, 9–11, 13, 17–18; John 15:9, 10; Jude 21).[47]

Carson warns against absolutizing or making one of these biblical ways of love a "controlling grid" in talk of God's love.[48] Each one is riddled with difficulties if taken to such extremes. For example, restricting God's love to mere general providence makes God's love too distant from the persons he created, which downplays the Bible's emphasis on God's indwelling Spirit residing in the hearts of his people. If an intra-Trinitarian model is emphasized, then all of humanity shares in this love, by merely *existing*,[49] which creates inconsistencies when the Bible speaks of wrath, love of the elect, and the cross. And God's specific love for his elect can promote a hyper-Calvinistic leaning, whereas conditioning God's love strictly through obedience leads to merit theology and an improper fear of the Lord.[50]

Oord's statement regarding the lack of an internally consistent definition of love raises the point that maybe one does not exist. Vincent Brümmer remarks that as soon as one observes all the difficulties that emerge in the various attempts by systematic theologians in distilling a concept of love from the Bible, it is readily apparent that "one unambiguous biblical concept of love in the Bible" is a "doubtful presupposition."[51] Formulating a definition that captures all the nuances of love in Scripture is, quite frankly, presumptuous. Oord concedes this point, in critiquing Anders Nygren's argument that *agape* is the appropriate form of Christian love, when he writes, "In sum, the Bible is far from uniform in its understanding of *agape*. . . . To be true to Christian scripture, we cannot talk about *the* biblical understanding of *agape*."[52]

Since the inception of the Christian faith, two millennia ago, an "internally consistent" definition of love has failed to emerge . . . *until* Oord? Many who have undertaken a study of the doctrine of love recognize the great diversity love has in the Bible, yet do, however, identify a governing theme in God's love.[53] With that said, we should take heed of the inherent

---

47. Carson, *Difficult Doctrine*, 17–21.
48. Carson, *Difficult Doctrine*, 21.
49. Process thought upholds this dynamic in God's relation to the world.
50. Carson, *Difficult Doctrine*, 23.
51. Brümmer, *Model of Love*, 31.
52. Oord, "Love Racket," 936n9.
53. Peckham, *Love of God*, 65, argues for a canonical view of divine love, but qualifies his view, stating that no single aspect "should be selected and declared to be the meaning of love" (Peckham's comment is actually addressed to Oord in his book). See also Newlands, *Love of God*, 18–19, who writes, "the centrality of the love of God has always been an interpretation of the New Testament record in terms of God's self-giving

problems associated in making one aspect of God's love in the Bible central, or rather, primary, in God. And Oord's aim in formulating a definition that provides a general meaning of love, serving "as a key aspect of an adequate theology . . . [and] generally descriptive of God's love" is risky.[54]

A Definition of Love

In *The Nature of Love*, Oord presents his definition of love: "To love is to act intentionally, in sympathetic/empathetic response to God and others, to promote overall well-being."[55] He further clarifies that God influences all loving actions, "purposefully done hoping to encourage, create, or sustain something good."[56] His definition of love applies to what he believes "should be regarded, generally speaking, as the love that both God and creatures express."[57] Oord says that the *imago Dei* in man establishes the basis for such a definition, creating a connection that "makes possible the use of love language to describe that which creaturely and divine love share in common."[58] He then details the components of his definition to clarify them further, which provides the basis for his theology of love to follow.

To promote overall well-being. This point he derives from his understanding of the *hesed* language tradition of Judaism, which is often translated as "steadfast love." *Hesed* love, he states, is "reserved for ideal ethical actions, or what the Hebrew authors called *righteousness*. . . . When I use the word *love*, therefore, I follow the practice of the *hesed* tradition."[59] He refers to Luke 6:35; Matt 5:44–45; John 3:16; 1 John 4:9. These texts demonstrate love as a blessing to others, Christian and non-Christian. Oord quantifies the love commandments as an example of God's general love for creation (Ps 145:9; 136:1; Exod 34:6) throughout the Bible (1 Thess 5:15; 2 Thess 2:16–17; Rom 12:21; 1 Cor 8:1b; 1 Pet 3:9; 1 John 3:16–17) to support his claim that "love entails doing good—i.e., promoting well-being."[60]

---

in the sacrifice of his son, and in Jesus' self-giving to God and mankind. Here is the true paradeigmatic [sic] structure of God's nature"; "[The] one great overriding theme [of the Bible]—namely, that the love of God is a love completely for the undeserving" (Morris, *Testaments of Love*, 271); "Do you wish to see God's love? Look at the cross" (Carson, *Difficult Doctrine*, 70).

54. Oord, *NOL*, 17.
55. Oord, *NOL*, 17.
56. Oord, *NOL*, 17.
57. Oord, *DL*, 178.
58. Oord, *DL*, 180.
59. Oord, "Love Racket," 928.
60. Oord, *NOL*, 19.

Furthermore, in promoting well-being, love promotes holiness—promoting *wholeness*. Holiness theology is a distinctive of Wesleyanism, Oord's theological heritage. Relational holiness is "our moment-by-moment response to God's love" where "each [Christian] sets out on an open-ended and largely unplanned adventure," choosing options "that produce happiness and wholeness" or "unjustified suffering and evil."[61]

The nature of well-being is that of peace—full-bodied *shalom*. Doing good and promoting well-being includes helping with living necessities, self-worth, medical care, and physical fitness. And it also includes encouraging Christians and promoting good Christian virtues.[62] Oord writes, "*Overall* also reminds us that justice plays an important role in love. When we become aware that doing good to one or a few obviously hurts the many or the whole, the justice of love demands we seek the common good."[63] And because God loves the world, *overall* denotes that love has a broader context. The loving reign of God has come; however, creatures must respond in love to contribute to his Kingdom.[64]

In sympathetic/empathetic response to God and others. Oord writes, "Love is inherently relational. Love takes at least two. . . . An act of love presupposes past relations and the possibility of future relations."[65] To sympathize, Oord writes, "is to be internally influenced by the other such that one's own experience is partially constituted by the other."[66] Sympathy and empathy are incorporated into his definition because they "remind us that a real relational bond exists between lover and others. This bond partly determines the existence of each person."[67] The strength of Oord's view is that he seeks to repristinate the relationality of God, which he says much of Christian theology has "underemphasized" or even "ignored."[68] Such an approach is helpful in that many who have a disdain for religion do so because of the unfortunate nominalist notions that pervade in a secularist view of deity. Oord wants people to see that God is personal and God is love, and "[w]e cannot understand love well when we ignore relationality."[69]

---

61. Oord and Lodahl, *Relational Holiness*, 75, 82–83.
62. Oord, *NOL*, 19.
63. Oord, *NOL*, 20.
64. Oord, *NOL*, 20.
65. Oord, *NOL*, 21.
66. Oord, "Love Racket," 926.
67. Oord, *NOL*, 22.
68. Oord, *NOL*, 22.
69. Oord, *NOL*, 22.

God is personal in his being and because he is love, "we love because he loved us first" (1 John 4:19). And from this passage, Oord holds to the "idea" theologians refer to as *prevenient grace*, in which God acts lovingly[70] first toward humans who are then empowered to *freely* respond in love. He sees "God [as] an actual, causal agent to whose noncoercive inspiration, or 'call,' creatures respond appropriately when expressing love." God *preveniently* "'walks ahead of us,' enabling us to choose salvation freely , . . relat[ing] to us by acting first in every moment to provide us with opportunities for action."[71]

Oord identifies and shows the inconsistency of various forms of love associated with relationships, sex and romance, devotion and worship, fondness and affection, and the church. While the love forms are imbalanced if taken to be absolute, Oord points out the profundity and uniqueness of expressing love within the church. Importantly, Oord states that "the person not engaged with others in the body of Christ stunts his or her capacity to love and feel loved."[72] In fact, Oord remarks on the impossibility of certain expressions of love, apart from a church context, because of the uniqueness of the body of believers (Col 3:14). And these love forms cannot be expressed unless one has responded in faith to Jesus Christ.[73]

To act intentionally. Love is intentional because the Bible commands the promotion of well-being and love toward one another. Oord writes, "The motive facet of intention says we must properly do good."[74] Human freedom, according to Oord, entails moral responsibility, and people have a choice to act good or evil. "To be free is to make choices that are not entirely dependent on external conditions that make it the case that one cannot do otherwise."[75] The deliberate nature in acting in love means such "actions contain decisions with some degree of freedom."[76] If love is coerced, then "love is meaningless."[77] A definitive element of intentional love is in the mode of self-sacrifice. Oord claims that it is wrong to define love as *exclusively* self-sacrificial; it is unbiblical.[78] Scripture affirms self-love. Since God loves all creatures, and since we are called to imitate God's love,

---

70. Oord, *NOL*, 22.
71. Oord and Lodahl, *Relational Holiness*, 81.
72. Oord, *NOL*, 25.
73. Oord, *NOL*, 26.
74. Oord, *NOL*, 27.
75. Oord, *DL*, 17.
76. Oord and Lodahl, *Relational Holiness*, 74.
77. Oord, *NOL*, 27.
78. Oord, *NOL*, 27.

then we must love ourselves.[79] Loving ourselves may best promote the common good.[80] Furthermore, Scripture advocates "friendship-oriented love," as in Paul's admonition to the Romans, where he expresses that true Christians express *philia* love not only to each other but to outsiders (Rom 12:10, 13; cf. 1 Tim 3:2).[81]

An intentional act of love, as in worship, Oord says, "confuses and confounds . . . and goes against the typical biblical practice of defining love in terms of 'doing good.'"[82] Furthermore, emphasizing that *action*, itself, is love contrasts the biblical notion of love as promoting overall well-being, in that such acts of love are either proper or improper, requiring an adjective before *love* in order to indicate which form it is. According to Oord, *love* should always be able to stand on its own; no adjective should ever be required before using love to denote the moral intentions of said actions. *Love*, "according to my definition and the dominant love language tradition in the Bible . . . is never impure."[83] "The virtuous Christian," writes Oord, "obeys the love commands of Jesus (John 14:23; 15:10). . . . The virtuous person enjoys a personal history of frequent intentional responses that promote the common good."[84]

Oord's intention behind giving love primacy in theology is because love is "at the heart of Scripture."[85] And unfortunately, Oord sees traditional theology has let love slide. As one who is a Reformed classical theist, one of the challenges to my tradition is that doctrinal rigor often times seems to have precedence over loving relations. I, too, agree with Oord that love needs to have *the* exalted place in theology, which spills over into the pews of the church, thus strengthening the loving relationships founded on *doctrinally* articulated biblical truth. I commend Oord for his attempt to establish a definition of love that reflects the heart of Scripture, thus ultimately the heart of God. However, there are some concerns that deserve critical attention.

---

79. Oord, *NOL*, 27–28.
80. Oord, *NOL*, 28.
81. Oord, *NOL*, 28.
82. Oord, *NOL*, 29.
83. Oord, *NOL*, 29.
84. Oord, *NOL*, 30–31.
85. Oord, *NOL*, 31.

A Definition of Love—Critical Evaluation

To restate Oord's definition of love: "To love is to act intentionally, in sympathetic/empathetic response to God and others, to promote overall well-being." Oord's definition of love raises a pertinent question: How did he formulate his definition? He acknowledges that "the Bible does not provide an internally consistent witness to love's meaning."[86] Therefore, Christian theologians, likewise, do not place love at the center of their theology. While his definition serves as a helpful guide, it lacks the capacity to properly convey the breadth of meaning and expression of love as demonstrated in Scripture. If the Bible does not have an internally consistent form of love, then Oord undermines his own case; how can he create one, if the Bible does not have one? What criterion is he using to adjudicate his definition, and *why*? With that said, he states that his definition takes into account the biblical witness to love, particularly demonstrated by Christ and the church, as well as what we understand of love through human experience and through the sciences.

Another concern is in Oord's starting point. While he says his definition takes into account the biblical witness regarding love, his appropriation of it as a general model, "descriptive of God's love,"[87] (which he affirms is univocal)[88] reveals that he actually starts not above—where God's love descends down to us; rather, he starts below, from a man-centered point of view.[89]

Robert L. Plummer, for example, in an expositional essay examining what the New Testament authors teach about the love of God, puts forth a somewhat similar working definition of love: "love is a relational and practical concern for another, rooted in the nature or disposition of the one loving and resulting in tangible expressions of that concern."[90] Plummer's general definition reflects the Scriptures' teaching on God's general providence (i.e., common grace). However, "the New Testament focuses on the effective, saving love God has for Christians."[91] The "New Testament authors consistently

---

86. Oord, *NOL*, 12.

87. Oord, *NOL*, 17.

88. Oord qualifies, however, "I stress that the degrees to which divine love is expressed are not the same as the degrees that creatures express love. But my definition of love is meant to apply both to God's love and to creature love." Oord, personal email to author, February 14, 2018.

89. Wells, *Whirlwind*, 85.

90. Plummer, "What Do the Apostles Teach?," 77.

91. Plummer, "What Do the Apostles Teach?," 78. In fact, Plummer remarks that according to Ephesians 2:4–7, the *sine qua non* of God's love is his regenerative work in the hearts of dead sinners, uniting believers to Christ, saving sinners from wrath and judgment, securing believers in union with Christ, and promise of eternal joy guaranteed by Christ's finished work on the cross.

look back to God's historical intervention" in the saving of *his* people through his Son's atoning death on the cross.[92] And thus, one can only experience God's love through *those* saving benefits secured on the cross. God pours out his love on those he redeemed through Christ's death (Rom 5:5; cf. Rev 5:9–10), giving them the Spirit—his love—in order to transform his people into a committed, holy priesthood (1 Pet 2:9–10). While limited to the apostles' teaching on the subject, Plummer nevertheless demarcates the varying aspects of God's love, even within that narrowed context.

The first aspect of Oord's definition, *to promote overall well-being*, comes from his understanding of the *hesed* language tradition of Judaism, in that it is attributed to proper action and is often translated as "steadfast love."[93] While this word carries with it a sense of doing good for others, Oord is missing the greater semantic significance that it has.[94] Translating *hesed* as "steadfast love" lands within the semantic range for *hesed*; however, it "most often serves as a substantive for grace in the Old Testament."[95] Exodus 34:6–7, which employs the word *hesed*, is God's statement of faith he declares to Moses, demonstrating his gracious nature toward his covenant people.[96] Deuteronomy 7:7–9, also, is another passage where *hesed* is used, indicating the steadfast nature of God's love, in which he swore an oath to Israel's fathers "because the LORD loved you" (v. 8); however, it is in the context of a covenant that God reserves and expresses this type of love. J. A. Thompson, commenting on verses 9–10, writes, "When men are in a relationship of *love* with Yahweh, they discover that [he] is faithful to His covenant relationship and loyal to His promises."[97] In his observation of

92. Plummer, "What Do the Apostles Teach?," 81.

93. Oord, "Divine Love," 94.

94. Gowan, *Exodus*, 236, who says while, "'Steadfast love' is probably the best we can do," notes that it "cannot be adequately translated by anything short of a paragraph."

95. Heath, "Grace," 372. It is also in the context of God's people, the faithful ones. See Childs, *Exodus*, 602.

96. Lofthouse, "Hen," 29–35. Swanson, "hesed," in *Dictionary of Biblical Languages*, notes a primary definition of *hesed*, referencing Exodus 34:6–7, is that of a loyal love, i.e., "a love or affection that is steadfast based on a prior relationship." And Steobe, "hesed," according to N. Glueck, whose definition has been a dominant one, says *hesed* "refers ... to a mode of behavior that arises from a relationship defined by rights and obligations (husband-wife, parent-child, prince-subjects)." Peckham observes that this *locus classicus* of the divine character shows that "God goes far *beyond* covenant responsibilities, or even moral expectations, by continuing in [*hesed*] toward a stiff-necked, rebellious, unworthy people who had forfeited all covenantal privileges." Peckham, "Concept of Divine Love," 355–56. Emphasis added.

97. Thompson and Wiseman, *Deuteronomy*, 131. Christopher Wright notes that God's faithfulness is imperative in this context because "Yahweh's claim to ultimate deity is founded on his action, and specifically his saving action (v. 8)." Wright, *Deuteronomy*, 116.

God's *hesed* love for his people, Daniel Strange remarks on the shadings of God's love captured in Psalm 136, demonstrating how creatures—from this one act of *hesed*—experience his love in different ways:

> Give thanks to the LORD, for he is good.
> His love endures forever. . . .
> who spread out the earth upon the waters,
> His love endures forever. . . .
> to him who struck down the firstborn of Egypt
> His love endures forever. . . .
> but swept Pharaoh and his army into the Red Sea;
> His love endures forever. . . .
> to him who led his people through the wilderness;
> His love endures forever. . . .
> to him who struck down great kings,
> His love endures forever. . . .
> He gives food to every creature.
> His love endures forever.[98]

Strange writes, "God's *hesed* for his people means that he strikes down mighty kings and kills kings of splendor, those who have been sustained by his common grace."[99]

While Oord lists a few texts to support his conclusions, he misses the crucial element of the *hesed* tradition as found in God's elective, covenantal love (specifically, God's extension of grace toward his people) *and* in his actions of wrath and judgment *because* of his love.[100] And while Oord affirms the role of justice in love, ultimately, he overlooks the fact that love demands justice for those who have reviled and turned away from God. He writes, "God's wrath and vengeance are not instances of punishment. They are the natural negative consequences that come from failing to cooperate with God's actions to promote well-being. God does not sentence people to eternal punishment. No crime deserves such punishment."[101] Such a statement intersects with the biblical data, demonstrating a time where God *actively* brings about

---

98. Ps. 136:1, 6, 10, 15–18, 25. Adapted from Strange, "Does the Love of God?," 157.

99. Strange, "Does the Love of God?," 157–58.

100. As Tony Lane observes: God's "wrath is his response to something outside of himself. . . . [W]rath is not fundamental to God in the same way love is. . . . [But], there is no true love without wrath." Lane, "The Wrath of God," 146.

101. Oord, "BYU Presentation." Oord affirms self-giving love even into the afterlife, and he believes "God will eventually woo all creation to eternal bliss of love."

judgment on sinners.[102] Holding to Oord's view downplays the personal and unjust nature of sin, in that all sin is against God (Ps 51:4; cf. Exod 10:16; Josh 7:20; Judg 10:10), and he is the one who establishes justice and carries it out. Two passages in the New Testament speak against this understanding of judgment: Acts 5:1–10, God striking down Ananias and Sapphira for lying to the Spirit; and 1 Cor 11:27–31, Paul's warning to those taking the Lord's supper in an unworthy manner, informing the Corinthian church that God has brought death to those who have done so.

The Old Testament, on numerous occasions, makes references to the "Day of the LORD."[103] And in the New Testament, Jesus spoke of the coming judgement—the Last Day—the great appearing of the Son of Man.[104] When Jesus returns, all the nations will be gathered before him, and he will separate the sheep from the goats—*his* sheep will inherit eternal life, the kingdom prepared for them; the goats will inherit eternal fire, "prepared for the devil and his angels" (Matt 25:31–33, 41). The author of Hebrews leaves no room for doubt: "[I]t is appointed for people to die once—and after this, judgement" (9:27). Christ's warning to fear God, not man, because "he has authority to throw people into hell after death," is a sobering reminder that God *alone* is the Judge of heaven and earth (Luke 12:5; cf. Matt 10:28). Not observing this fact fails to justly appropriate humanity's due penalty for sin,[105] which only heightens the contrast of the great love God has shown his saints in removing that penalty through the blood of Christ.

While Oord espouses that hell is not a place,[106] Jesus' words in Matthew 25:46 imply each outcome is not only experiential but also having a location. The context of Matthew 25:31–46 (and the wider context of Jesus' Olivet Discourse, 24:1—25:46) is a build-up, showing a progression of events leading

---

102. Oord, *NOL*, 156.

103. Cf. Isa 13:6, 9; Jer 46:10; Ezek 30:2–3; Joel 1:15; 2:1, 11, 31; 3:14; Amos 5:18; Obad 15; Zeph 1:14–16; Zech 14:1.

104. Cf. John 6:39; Rom 2:5; 1 Cor 1:8; 5:5; Eph 4:30; 2 Thess 1:10; 1 Pet 2:12; 2 Pet 3:12; Rev 6:17; 16:14.

105. Paul assumes as such, in that his parenthetical statement in Romans 3:5–7, responding to the human way of thinking about the problem, explaining that God's response to sin with wrath is a *righteous* action on God's part. Paul is responding to objectors who insinuate God is unjust, making the point that God is not unjust to inflict wrath on his own people; otherwise, as Judge (Gen 18:25) how else would he judge the world? So also, Moo, *Romans*, 192. And Morris observes, "The final judgement is not something that must be argued for. It is something that may be argued from." Morris, *Doctrine of Judgment*, 55.

106. Oord just recently affirmed as such, whereas, previously, he left the location of hell up to discussion, focusing rather on the experience of hell in this life and the next. Oord, *NOL*, 156.

up to the Day of LORD—*the* Day of judgment. One of two destinations await all of humanity—eternal life or eternal punishment. The syntax of the Greek "life" and "punishment" are both modified by the adjective "eternal,"[107] in which, "[t]here is not the slightest indication in the words of Jesus here that the punishment is not coeval with the life."[108]

Oord's further remarks regarding well-being as *shalom* prioritize temporal needs rather than spiritual needs. If such describes God's love, then, using Oord's definition, that promoting well-being includes helping with living necessities and medical care, it is difficult to reconcile such a definition with Christ's purpose in making Paul his "chosen instrument" to whom "I will show him how much he must suffer for my name" (Acts 9:15). Furthermore, the fate of those who follow Paul's path—to live a godly life in Christ—will suffer persecution (2 Tim 3:12),[109] raises the objection that such a definition does not accurately represent God's love. One could easily think that God does not regard one's well-being if the result of following Christ leads to a diminished state (or even a fatal state) of well-being. But, as Gerald Bray reminds us, that is the Christian life—like a sheep led to the slaughter (Rom 8:36), "all for the sake of their commitment to [Christ]. These things are not the exception, not a tragic aberration in the life of the believer, but the norm which the Bible tells us to expect."[110]

in sympathetic/empathetic response to God and others. While Oord looks to 1 John 4:19 to support his definition, what informs his interpretation of this text is his adoption of the doctrine of *prevenient grace*. Prevenient grace is "divine grace . . . that comes before from God in advance of human response."[111] This will receive further treatment in chapter 5. For now, I will just pose the question, which forms the basis of my objection: What is the purpose/function of prevenient grace as a requirement for one to have faith if man is given libertarian free will to choose to have faith in God?[112]

---

107. In the Greek: *eis kolasin aiōnion*, . . . *eis zōēn aiōnion* are mirrored phrases, which literally read, "to punishment eternal . . . to life eternal." While *kolasis* is simply punishment as consequent, "infliction of suffering or pain in chastisement." BDAG, 555. Matthew's insertion of the adjective, *aiōnios*, Leon Morris notes, pertains to an age; an age without beginning or end. Morris, *Matthew*, 641n79.

108. "Matthew 25:46," in Robertson, *Word Pictures*.

109. Recall Paul's persecution in defense of his apostolic ministry (2 Cor 11:21–27).

110. Bray, "Love of God," 8.

111. Thorsen, *Calvin vs. Wesley*, 47.

112. As will be observed in chapter 5, Oord sees God's grace as *necessary* grace, in a manner that moves beyond an Arminian/Wesleyan view of grace.

With that said, due to recent attempts to define love exclusively as relationship in the Christian faith, Oord terms "the mutuality tradition,"[113] his statement raises a concern as to the nature of love in relationships. Theologian Vincent Brümmer says, "Love must by its very nature be a relationship of free mutual give and take, otherwise it cannot be love at all."[114] However, Oord objects to Brümmer's statement because it "wrongly implies *all* relationships are loving. It regards relations themselves as love."[115] I do not think Brümmer's statement carries with it the implication that Oord observes. Kevin J. Vanhoozer, however, rightly seeing the problem in Brümmer's definition, remarks:

> If love *is* the relationship, then it follows that the notion of unrequited love is impossible. For if love's overture is unrequited, then there is no reciprocity, and where there is no reciprocity there is no free mutual giving and taking, no relationship—no love. If Brümmer is correct, then it becomes difficult in the extreme to know how to love one's enemies.[116]

Oord's reason for rejecting Brümmer's statement is problematic. He says, "It [the *mutuality tradition*] ignores the biblical command that sometimes love requires our severing relationships with that which causes evil (2 Tim. 2:22)."[117] However, he stretches the context of this passage to support his conclusion. Paul writes in 2 Timothy 2:22, "So flee youthful passions and pursue righteousness, faith, love, and peace, along with those who call on the Lord from a pure heart." The context of the passage pertains to the pattern of godliness a shepherd should exude. Paul was not commanding him to sever relationships that create evil; rather, he was calling him to flee passions of the flesh as compared to those who oppose him, who do not demonstrate such qualities, so that no one would render him unfit in his youth to be a shepherd (cf. 1 Tim 4:12).[118] Love—as expressed in Jesus Christ—opposes severing

---

113. Oord, *NOL*, 22.
114. Brümmer, *Model of Love*, 161.
115. Oord, *NOL*, 22.
116. Vanhoozer, "Introduction," 19.
117. Oord, *NOL*, 22.
118. Mounce, *Pastoral Epistles*, 533, writes, while the emphasis could certainly pertain to "sensual lusts of the youth," the verses following it do not speak to that fact. Therefore, the "emphasis is on Timothy's youthful temperament and the possible difficulty of avoiding arguments and being gentle in instruction."

relationships;[119] rather, love creates relationships through the reconciliatory work of Jesus Christ (Rom 5:8–11).[120]

The last part of his definition of love is *to act intentionally*. Oord uses the word *intentional* "because it has three facets of meaning: deliberateness, motive, and freedom."[121] Oord's belief that the act of love in worship "confuses and confounds" and "goes against *the typical biblical practice* of defining love in terms of 'doing good'" is troubling (emphasis added). His assertion demonstrates the pitfalls in attempting to make a strict definition of love from Scripture. He dismisses other expressions of love that do not fall within the guidelines he has prioritized in his definition.

An undeniable fact in Scripture is that worship is not optional: "Love the LORD your God with all your heart, with all your soul, and with your strength" (Deut 6:5). Scripture says this is "*the* greatest and most important command" (Matt 22:38, emphasis added). The evidence of genuine religion is worship from the heart; the Lord does not desire sacrifices and offerings but a broken spirit and humble heart (Ps 51:16), which only comes from true love for God and manifests itself in obeying his commands (John 14:15, 23–24; 15:10–14). And the foundation for true worship is based on forgiveness[122] (e.g., the woman's overflowing expression of love to Jesus was because "her many sins have been forgiven" Luke 7:43–50.). It is the magnification of the glory of God, fitting for those whom God has lavished his grace and goodness upon, to be holy and blameless before him, done all "to the praise of his glorious grace" (Eph 1:6, 12, 7). The exhortations to worship abound in the Bible.[123]

If, as Oord claims, love is the metaphysical attribute of God—the starting point of all theology, and the greatest command in Scripture, permeating every aspect of a believer's life (Deut 6:5–9), then it seems that worship is the expression of love that matters most to God. While *love* is not the word

---

119. No doubt, "Bad company corrupts good morals" (1 Cor 15:33). There are relationships that can be unhealthy, promoting a love of the world, which belong to the devil (1 John 2:15–17; cf. 2 Cor 4:4).

120. Vanhoozer arrives at the same conclusion. As it pertains to how one would love one's enemies without reciprocation and relations, he sees that "[t]he only alternative would be to argue that God's love is of such a nature that it unilaterally creates relationships that invariably elicit a genuine response on the part of the beloved. But that is another theological controversy." Vanhoozer "Introduction," 19. And in his footnote, he writes, "I refer, of course, to the notion of irresistible grace. It may also be the heart of the issue." Vanhoozer "Introduction," 19n55.

121. Oord, *NOL*, 27.

122. MacArthur, *Worship*, 53. In fact, all of Ephesians 1 attests to it.

123. To list a few: Ps 27:4; 29:2; 66:4; 71:8; 84:1–3, 10; 95:6; 96:9; 99:5; 132:27; Isa 12:5; John 4:24; Rom 12:1; 1 Pet 2:5; Heb 13:15; Rev 4:11.

generally used in passages speaking of worship, the impetus of love is behind the act of worship. We worship and praise that which we love and adore most, revealing where our heart is (Matt 6:21). When God is adored, true worship comes forth. And that is what God desires from his people.[124]

Oord's conclusions reveal the pitfall in making one aspect of love the general definition of love, and also, referring to his definition as the typical biblical practice. In so doing, he dismisses the various nuances of the love themes in Scripture. Oord says using the word as it pertains to worship is confusing. But the biblical witness reveals that the primary error leading to Israel's decline was that they were *confused* in their worship because they did not direct their love and affections toward the One, true Lord. If they followed Deuteronomy 6:4, they would have understood what true worship looks like: genuine obedience that flows from the heart. Oord's definition of love suggests that the biblical model of love = benevolent love. Oord mistakes God's love as primarily to *promote well-being*. In intending his definition "to be generally descriptive of God's love,"[125] Oord does not do justice to the biblical testimony of the loves of God, particularly in how God specifically enters into a covenant love with his people (Gen 15; Exod 2:24; Lev 26:9; Deut 7:12).[126]

Oord's definition of love is problematic, in that it fails as the "typical biblical practice" of 'doing good' regarding those who die in their sins, never having heard the gospel message. But there are plenty who have died in their sins, never hearing the Word through which faith comes (Rom 10:17).[127] Ultimate care for one's well-being should extend beyond the temporal world. And since God did not reveal the only hope for salvation—eternal well-being—to all of creation, God either had different intentions or God was unable to fulfill his intention of revealing his Son to every person that ever existed.

---

124. In fact, the Lord brought judgment on Israel because they did not serve the Lord with joy and gladness from a heart satisfied in God (Deut 28:47–48).

125. Oord, *NOL*, 19.

126. Cf. 1 Kgs 8:23; Isa 54:10; Dan 9:4

127. To answer this objection, Oord would most likely place the blame on mankind failing to bring the message to the lost because it chose not to cooperate with God. However, the Old Testament narrative has a foundation in holy genocide (the book of Joshua), in which God's "promotion of good" comes about through eradicating the Canaanites. Oord "take[s] the bolder stance that the Israelites who believed God desired genocide misunderstood God. I claim this based on my reading of the Bible's more prominent claims about God's love for all, including enemies, and the fullest revelation of divine love in Jesus." Oord, personal email to author, March 22, 2018.

As it pertains to the unredeemed, Oord does not portray their fate as the Bible does. He offers little discussion in regard to eschatology.[128] But his love-theology requires a "participatory eschatology." God's love cannot coerce, so even the dead cannot be forced into eternal bliss; therefore, God's love "invites creatures to participate in securing victory."[129] In the few pages he devotes to the subject, he shies away from such language of "judgment" or "damnation," reserving it only when speaking of "[a] predestining God [who] does not love steadfastly" and "arbitrarily chooses some for salvation and others for damnation."[130] While he speaks of hell, he uses obscure language, making it seem mythological, almost denying its reality. He notes the infrequent usage of "hell" in Scripture but states that Christians have always "affirmed some form of negative consequences for sin."[131] However, Oord's manner of speaking of "negative consequences" disassociates God from those consequences, as the one who administers them.

Consistent with his aim to keep God off the dock, he concludes that creatures, within the freedom a loving God has given them, can inappropriately respond to the calling of God and choose hell. Hell is the "negative consequence . . . that comes from choosing less than the loving best to which God calls."[132] In a recent blog article discussing *The Uncontrollable Love of God*, a reader posted a comment, asking Oord if he believes in hell and if so, does he believe it is eternal, conscious punishment. Oord responded, stating,

> I think hell is a state of disobedience that involves suffering the natural negative consequences of failing to cooperate with God's love. . . . I don't think God condemns the disobedient to eternal conscious torment. But neither do I think God coerces free agents to cooperate in enjoying abundant life. I think God everlastingly pursue [sic], calls, and invites—in this life and the

---

128. As it pertains to eschatology, Oord adopts a "participatory eschatology, whereby creaturely participation is essential for bringing about God's desired ends"; thus, affirming "the 'co-workers' intuition of postmillennialism, without requiring belief in millennialism itself." Oord, "BYU Presentation." See Oord, *NOL*, 152–56.

129. Oord, *NOL*, 152.

130. Oord, *NOL*, 155–56. In the survey of Oord's primary works examined in this study, he refrains from employing the words "damnation," "judgement," and "condemnation" eschatologically speaking as it pertains to God's response to sinners. In Oord, *ULG*, 121, the subject of hell is mentioned once, and it is a quote from another source. His dissertation references 'judgement' once, and it is in a quote of Calvin. And in a footnote, he makes one reference to hell, stating: "God will not control the individual's decision whether to spend eternity in heaven or hell." Oord, *ULG*, 272n80.

131. Oord, *NOL*, 156.

132. Oord, *NOL*, 156.

next—but any person can continually say "no" to God's invitation. Saying "no" to God's love means enduring the natural negative consequences that come from rejecting God's invitation to enjoy well-being.[133]

It seems that Oord rejects the notion of God as a righteous judge against those who freely sin. However, via personal correspondence, Oord clarified that he affirms God as judge and the condemnation of sinners, but God does not condemn sinners for eternity.[134]

While Oord states that God *does* judge those who reject his love, in the end he believes that all of creation will be "wooed" to eternal bliss of love. If that is the case, the apex of God's love in the sending of his Son loses its necessity to save sinners in *this* life. Salvation is just a waiting game; eventually, God's persuasive power will draw all of creation into relation with him. Oord's expectation that God will "woo" everyone in the end reveals that he holds to a form of determinism; his form of it just includes all of creation, rather than the elect people of God. Ultimately, Oord's definition of hell is inconsequential because in the end, according to Oord, no one actually ends up there. Such a view is in stark contrast to the biblical story.

A Theology of Love

While Oord provides a definition of love in order to construct a proper theology of it, he examines the well-known works on Christian love by Anders Nygren, St. Augustine, and Clark Pinnock. He highlights helpful contributions from each theologian, providing critiques as well, and proposes a new model of love he terms *Essential Kenosis*, which also serves as his model of divine providence and his solution to the problem of evil.[135] Anders Nygren's views of love are most significant to the critical discussion of this study, so only Oord's survey and engagement of Anders Nygren will be evaluated.

---

133. Discussion post made by Oord in Roberts, "What If God?"

134. Oord states that he does "believe in a God who judges. . . . God condemns those actions that do not promote wellbeing, i.e., not loving." Oord, recorded message to author, December 13, 2017.

135. *Essential Kenosis* will be examined in chapter 5.

Oord's Exposition of Nygren and Agape Love

Anders Nygren, in his very influential study on the Greek word *agape*, *Agape and Eros*, concludes that *agape* is *the* Christian form of love.[136] His teaching on divine love is one of the strongest motivating factors behind Oord's aim of redefining a Christian doctrine of love. Therefore, Nygren's views have importance in the discussion. Oord is highly critical of Nygren, some of which is justified. While Nygren's strong assertion of the uniqueness of *agape* as "the Christian fundamental motif *par excellence*"[137] resonates with Oord, he rejects Nygren's thesis that *agape* is the only authentic form of Christian love.[138]

At the start, Oord contends that Nygren's lens of reading Scripture "is not usually helpful . . . [and that] his theory of *agape* does not fit the biblical witness well."[139] Beginning with Nygren's content on the idea of *Agape*—that of divine love, Nygren identifies four features that describe the content of divine love, on which Oord comments, "[t]he first two aspects reveal that those God loves do not draw out God's love. . . . The second two aspects . . . underscore the unilateral nature of *agape* as the only Christian love."[140] Oord's observations conflict with his own view of divine love which is a mutual give-and-take relationship, where creatures affect God, and that *agape* is *not* (unilaterally) the only form of Christian love.

---

136. Oord, NOL, 33.

137. Nygren, *Agape*, 41. Quoted in Oord, NOL, 35.

138. Oord, "MTP," 7. He also states that he rejects "Nygren's all-determining and impassible God." Oord, "MTP," Abstract. Others have also observed the flaws in Nygren's word-based reductionistic approach, leading to misperceptions of the love of God. Carson, "Love," remarks that Nygren's analysis of love with reference to the three Greek words, *eros, phileo,* and *agape* fails in consistency because the words used in Scripture, contextually speaking, often times do not have the same meaning as when standing alone. So also, Agan, "Christian Walk," 191; Badcock, "Concept of Love," 37. However, barring Nygren's flawed reductionism, his attention to *agape* as crystalized by the gospel and the New Testament context carries a significant element in making God's redemptive actions in Christ unique to the faith, as compared to an egocentric love as understood in *eros*. Peck, "Agape," 137. Furthermore, contemporary critics challenge Nygren's thesis, theologically speaking, insisting that his emphasis on *agape* as a unique form of grace-dispensing love originating in God, which he expresses toward the unlovable, misses the importance of relational exchange and mutuality. "These critics suggest that to embrace the ideal of agape, with its intrinsic structure of condescending bestowal, is, in fact, to prevent the direct mutuality [as *philia* denotes] that is accessible only through acknowledgement of our own vulnerability." Grant, "Agape," 9. According to Grant, it appears that in the "Enlightenment Agape," *philia* displaces the New Testament agape.

139. Oord, NOL, 34.

140. Oord, NOL, 35–36.

Agape Is Spontaneous and 'Unmotivated'

Nygren sees that *"agape is spontaneous and 'unmotivated.'"*[141] Nygren's emphasis on *unmotivated* is purposed to eminently denote that God's love "is to be ground in God himself."[142] Nothing extrinsic to God establishes the foundation of love by which he displays it. Divine love must be *divine*, through and through.[143] And therefore, it is spontaneous. God, writes Nygren, "does not look for anything in man that could be adduced as motivation for [him to love]."[144] Regarding this essential aspect, Oord concludes, according to Nygren, "Nothing . . . praiseworthy exists in creation that might inspire God to love."[145] However, Nygren did not use the words "praiseworthy" or "inspire."

In looking carefully at what Nygren did say and the context, his point was to emphasize that God's love is *his* love. And his love does not depend on something outside of himself to motivate him to love. Contrary to Oord's presentation of Nygren's view of God's love, Nygren's statement expresses God's praiseworthiness. First, if God needed something praiseworthy to motivate him to love, though God alone is praiseworthy, then God's love is not perfect; it is contingent, not *divine* and unique to God. And second, Nygren's intention was to contrast divine *agape* love with the motivated love forms found in humans, which "directs love to the righteous, to those who deserve it."[146] The love of God revealed in Christ does not go to the "worthy," the religious one; rather, it goes to the sinner, the unworthy one. Nygren writes, "If God's love were restricted to the righteous it would be evoked by its object and not spontaneous; but just by the fact that it seeks sinners, who do not deserve it and can lay no claim to it, it manifests most clearly its spontaneous and unmotivated nature."[147]

---

141. Nygren, *Agape*, 75.

142. Nygren, *Agape*, 75.

143. To say something is divine, through and through, underscores the classical doctrine of divine simplicity. God's love is perfect, motivated only by God's own self.

144. Nygren, *Agape*, 75–76.

145. Oord, *NOL*, 35.

146. Nygren, *Agape*, 76.

147. Nygren, *Agape*, 76–77.

Agape Is "Indifferent to Value"

Second, *agape is "indifferent to value."*[148] Oord understands this to mean that "Nothing valuable . . . exists in creation that might inspire God to love."[149] Oord overlooks the manner of Nygren's careful explanation intended to reflect the impartiality of God. God's indifference is not a lack of interest or sympathy, as it seems Oord intends to convey; rather, Nygren writes,

> *any thought of valuation whatsoever* is out of place in connection with fellowship with God. . . . But when God's love is shown to the righteous and godly, there is always the risk of our thinking that God loves the man on account of his righteousness and godliness. But this is a denial of Agape. . . . God's love allows no limits to be set for it by the character or conduct of man.[150]

As alluded to earlier, Nygren's essential aspects of *agape* highlight the *praiseworthiness* and *valuableness* of *God's* love, in contrast to Oord's emphasis on the value and praiseworthiness of God's *creation*. Oord writes that it is important to distinguish between the modes of God's love as necessary, which means "that the particular form God's love takes is dependent upon creaturely actions and responses." We do not need to embrace Nygren's view of creation as "value-less."[151]

While Oord observes Nygren's remark about God seeking those who do not deserve love, he separates it from the context. Again, Nygren's point was to establish that God's love is not like human love that loves the righteous, those *deserving* of love,[152] but rather, divine love loves the sinner, those *undeserving* of love (i.e., according to a creaturely manner of love). Nygren expresses the important sentiment in the New Testament that Jesus came to "bring a new fellowship with God."[153] While Christianity and Judaism have a historical and religious-ethical connection, Nygren writes it is a "fundamentally different thing from Judaism."[154] Jesus' words in Mark 2:17, "I didn't come to call the righteous, but sinners," turned "the entire scale of Jewish values upside

---

148. Nygren, *Agape*, 77.
149. Oord, *NOL*, 34.
150. Nygren, *Agape*, 77.
151. Oord, *NOL*, 55.
152. Nygren, *Agape*, 76. Nygren qualifies it as "the ordinary sense."
153. Nygren, *Agape*, 68.
154. Nygren, *Agape*, 68.

down."¹⁵⁵ Oord asserts that for Nygren, this passage "confirms his views that creatures have nothing of value to motivate God's love."¹⁵⁶

However, that is not Nygren's purpose. Rather, he uses it to identify the stark contrast between "a sinner" and "the righteous." The *value* Oord references in Nygren has to do with the Jewish understanding of *righteous* according to "the legal scheme" of the Covenant, where "such love" (e.g., Jesus coming to sit and dine with sinners in fellowship; cf. Ps 26:4–5) had no place, where "fellowship with God [was] in terms of law and justice." God shows his love to the one who fears him, "the righteous, not to the sinner,"¹⁵⁷ according to the stipulations of the covenant.

Oord assesses Nygren's claims that fellowship with God rests solely on God's initiating *agape* and that receivers of his love do not have value in God's decision to initiate fellowship. Oord refers to Matthew 9:23, a parallel verse to Mark 2:17, of which he points out is a reference to Hosea 6:6, "I desire faithful love and not sacrifice, the knowledge of God rather than burnt offerings." This passage, Oord claims, "implies the God of the Old Testament is also concerned with sinners."¹⁵⁸ Oord maintains that Matthew 9:23 directly refutes Nygren's assertion that humans cannot love; the biblical idea of God desiring that *we* love conflicts with Nygren's proposal.

With that said, while Oord has grounds to challenge Nygren on his view of *agape* as a purely *divine* form of love, Oord is missing the greater theological point. The wider context of the Matthew and Mark passages is that in Jesus' claim as the Son of Man, having the authority to forgive sins, the Pharisees and the teachers of the Law were wondering why Jesus would sit and dine with *sinners*, those who were violating the Law of Moses, rather than *the righteous*, those like them. According to the Law, they had *value* from the standpoint of being more worthy of receiving God's favor.¹⁵⁹ Nygren's point was *not* that God lacked a concern for sinners, as Oord claims; rather, Nygren was emphasizing the unique expression of God's love "that was bound by the limits of the Law and the Covenant,"¹⁶⁰ now revealed in the person of Jesus who comes to have fellowship with sinners, the unworthy, which *the righteous* (the Pharisees) did not consider themselves to be. Again, it was a radical change in what the Jews expected of one claiming to be from God.

155. Nygren, *Agape*, 68.
156. Oord, *NOL*, 42.
157. Nygren, *Agape*, 71.
158. Oord, *NOL*, 43.
159. Nygren, *Agape*, 75.
160. Nygren, *Agape*, 71.

Oord does express his agreement with Nygren on God's unmotivated love, complimenting his views, stating that God's eternal nature as love is "an essential aspect to God's essence."[161] However, because Oord sees love as God's essential nature, God, then, must love all of creation. Nygren distinguishes God's essential nature of love from the point of God's independence from something contingent to stir God's love into action.

Agape Is Creative

The third of Nygren's essential aspects is "*agape is creative*." This aspect builds off of the first two, in that because God's love is spontaneous and unmotivated (i.e., not dependent on the object to stir up something in God *to* love), agape love is creative in that "it does not recognize value, it creates it."[162] It is value-creating because the "man loved by God has no value in himself; what gives him value is precisely the fact that God loves him."[163] The creative aspect of *agape* points back to the *uniqueness* of God's love, which does not love what is worthy of love, in contrast to human love, which loves what *is* worthy of it (according to a fractured, human view of value). Nygren's point purposed to challenge modern theology's obscuring of God's *unique* love, which replaced it with the "'infinite value of the human soul' as one of the central ideas of Christianity" that "connected it with the idea of 'God's fatherly love.'"[164] Such thought stems from the theological liberalism of Adolf von Harnack, whose idea of religion makes man the emphasis, whereby God loves man because of *man's* "matchless value."[165] The "destructive effect" of this concept on divine love, writes Nygren, means that "God's love would not in the last resort be spontaneous" because the motive is the "infinite value inherent in human nature.... The forgiveness of sins would then imply merely a recognition of an already existing value."[166] Forgiveness of sins is a gift; it looks past man's faults, emphasizing the infinite value of the gift giver, through whom, in the forgiveness of sins, we see the "*creative work of Divine power*" (e.g., Jesus' healing of the paralytic; Mark 2:5–12).[167]

---

161. Oord, *NOL*, 55.
162. Nygren, *Agape*, 78.
163. Nygren, *Agape*, 78.
164. See Harnack, *What Is Christianity?*, 51, 63.
165. Nygren, *Agape*, 78–79.
166. Nygren, *Agape*, 78–79.
167. Nygren, *Agape*, 80.

Agape Is the Initiator of Fellowship with God

The last essential aspect is that "*agape is the initiator of fellowship with God.*" Oord understands this to mean that "agape initiates any fellowship that exists between God and creatures. . . . Unless God initiates and creates value, nothing would exist that God could appreciate."[168] The fourth point is the capstone of Nygren's view of divine love in that it identifies that all of man's ways to seek God are futile. Nygren writes, "Agape is completely revolutionary" in that the "way of righteousness" and "self-abandonment" are "incapable of leading to the goal; it follows that *there is from man's side no way at all that leads to God.*"[169] Going back to what Nygren said earlier, *agape* does not love the worthy, the righteous; rather, it loves the sinner, which in man's eyes is not worthy of love. As observed in the New Testament, the pharisees thought they were "loved" by God because they approached him by the "way of righteousness," thinking they were valued *because* they exemplified righteousness (i.e., an external keeping of the law; cf. Luke 18:9–12; John 9:16; Gal 2:15). But that is not *God's* way of fellowship; rather, God's way of forgiveness is what enables fellowship (cf. John 14:6).[170]

Oord says Nygren is right to affirm that "God always makes the first move to establish right relationship. . . . We rightly call the idea that God initially acts to make fellowship possible 'prevenient grace.'"[171] Oord prefers *prevenient* grace over predestination because he does not accept arbitrariness in God's love. However, Oord does not demonstrate it from the texts he cites;[172] rather, he assumes it, and then he refers the reader to various scholarly writings.[173] A proper relationship with God, says Nygren, relies on "a purely theocentric love, in which all choice on man's part is excluded."[174] To Oord, because of the primacy of God's love, predestination, election, and coercion are excluded. If one is responsible for one's actions, one must have "response-ability."[175] Through prevenient grace, God empowers humans to respond in love to his call. "God initiates relationship moment by moment and creatures freely respond. Divine love initiates fellowship. God enables creatures to respond freely."[176]

168. Oord, *NOL*, 36.
169. Nygren, *Agape*, 80.
170. Nygren, *Agape*, 80.
171. Oord, *NOL*, 52.
172. Oord, *NOL*, 23, 129, cites 1 John 4:9 and Phil 2:12b–13.
173. Oord, *NOL*, 52n82.
174. Nygren, *Agape*, 214. Quoted in, Oord, *NOL*, 53.
175. Oord, "MTP," 150.
176. Oord, *NOL*, 53.

Nygren's understanding of man's inability to love God, likewise, extends to man's inability to influence God. An essential element in a divine-love theology (and in relational theism in general) is a creature's ability to influence God (i.e., man's ability through his actions toward God, resulting in God responding to him or causing within God varying emotional states based upon those actions, as common within creature-creature relations). Oord objects to Nygren's claim, noting that Scripture proves otherwise. The Apostle Paul's admonition that Christians be cheerful givers, stems from God's loving those who do so (2 Cor 9:7), thus demonstrates, says Oord, "[h]uman activity, motivates, at least in some way, God's love."[177]

Nygren's Error

While *agape* love is a paradigmatic component of Christian theism, Oord concludes that Nygren's view of *agape* does not have biblical support.[178] Oord critiques Nygren's interpretation of various passages in the Gospels and Pauline texts, showing the inconsistency in Nygren's assertion that *agape* is unique, in that such passages, though using the word *agape* nevertheless take the form of *eros*, a motivated love. Oord's critique is warranted, as others have also concluded, in that Nygren does not consistently take into account the context of passages, resorting to reductionism, thus undermining his *agape* theology.

One stand-out example is that of John 3:35 and 5:20, where in both passages the Father says he loves the Son but uses *agapao* in 3:35 and *philia* in 5:20.[179] There are other meanings of love expressed in Scripture, the forms *philia* and *eros*.[180] Oord observes that biblical translators often translate the word *agape* with *eros* meanings. Biblical texts such as 2 Timothy 4:8; 4:10; John 3:19; 12:43; Hebrews 1:9; and Revelation 12:11 though employing the word *agape*, Oord says, are translated with English phrases implying an *eros* meaning.[181] The Apostle Paul uses *philia* in his exhortations that Christians should express *philia* to what is good (Titus 1:8) and to others (1 Tim 3:2), for *philia* is a defining mark of a true Christian (Rom

---

177. Oord, *NOL*, 46.

178. Oord, *NOL*, 49.

179. Oord, *NOL*, 50. This is also one of the key examples cited in Carson, "Love."

180. *Philia* is an "affection for friends . . . or a liking of something" and *eros* is an "attraction of desire . . . especially in sexual love." Baker, "Love," 472. However, the word *eros* is not found in the New Testament; rather, Oord states, *eros-love forms* are present in Scripture. Oord, *NOL*, 49.

181. Oord, *NOL*, 50.

12:10, 13). And in the last days many will be lovers of themselves and not *philia* toward God (2 Tim 3:4) who showed *philia* toward mankind in the saving love of Christ (Titus 3:4).[182]

While Oord appreciates the inroads Nygren made in his treatment on love, he does not agree with his thesis of the primacy of *agape* love as *the* definitive form of Christian love.[183] The writers of Scripture use different words to express different aspects of love and Christians need to express those aspects of love in accordance with how they are used in Scripture. Furthermore, while the examination of Nygren's thesis yielded inconsistencies in his claim, his study of *agape* love provided a context to support the thrust of Oord's thesis that *agape* is an "in spite of" love.[184] Oord finds it is best to provide a definition that complements what a theologian embraces, which must correspond with the biblical witness, and define *agape*, not as a mode of love, but rather as a form of love.[185] For Oord, *agape* is a "form of love that promotes, extends, or attempts to establish *shalom* in response to that which promotes sin and evil; . . . agape [is] *acting intentionally, in response to God and others, to promote overall well-being in response to that which produces ill-being.*"[186]

Some Concluding Thoughts on Oord's Reading of Nygren

Oord's critiques of Nygren are shared by many. I, too, agree with Oord and other critics that Nygren's conclusions based on his methodology is flawed. However, while Nygren's method is problematic, his theological conclusions regarding the uniqueness of God's love—*conceptually speaking*—in contrast to love as understood in a fallen world (*eros* love) is valid. A standard work in lexical and exegetical studies observes that "[t]he vast majority of the New Testament's use of the word *agapao* is used with reference to a distinctive of Christian virtue, but this fact witnesses to the significance of the theological *concept*, not to any positive qualities inherent in the *word* itself."[187]

---

182. Oord, *NOL*, 51.

183. The introductory section for "agapaō," Silva, 1:107, remarks, "One should not infer that this word has some kind of intrinsic 'divine' meaning, as though the terms themselves indicate selfless, sacrificial, pure love."

184. Oord, *NOL*, 56.

185. Oord, *NOL*, 56.

186. Oord, *NOL*, 56.

187. Silva, "agapaō," 1:107. Further noted is "that the New Testament never uses the noun *agapē* in negative contexts," but rather most often "related to the phrase [*hē agapē tou theou*], 'the love of God,' incl. the love for fellow believers—and even for one's enemies—that the presence of God evokes. This usage brings [*agapē*] very close to

Leon Morris observes that the newness of *agapao* was not in the verb form, but rather in the noun form,[188] in which the New Testament authors and the early church understood and used in a manner denoting the unique love of God as manifested in Christ. The concept made the word significant, not the other way around. Carl Henry speaking to the uniqueness in God's love manifested through the Spirit in the hearts of believers, quoting Emil Brunner, writes, "It is not that we already know what 'love' is,[189] and can then apply it to God. . . . Rather, . . . the *idea*, the understanding of love—the Agape of the New Testament can only be understood from what *happens* in revelation."[190] This revelation diffuses true love into the human soul, creating hearts that manifest the love of God to the world, our enemy. The uniqueness of divine love in contrast to human love is that God has the desire to love and redeem the unlovely, whereas human love rarely has such affections for the unlovely; rather, human love prefers the good or the beautiful.[191] God's love perfects the imperfect through Christ (Eph 1:4; 1 Cor 6:11)—the creative element of divine love. The content of divine love, "cannot be projected from the finite, sinful nature of man"; rather, it is only knowable through God's self-revelation.[192]

Because Scripture expresses various forms of love, it is important that when speaking of love, we do so in proportion to the biblical context.[193] We must pay attention to the manner in which the biblical authors used the words to express love, understanding how they function—thematically, canonically, and ethically. Critiques can be given of Oord's theological

---

concepts like faith, . . . and grace, . . . all of which have a single point of origin in God alone."

188. Morris, *Testaments of Love*, 126.
189. Torrance, "Is Love?," 130,
190. Brunner, *Doctrine of God*, 185, quoted in, Henry, *God*, 6:342.
191. Danaher, "Human and Divine," 34.
192. Henry, *God*, 6:342.

193. Peckham observes that "the meaning of the *agapao* and *phileo* word groups, as used in the New Testament, overlap in nearly every respect. Both terms are used to describe the Father's love for the Son (John 5:20 cf. John 3:35), the Father's love for the disciples because of their love for Jesus (John 16:27; cf. 14:21, 23), Jesus's love for humans (Rev 3:9, 19), Jesus's love for individuals (John 11:36; cf. 11:5), human love for other humans (John 15:19; cf. 15:19), human love for their own life (John 12:25; cf. Rev 12:11) and both terms describe the disciple whom Jesus loves (John 20:2; cf. 13:23). Furthermore, both are used of preferential love (Matt 10:37; John 11:5; 13:1), misdirected love (Matt 23:6; Luke 20:46; 22:15; Rev 22:15; 2 Tim 4:10; cf. Prov 21:17), conditionally reciprocal divine love (John 14:21, 23; 16:27), emotion and/or passion (John 11:36; 13:1; compare Jas 4:4), pleasure, enjoyment and/or evaluative love (Matt 3:17; Col 3:19; compare Gen 37:3–4) and other insider love (John 13:1; 15:14–15), and love that includes discipline (Rev 3:19; Heb 12:6)." Peckham, *Love of God*, 76.

conclusions based on his interpretation of the passages Nygren used to form his *agape* theology (i.e., soteriologically speaking). For example, Oord's conclusion touches on a point he seems to either not fully realize or chooses not to embrace: man's fallen nature and his state of enmity with God. Having a biblical anthropology as such places a strong emphasis on the nature and role of God's grace in redemption, which is why Nygren makes the important distinction of God's unilateral regenerative work in the sinner that makes the impossible—man's desire for God and the true good (Rom 3:9–11)—possible. While Oord's criticisms of Nygren's theological conclusions as derived from his reductionist methodology of *agapao* are in fact warranted, Oord's conclusion that Nygren's theological judgements form an inadequate form of *divine* love is not persuasive.

God's Necessary Love for the World

Oord says unless God is essentially related to creatures, then there is no guarantee that God loves them. Oord writes, "A God who may or may not love us could just as easily hate us."[194] Chapter 2 of this study addressed the philosophical and theological problems with holding to an essentially related view of God and the world. Here, I want to offer a biblically justified response to Oord's question, in that one can, apart from his logic, affirm God's necessary love.

Oord sets up the question of God's love for the world by means of a diagnostic test. He first asks: "*Could* God stop loving us?" And the second question is: "*Would* God stop loving us?" Oord says most people answer "yes" to the first (Oord does not agree) and "no" to the second (Oord does agree). The reason most people say "yes" to the first question, says Oord, is because "most think God's love for the world is freely chosen in all respects and that God could decide to stop loving creatures if God chose to do so."[195] Traditional views of God say that he sovereignly decided to create, and God is free to do as he pleases.

For the second question, Oord says almost everyone answers "no" because "people who think God *could* stop loving us, however, have no justification for thinking God *would not* stop loving us." Such people have no grounds to hold to that claim *unless* God's eternal nature includes love for the world. And then he sometimes asks a follow-up question: "*Why* are you so confident God would always love us?"[196] Oord says that most people

---

194. Oord, *NOL*, 110.
195. Oord, *NOL*, 111.
196. Oord, *NOL*, 112.

are confident that God will keep loving them, otherwise God would not be acting like God. And such an answer is revealing in what people really think about God: his "love for the world is an essential element in God's nature."[197] Most people affirm God's freedom to love and also affirm that love is his essence and thus cannot *not* love. Therefore, writes Oord, "they need another way to do so." And that option is to affirm God's essential love for himself and all others—"members of the Trinity and the members of creation—because God's nature is love."[198]

Oord claims this option provides stronger grounds for us to trust God because affirming that God's love for the world is contingent is therefore arbitrary. The problem is that Oord does not make a distinction in God's love for the elect and those of the world,[199] as Scripture does. He blurs the lines between God's love for Christians and the world. For example, Oord writes,

> Because God loves the world (Jn 3:16) and desires to redeem all creation (Rom 8:19–22), all creatures are recipients of divine love. God acts variously to establish the reign of love throughout all creation as the Great Lover of us all. . . . The love of God is shed abroad because the Spirit cares about each creature and the common good (Rom 5:5). Abundant is the love God lavishes upon creation (1 Jn 3:1).[200]

I have a few concerns with Oord's interpretation, in that that for him, *divine love*, is intra-Trinitarian love.[201] All creatures, Oord writes are recipients of *that* love. Neither Scripture nor the Christian tradition affirm that God has manifested his triune love to all of creation. And in Oord's remark about God shedding the love of the Spirit to each creature for the common good, his citing of Romans 5:5 misses the mark. Paul is speaking of believers in the context of them having righteousness and peace because they have "obtained access [to God] through Christ by faith" (Rom 5:1–2). Paul concludes his argument in 5:5, stating that Christians have obtained access to God through Christ because he has given his Spirit *to them*. Paul's audience is the church, not the world.

And then Oord's last sentence, referring to 1 John 3:1 to support his view that God has lavished his abundant love on creation, also, widely misses the mark. The apostle John writes, "See what great love the Father has given

---

197. Oord, *NOL*, 112.

198. Oord, *NOL*, 113.

199. An Arminian affirms that God loves the world, according to John 3:16; however, he does make the qualitative distinction between his church and the world.

200. Oord, *ULG*, 166.

201. Oord, *NOL*, 139.

us that we should be called God's children—and we are! The reason the world does not know us is that it didn't know him." More so than the last text, this passage speaks directly of God's love of his children, which greatly conflicts with Oord's argument about God's love of creation. And in one last example, Oord cites Romans 11:29, where Paul says God's gifts are "irrevocable" to support Oord's argument that God gives freedom and agency to all of creation. But that is not the context; Paul was speaking about God's promises to Israel because it seemed that God's shifting his love toward the Gentiles meant his rejection of Israel.[202] Oord refers to the Bible often in his writings, but his process philosophy does not allow him to affirm a love of God that is selective or specific to certain aspects of his creation.

Robert Plummer's essay on love in the New Testament (as observed in chapter 3) demonstrated that it focuses on the effective, saving love God has for *Christians*, not the world. While John 3:16 captures God's benevolence for the world, as it is *his* world, the focus of Christ's love centers on his bride, the church. And the promise that guarantees God's love for the world, is actually only a guarantee that God made for *his people*, secured in Christ's death (John 10:14–18). The willingness of the Son to go to the cross for the salvation of sinners, those whom the Father gave to the Son (John 19:6; 9–10) and sealed with the Holy Spirit (Eph 1:13–14; 4:30; 1 Pet 1:5), is the work of the triune God to redeem his elect, those chosen "from before the foundation of the world to be holy and blameless in love before him" (Eph 1:4).

About halfway through his letter to the Romans, Paul speaks of the triumph that believers have in Christ. And to secure that triumph, Paul does not turn his audience's attention to God's essential nature of love for the world. Rather, he turns their hearts to the cross. To those who are fearful of death and persecution and with trembling hearts, Paul says:

> If God is for us, who is against us? He did not even spare his own Son but offered him up for *us all*. How will he not also with him grant *us* everything? Who can bring an accusation against *God's elect*? God is the one who justifies. Who is the one who condemns? Christ Jesus is the one who died, but even more, has been raised; he also is at the right hand of God and intercedes *for us. Who can separate us from the love of Christ*? Can affliction or distress or persecution or famine or nakedness or danger or sword? As it is written: Because of you we are being put to death all day long; we are counted as sheep to be slaughtered. No, in all these things we are more than conquerors through him who loved us. *For I am persuaded that neither death nor life, nor angels nor rulers, nor things present nor things to come, nor powers,*

---

202. Oord, *ULG*, 169.

> *nor height nor depth, nor any other created thing will be able to separate us from the love of God that is in Christ Jesus our Lord.* (Rom 8:31–39; emphasis added)

The emphasized portions highlight the eternal love of God manifested toward *his* people, stating that *nothing* in all of creation can separate God's love from *them*. In reviewing Oord's diagnostic questions, a believer has solid ground—the Word of God—to stand on when he answers that God cannot and will not stop loving him, and that foundation is the love of God manifested in Christ Jesus. Romans 8:31–39 is how *God* demonstrates his never-ending love to his elect.

While Oord speaks of believers experiencing a renewal in God's image, painting a wonderful picture with various biblical texts of sanctification and eternal security *for believers*,[203] he breaks away from Scripture in expressing that God's steadfast love is for all of creation, without distinction. Oord even cites Romans 8:39, to support his statement that "we need not fear that the God whose nature is love will stop loving us." But he grounds this in God's essential nature of love that has been creating and relating with some creation, rather than God's Word, which says he has chosen a people for himself, specifically revealing his redemptive love to them.

Conclusion

The aim in this chapter was to provide an account of Thomas Oord's divine-love theology, followed by an evaluation and critique. Most alarming was Oord's admission that the Bible does not articulate an internally consistent definition of love, yet he attempted to formulate one, which he believed dominated the biblical witness. However, that does not mean Oord should be held in contempt for developing a model of love. In the attempts by others in constructing models of divine love, all of them most certainly have aspects deserving of critique.

An examination of Oord's works demonstrated his attempt was inadequate because of his failure to take into account the diverse elements of love found in Scripture, due to his operating with a contrived philosophical definition of love rather than an exegetically derived definition. In his treatment of Anders Nygren, while properly identifying the errors in Nygren's methodology, he dismisses Nygren's *agape* theology of love because of its conduciveness to particular doctrines Oord rejects: a view of *agape* love defined as God's unilateral spontaneous love of mankind

---

203. Oord, *NOL*, 120.

grounded *in* and motivated *by Godself* and not in the worth or value of humanity. And though he proposes that *prevenient grace* is a more favorable view that better accounts for "the centrality of God's love and of creaturely responses,"[204] he does not argue for it exegetically.

Other theologians, observed in this chapter, who endeavored on a similar study, recognized the complexities in formulating a doctrine of love[205] due to the diverse uses found in Scripture. Such affirmations led them to conclusions that embraced a multifaceted definition. While Oord recognizes that love is "multidimensional,"[206] his definition, *to act intentionally, in sympathetic/empathetic response to God and others, to promote overall well-being*, is quite selective, thus truncating his study of love, limiting the scope needed for such a significant task. Furthermore, Oord's overlooking the context behind Nygren's essential statements about divine love seem to demonstrate an arbitrariness in Oord. The data must guide the development of the thesis; the thesis does not develop the data.

---

204. Oord, *NOL*, 52.

205. For example, in Psalm 136, which we observed earlier, because of God's *hesed* love for Israel he strikes down all of Egypt's firstborn and mighty great kings, those he also sustained through benevolent love. Such an instance shows preferential treatment of Israel over other people. And as Deuteronomy 7 shows, God's loving Israel was not because it did anything great to deserve it, but rather, "The LORD had his heart set on you and chose you . . . because the LORD loved you and kept the oath he swore to your fathers" (vv. 7–8). Oord said he follows the *hesed* love tradition, but nowhere does he acknowledge or approach such texts that veer off from his definition of love, though are part of that same tradition.

206. Oord, *NOL*, 121.

4: Scripture and Metaphysics

A Process Approach

CENTRAL TO THE PROBLEM of coherence in Oord's theology with Scripture is the role of metaphysics. While Oord claims that his theology, his "arguments, hypotheses, and theories rest primarily . . . on the witness of Scripture," and I believe Oord is sincere, my argument is that his process metaphysic is the adjudicator of his interpretation of Scripture. And therefore, many of his interpretive conclusions are inconsistent with Scripture and the historic Christian tradition. In this section, I will identify key metaphysical aspects of Oord's process thought in contrast to classical metaphysics. While we all lean on a particular metaphysic in theological formulation, I maintain that Scripture more consistently agrees with a classical view than a process view.

Oord writes, "A robust theistic metaphysics proposes that God's loving nature serves as the source and standard for all goodness in the world."[1] More definitively[2] the "self-giving, others empowering love of God revealed in Jesus Christ [is] logically primary in God's eternal essence."[3] And imbedded in God's loving nature is that "God's love is uncontrolling."[4] For Oord, love *cannot* coerce; applied to God, it means God cannot control others. Since God always loves, yet evil occurs, it is because "God *cannot* unilaterally prevent genuine evil."[5] Oord agrees with the common Christian view as expressed in John 4:24 that "God's essential 'being' or 'constitution' is spiritual."[6] And, accordingly, Oord's understanding of God as "omnipresent and incorporeal spirit" means that God cannot metaphysically control

---

1. Oord, *ULG*, 77.
2. Oord cites John 15:5; Acts 17:28; Phil 4:13; 1 John 4:19.
3. Oord, *ULG*, 160.
4. Oord, *ULG*, 183.
5. Oord, *ULG*, 167.
6. Oord, *ULG*, 176.

others because he "does not have a localized divine body to thwart evils through direct bodily impact."[7] Rather, God relies on persuasion.[8] God's steadfast love of all creation means that "God cannot present forms of existence that would be unloving."[9] Locating love as the logically primary metaphysical attribute in God means his "actions originate in love."[10] Citing 1 John 4:8, 16, Oord writes, "'God is love' means . . . God relentlessly expresses love in the quest to promote overall well-being."[11]

For Oord, God's relation to the world is essential.[12] This statement is important to a process construct. In contrast, classical theism posits that the only *essential* relation for God is the intra-Trinitarian relations of the Godhead. Oord, however, says the Bible affirms that God has always been creating from something; therefore, "it makes more sense to say that God necessarily exists *and* necessarily relates to creatures."[13] God's work of creation is good and is an activity that God continues doing (Gen 1:4, 10).[14] Oord prefers to use what he believes is a more biblical designation, *almighty*, instead of the non-biblical term *omnipotent* in reference to God's power.[15] "God is the ultimate source of might; . . . he supplies power for all others, thereby empowering them to be or act."[16] God enables creatures to act, in that he shares his power with them, providing the "fundamental energy" needed for creatures to exist and act. Citing Romans 8:28, Oord writes, "We can be God's partners and co-conspirators by following the Spirit's lead. God's collaborative love seeks all who want to work for well-being, which is God's purpose."[17] Oord links this view of God to the Wesleyan tradition, which terms it "prevenient grace." This perspective of God's power states that "God's loving power precedes and makes possible creaturely responses."[18]

---

7. Oord, *ULG*, 188.
8. Oord, *ULG*, 179.
9. Oord, *ULG*, 200.
10. Oord, *ULG*, 165.
11. Oord, *ULG*, 161.
12. Oord, "God Always Creates," 114.
13. Oord, "God Always Creates," 114.
14. Oord, *ULG*, 165.
15. However, one is the German and the other the Latin version of the same idea. Both are in English so neither is "biblical"; both are translations of the same biblical word.
16. Oord, *ULG*, 190.
17. Oord, *ULG*, 165.
18. Oord, *ULG*, 190.

The fundamental metaphysical aspects in Oord's view of God are:[19] (1) God must love; it is his preeminent attribute. (2) God promotes overall well-being through full-orbed love. (3) God *cannot* unilaterally prevent genuine evil. (4) God's love necessarily means he must give freedom, even to those who use it wrongly. (5) God has pervasive influence, but he cannot control others. (6) God necessarily gives agency and self-organization, which means "God *cannot* interfere with the lawlike regularities" he has given to creation.

Oord claims that his metaphysical framework better supports the view that God essentially loves creation. In fact, it is entirely accurate to state that the process metaphysical *mantra*, the key distinction between process theology and classical theology, is that "God essentially and everlastingly loves creation."[20] Whitehead writes, "Metaphysics requires that the relationships of God to the world lie beyond the accidents of will, and that they be founded upon the necessities of the nature of God and the nature of the World."[21] In other words, in order for God to love *necessarily* he must not be able to *not* love *necessarily*.[22] Therefore, the metaphysical guarantor that necessitates God's love for creation is one of nature not of arbitrary choice. A corollary of this underlying metaphysical necessity is why Oord (and the process tradition) cannot affirm the traditional Christian view of creation, *creatio ex nihilo*; it "provides no grounds to trust that God will continually love us. . . . God's love for the world may or may not be so. It is arbitrary."[23]

At its foundation, process philosophy "is a form of *naturalistic* theism."[24] It denies miracles, in the supernatural sense. It sees that the world is an organism or God as mind and the universe as his body, which functions according to the laws of nature. Hence, it is grounded in naturalistic metaphysics, where nothing occurs apart from the law-like principles of the natural world, of which God is essentially a part. And from a naturalistic construct, supernaturalistic readings of Scripture have to be discarded or reinterpreted in a manner that violates the context of the text.

Oord, however, does believe that "God sometimes acts miraculously."[25] But the problem for Oord with adopting a definition of miracles as "God's

---

19. Summarized from Oord, *ULG*, 160–74.
20. Oord, "God Always Creates," 118.
21. Whitehead, *Adventures*, 215.
22. While I agree with the emphasis on God's loving nature being a necessary aspect of his nature, my concern is that process theism denies God the ability to not love at all.
23. Oord, "God Always Creates," 119.
24. Griffin, "Process Philosophy," 135.
25. Oord, *ULG*, 192.

intervention in the natural processes of life," is the word *intervene*.[26] For Oord this is problematic because it assumes that "God resides outside nature and its causality.... It implicitly denies divine omnipresence."[27] Furthermore, if God inserts himself into his creation to perform a supernatural action, one may conclude that God acted in a manner that entirely controlled a thing or outcome, working around the natural causes he established. If this is the case, then, Oord writes, "The God who could control in this way, should have miraculously prevented all genuine evils."[28] For the reasons noted above, Oord defines a miracle as "an unusual and good event that occurs through God's special action in relation to creation."[29]

While I am appreciative of Oord's desire to express the loving nature of God, our expression of God's love must be shaped yet confined to the pages of Scripture. Oord has made some statements that resonate with the Christian tradition about God's love; however, much of what he has stated about God's love seems rather contrived. After sketching out a classical metaphysic, I will interact with Oord's interpretation on a few passages that pertain to miracles. Chapter 5 of this study will expound further on the inconsistencies of a process metaphysic and congruency with Scripture within a doctrine of providence, while demonstrating the greater consistency of classical metaphysics with the teachings of the Bible.

A Classical Approach

Classical theism makes contemplation of the triune God the *key* to understanding God himself, as revealed in Scripture. Located in the Christian doctrine of God, theological interpretation is "appealing to the specific understanding of God that is derived from the prophets and the apostles of Holy Scripture by means of exegesis. It is an appeal to the Holy Trinity."[30] A classical view starts with: God has spoken. God has revealed himself beyond the empirical; he has revealed himself through his divine breath, his Word and his *written* Word.

While his power and divine nature is known from what is seen in creation, the things he has made (Rom 1:19–20),[31] his special, inspired

---

26. Oord, *ULG*, 194–95.
27. Oord, *ULG*, 195.
28. Oord, *ULG*, 197.
29. Oord, *ULG*, 196.
30. Carter, *Interpreting Scripture*, 33.
31. Levering writes, the apostle Paul observes that "when one moves intellectually from contingent creatures to uncreated cause," the existence of God is apparent. Levering, *Scripture and Metaphysics*, 60.

revelation is seen in the Word become flesh (John 1:14). And following Christ's ascension, though he left earth, he did not leave his children as orphans (John 14:18). He poured out his Spirit, whom "the world is unable to receive," to teach *his* children "all things." (John 14:17, 24). From the biblical text, the church has described God as Spirit (John 4:24), eternal (Ps 90:2), immutable (Ps 102:26, 27), omnipresent (Jer 23:24), omniscient (Ps 147:5), omni-sapient (all-wise) (Rom 16:27), omnipotent (Job 26:15), holy (Exod 15:11), all-good (Mark 10:18), omnibenevolent (1 John 4:8), and sovereign over his creation (Ps 103:19). These are just a sampling of passages to support these ascriptions of God.

While I list these as classical expressions of God, apart from divine sovereignty,[32] Oord also excepts these designations. However, Oord modifies some of these descriptors. He affirms immutability in the sense that God's nature or essence is immutable, but God's experience is mutable. And when Oord speaks of God being eternal, he is also referring to God's loving nature being eternal. God's experience is "everlasting, in the sense of being in all times. . . . A time-full rather than timeless God interacts in a time-full world."[33] Creatures have the freedom to love or not love, but God's eternal nature of love means love in God "is preeminent and necessary."[34] Oord's understanding of God as omniscient means "God knows what can be known, which does not amount to exhaustive foreknowledge."[35] So, while Oord has reservations about some of the classical expressions of the divine nature, we can see that there is a shared consensus on most because of the place of Scripture in our Christian theology. However, variations arise due to different metaphysical starting points.

God is transcendent yet pervasively immanent. Wherever we go, God is there (Ps 139:7–8). God's revealing himself to Moses at the burning bush as "I AM" (Exod 3:14) displays God's uniqueness. In God expressing himself in verb form, the deepest meaning to be drawn is that "I am myself."[36] The

---

32. Oord says that making love logically paramount "does not mean we disregard other divine attributes, such as sovereignty." Oord, *ULG*, 163. However, Oord does not affirm a view of divine sovereignty that says God can unilaterally act in a manner that controls, coerces, overpowers, or prevents any creaturely act or any aspect of creation. In fact, "God *cannot* unilaterally prevent genuine evil" (167). Because "if love comes first, God *cannot* exercise meticulous providence or determine everything" (147). Oord says those who affirm that "God rules through sovereign power . . . are in error." Oord, *GC*, 183. Oord does not see divine sovereignty as overpowerment but rather God's empowerment of creation toward well-being. Oord, *ULG*, 160.

33. Oord, *NOL*, 77–78.

34. Oord, *ULG*, 61, 161.

35. Oord, *NOL*, 90.

36. Aquinas writes, "*HE WHO IS* . . . does not signify form, but simply existence itself." Aquinas, *ST*, 1.13.11.

divine being is not like created being; rather, in stating "I am who I am," God is saying that he is "a self-contained, incomprehensible being."[37] How are we to speak about God? God is not just an upgraded version of mankind; rather, he is utterly different. But in God revealing himself to his creation, he also gives his creation a language to express and convey thoughts to each other and to God. The infinite God has given finite man analogical language to speak, not comprehensively, but, *truly* of God.[38] Scripture is *ontological* in the sense that it is God's communicative presence.[39]

Revelation demonstrates God's distinction from his creation. The doctrine of *creatio ex nihilo* is instrumental in supporting this claim, in that Scripture teaches that God is the one who causes all things to be. Contrary to process theology, God creates and relates not by necessity but according to his will (Rev 4:11).[40] And because God is Creator, he creates as he determines, and he upholds all things by his powerful word (Heb 1:3).[41] As a prime example within the classical tradition, Matthew Levering traces out Aquinas' connection between his exegesis and metaphysics. First, he notes God's naming himself by means of the verb "to be," signifying his being and simplicity, his sheer presence and encompassing existence in all tenses of time and outside of it. And second, because we *cannot* determine any sort of *mode* of the divine being, "to be" then reveals himself as "YHWH," which narrows down the broad reality of divinity. And third, he calls himself the "God of your fathers, the God of Abraham, the God of Isaac, the God of Jacob."[42] And in going from sheer existence to divine persona, "the God of Israel associates his historical salvific activity with his metaphysical reality."[43] Though many are critical of Aquinas'

---

37. Childs, *Exodus*, 76. Terrence Fretheim, more sympathetic to a relational view of God, sees Exodus 3:14 not as a mere statement of being; rather, the force of the text is that "God will be faithfully God for [Israel]." Fretheim, *Exodus*, 63.

38. Carter, *Interpreting Scripture*, 49.

39. Webster, *Holy Scripture*, 2.

40. Cf. Dan 2:20–23; 4:35; 5:23; Prov 16:4.

41. Cf. John 1:3; Col 1:16–17.

42. Weinandy notes, "What equally needs to be grasped is that, while an intimate covenantal relationship was made with the Israelites, which specified his loving presence and commitment, yet it was *the one God*—Yahweh—who established such a covenant. . . . Yahweh in his oneness is unique, and because he is the one God, the Israelites ultimately came to believe that he is the only God. Moreover, being the one God radically differentiates him from all else, even from the false and specious gods." Weinandy, *Does God Suffer?*, 44.

43. Levering, *Scripture and Metaphysics*, 63.

'substance' and 'being' metaphysics, he demonstrates in his theology "that biblical exegesis requires metaphysical analysis."[44]

A Challenge to Process Metaphysics

Miracles is a helpful, evaluative point of intersection between the two competing metaphysical views. Below, I will challenge Oord's interpretive understandings of passages he cites to support a process understanding of miracles.

Oord's View of Miracles

Oord's process metaphysic sees that creation must function according to law-like regularity, to what we can perceive with our senses (and scientific instruments). Therefore, when Scripture speaks of divine activity that defies the law-like regularities of nature, process metaphysics seeks an alternative explanation that corresponds with the laws of the natural world.[45] Empirical has the upper hand over the spiritual.

Oord defines a miracle, or "special divine action," as "an unusual and good event that occurs through God's special action in relation to creation."[46] God's "special divine action . . . takes into account the relevant ways creatures have acted in the past and might act in the future."[47] God's uncontrolling love means that God never coerces or controls any part of his creation, as many understand is what happens when God performs a miracle. Rather, God, based on "the past actions of other creatures and entities pertinent to the person or place, . . . provides new possibilities, forms, structures or ways of being to creatures."[48] If creatures and creation respond well to God's invitation, then miracles occur.[49] Creaturely cooperation is needed in order for miracles, such as parting the waters at the Red Sea, the resuscitation of Lazarus, turning water into wine, the flood in Genesis 7 that brought great harm to creatures, and striking dead Ananias and Sapphira (Acts 5), to occur.[50] Oord says that while many see that mir-

---

44. Levering, *Scripture and Metaphysics*, 151.
45. Oord, *ULG*, 49.
46. Oord, *ULG*, 199, 196.
47. Oord, *ULG*, 200.
48. Oord, *ULG*, 199–200.
49. Oord, *ULG*, 200.
50. Oord, *ULG*, 213.

acles are due to God coercing and controlling the elements of his creation, "the Bible gives no explicit support to the view that miracles require divine control."[51] So then, how does God bring about miracles without controlling the elements of his creation?

A naturalistic explanation of the parting of the Red Sea, Oord writes, is that violent winds blew the waters apart allowing for the Israelites to pass through. This "explanation is plausible and should be taken seriously" because parts of the Red Sea have been dried by such winds.[52] A supernaturalistic explanation assumes God's coercive power over the natural elements and processes within creation. However, controlled intervention is improper because this logically gives primacy to power, not love in God. So then, how did God accomplish the parting of the Red Sea? Oord says that God is able to coordinate random and/or spontaneous events within various levels of existences, simple to complex, creaturely and non-creaturely. And "this coordination is possible because of God's omnipresence and complete knowledge of what has occurred and is occurring."[53]

In the resurrection of Jesus, Oord points out that dead bodies have "agency, value, relationship, or freedom . . . and exist in a different state of being."[54] Therefore, the divine action involved in raising Christ from the dead was not one of coercive force. Rather, the noncoercive, kenotic love of God provided agency to Jesus, who, after being crucified, both his body and spirit, "cooperated with God's empowering love to raise him from the dead."[55]

For Oord, God's nature of love in giving law-like regularities to what he has made means he cannot break, intervene, or supersede those natural laws.[56] God is always ready and active, "exerting causal influence in all aspects and levels of nature."[57] Therefore, God's activity is always at work within creation. Oord does not define a miracle as God's special acting in creation that guides or moves some part of his creation not in accordance with the laws assigned; for him God does not act in that way. Again, Oord does not deny miracles; rather, he defines them differently because God is completely

---

51. Oord, *ULG*, 201.

52. Oord, *ULG*, 207–8. I will respond to Oord's explanation of the Red Sea account in chapter 5 of this study.

53. Oord, *ULG*, 209.

54. Oord, *NOL*, 151.

55. Oord, *NOL*, 152.

56. Oord, *ULG*, 174.

57. Oord, *ULG*, 208.

influencing his creation at every level of existence, never having to transcend his natural presence in creation to supernaturally act.[58]

A Critical Response

While Oord's view accounts for miracles, he makes "the metaphysical claim that miracles *always* involve actions from both the Creator and creatures/creation."[59] Scripturally, Oord identifies passages in the New Testament of miracles that involve creaturely contribution. For example, Peter's walking on water ended when his faith decreased (Matt 14:22–33). The Gospels have multiple accounts of Christ performing miracles or not performing miracles based on creaturely factors, demonstrations of faith (Matt 8:5–13; Mark 2:1–12; 6:56). However, when it comes to Jesus' performing nature miracles (e.g., calming the wind and the waves), Oord attributes the manifestation of the miracle to "aggregations of entities without the capacity for faith—amassed water molecules—not personal agents with free will."[60]

Oord's metaphysic of the natural world, in that nothing can happen that cannot be accounted for in the natural ordering of things, ultimately guides his interpretation of such passages.[61] Oord's claims that miraculous healings only occur through creaturely cooperation and that disbelief, a form of noncooperation, prevents miraculous healings. To support his claim, Oord cites Mark 6:5–6, emphasizing that Mark said Jesus *could not* do miracles because of their unbelief. However, the passage states, "He was not able to do a miracle there, except that he laid his hands on a few sick people and healed them."[62] According to Oord, "healings are the most common forms of miracles mentioned in the Bible."[63] So, Jesus *was* able to perform miracles. But what about the passage as a whole? A more plausible and consistent interpretation is that Jesus did not do it under these

---

58. Oord and a classical view find agreement on this point.
59. Oord, "Miracles," 207.
60. Oord, *ULG*, 206.
61. Oord writes, "In a universe of cause and effect, divine efficient causation is a direct objective cause of the same metaphysical kind as creaturely causes. No appeal to mysterious divine action is necessary; special pleas to inexplicable supernaturalism are not required. God's influence on creatures breaks no theoretical principles pertaining to the metaphysical laws that apply to all existents. Whitehead's plea that we not treat God as an exception to the metaphysical principles is heeded." Oord, *DL*, 194.
62. In the parallel passage in Matthew, the author writes, "And he did not do many miracles there because of their unbelief" (13:58).
63. Oord, *ULG*, 202.

circumstances because he did not want to do them.⁶⁴ Obviously he performed some healing miracles, to those who may or may not have been believers. But his hometown, as a whole, was full of rebellious hearts.⁶⁵ Therefore, his not performing "a miracle" should be understood from the context of Jesus' ministry, not Jesus' ability to work miracles.⁶⁶

When it comes to Peter sinking in the water due to his lack of faith, other than acknowledging Jesus' miraculous walking on water, Oord does not apply his cooperative interpretation to that event. He offers an explanation of Peter's sinking, suggesting that Jesus did not cause (divine control) the water molecules to amass to hold up Peter; if so, Peter should have been able to stay afloat, despite his lack of faith.⁶⁷ But what about Jesus? He was walking on water. Was his faith keeping the water molecules intact to support his weight? Or did Jesus walk on water because, as the Creator, he can control the elements of the world according to his purposes? And then, in regard to Peter, in understanding Jesus as Creator, a more appropriate explanation is that Peter sank because the Lord perceived his lack of faith (Matt 12:25; Mark 2:8) and loosened the water molecules so that Peter would sink.⁶⁸

While Oord's view accounts for miracles as unusual events, a miracle from his view is not a supernatural act;⁶⁹ rather, it is a special, natural act. Oord writes, "Miracles remind us that a loving God is at work in the world," where "God's kenotic and noncoercive love makes a real and sometimes astonishing difference in our lives."⁷⁰ When creatures "respond well to God's loving activity, miracles can occur."⁷¹ The metaphysical assumption that God cannot control any part of his creation—a process construct—controls Oord's interpretation of miracle passages, and it restricts his interpretation from following the point of the author in the biblical text.

---

64. Hendriksen, *Mark*, 224.
65. Edwards, *Mark*, 174.
66. Lane, *Mark*, 204.
67. Oord, *ULG*, 204.
68. Interestingly, the resurrection of Lazarus (John 11) is absent from Oord's published books and articles. Oord, *NOL*, 151.
69. I define supernatural act as a divine special action where God directly or immediately modifies the order of nature to fulfill his purposes, as revealed in Scripture. Geerhardus Vos identifies supernatural acts in Scripture not just as a reordering of natural law, but in the prediction and conjunction of "two (possibly both natural) events coming together in time, and which in the last analysis is reducible to the omniscience of God, showing His supernatural presence in the course of things as clearly as the sign of omnipotence." Vos, *Biblical Theology*, 231.
70. Oord, *NOL*, 148.
71. Oord, *NOL*, 150.

A classical view understands miracles as an extraordinary act God performs by direct action, expressing divine volition that modifies the natural order (Ps 104).[72] As the omnipresent, incorporeal Creator, he operates on a completely different plane of reality. He is above his created order; therefore, when acting directly as an immediate cause,[73] he is working supernaturally. He does not have to abide by naturalistic rules; rather, to perform a miraculous activity, God "simply causes something to happen that is not comprehensible to our scientific classification of natural laws, because all we can study are the regularities of nature, not the exceptions."[74] Natural processes are deterministic.[75] But because creation lives and moves and has its being *in God* (Acts 17:28; cf. Col 1:17), God as the omnipresent, omnipotent, and infinite essence does not have to perform according to a mechanized naturalistic view of things.[76]

Conclusion

What was outlined in the previous few paragraphs identify the contradistinction between process and classical metaphysics. The former, as Oord contends, starts with revelation but rests on experience, as the arbiter of interpretation; the latter (i.e., classical) starts with revelation aided by a metaphysical grammar,[77] functioning in a manner that allows it to rest on revelation, thus *informing* and orienting one's experience of the divine and the Christian life, without any appearance of contradiction or

---

72. Aquinas defines miracle as something "done outside the order of any particular nature," specifically something done "against the order of the whole created nature" of a thing. Aquinas, *ST*, 1.110.4. John Frame, aiming to be as biblical as possible, defines *miracle* as "an extraordinary manifestation of God's covenant lordship." Frame, *Systematic Theology*, 124.

73. God's use of secondary causes, mediately in creation, is a natural operation.

74. Carter, *Interpreting Scripture*, 53.

75. Vicens, "On the Possibility," 318. I appeal to Vicens's definition of *determinism*, which is "every event is necessitated by antecedent events and conditions together with laws of nature, which remain constant until the end of the world." But God's complete pervasiveness in creation, as the one who upholds all things by the power of his Word (Heb 1:3), has the ability, as Scripture reveals, to modify the deterministic and/or law-like regulative aspects within creation to serve his purposes (e.g., 2 Kgs 6:1–6).

76. Bavinck, *Reformed Dogmatics*, 2:610, writes, "In miracles God only puts into effect a special force that, like any other force, operates in accordance with its own nature and therefore also has an outcome of its own." Though God built laws into his creation, he is not dependent on causes; rather, creation depends on them.

77. Stephen Holmes speaks of Trinitarian theology in this manner, explaining that the aim in articulating the threeness of God without compromising the doctrine of simplicity was that of grammar not logic. Holmes, *Quest for the Trinity*, 109.

incoherence.[78] Both views develop a highly contrastive metaphysical understanding of the nature and being of God. But both are claiming biblical fidelity over the other.[79] While we cannot rid ourselves of metaphysical presuppositions, we must allow Scripture to reform those presuppositions.[80] Augustine is a representative case to trace out this metaphysical reshaping through divine revelation, in John's prologue.[81]

When John writes that the Word was with God and *is* God, having created all things, designating that the Word is not part of the *created* order (1:1–3), we are tasked with conceptualizing a metaphysical reality from which the Word comes.[82] And then when John says that "in him was life" (1:4), serious ontological implications follow that are antithetical to a material understanding of the world. This was Augustine's dilemma in his early days when moving from Manichaeism to Christianity.[83]

Manichaeism lacked an ontological conception of God that made a distinction between God and the material universe. Cosmic dualism was its solution. However, it created an ontological paradox.[84] The problem for Augustine was trying "to conceive of God as both *real* and also as *not* in any way part of the material universe."[85] It was not until he came to understand,

78. This is not to say that Scripture does not inform and orient Oord's views of the Christian life and experience of the divine. However, my argument is that Oord's philosophical and metaphysical assumptions of what God can and cannot do direct that experience, which leads him to overlook important texts and themes in the Bible. For example, while he has a brief half-page section on a Christian's renewal in God's image in *NOL* (120), Oord's view of God's love leads him to reject views of election and predestination of individuals or groups. Rather, God "pre-decides the characteristics of those conformed to the image of his Son (Rom 8:29, 30)." Oord, *NOL*, 157n63. In a cursory reading of those passages, nowhere does Paul speak of God pre-deciding one's characteristics. Even then, since Oord claims humans are completely and undecidedly free, then he would need to explain how God pre-decides one's characteristics. Oord does not offer exegetical support for his interpretation. Because Oord's view of God's love is that it necessarily extends equally to all of creation, God's choosing or electing of individuals or a group does not have a place in his theology, even though Scripture has explicit examples of God doing the very thing Oord denies (e.g., Deut 7:6–8; 10:14–15; Rom 8:33; Eph 1:5, 11; 2 Thess 2:13; 2 Tim 1:9; 1 Pet 2:8–9).

79. Both views affirm that God is Spirit. However, the stark contrast lies in *what* and *how* God as Spirit acts.

80. Carter, *Interpreting Scripture*, 62.

81. Some of the material in the following section is drawn from Carter, *Interpreting Scripture*, 61–91.

82. That is not to say that God comes into a material world; rather, the designation is merely conceptual. He is everywhere present.

83. See Augustine's thoughts on this in his *Confessions*, books 5 and 7.

84. Carter, *Interpreting Scripture*, 68.

85. Carter, *Interpreting Scripture*, 69.

through Platonism, the concept of *spiritual substance* that his exegesis then had a platform on which to stand. He could now say that God is a real *thing*, a spiritual substance, but not a *material* thing, like the created universe.

However, Platonic thought only enabled him to perceive of God from afar. Holy Scripture *revealed* the triune God, manifested as Father, Son, and Spirit. Scripture revealed the glorious Christ, as fully God, entering into his own creation, taking on flesh, dying in the flesh, and being resurrected by the eternal Spirit in glory.[86] If there is no ontological distinction between God and the universe, such words are meaningless. Only a God who is a spiritual substance could be perfect, immutable, and eternal, thus establishing the basis for Augustine's (i.e., classical theism) theological metaphysics.[87]

Augustine was not a Platonist who tried to shape Christianity around it; rather, he was a Christian who carried "the gold" (i.e., Platonic concepts) away from Egypt, to properly distinguish it from every other religion (i.e., Manichaeism), in that he could now *metaphysically* articulate in a coherent and consistent manner the reality of God (e.g., Rom 1:19–20) and, most importantly, his triune revelation (e.g., John 1:1–18). As Paul recognized the "gold" when quoting an Athenian poet saying, "For in him we live and move and have our being" (Acts 17:28), Augustine, likewise, took the "gold" belonging to God in the Platonists of his day. Many religions have traces of precious metals in their content, which belong to God, however, they only use those metals to extol idols because they have "exchanged the glory of the immortal God for images resembling mortal man, birds, and four-footed animals, and reptiles" (Rom 1:23).[88]

Augustine did not always get things right; however, Scripture reigned in his theology. But does it reign with Oord? I do not think it does, hence the reason for my critique. Oord, in some ways, is like an Augustine or an Aquinas (not that he would say that); however, unlike Augustine, Oord's theology–philosophy synthesis is unable to uphold the central Christian truths of the historic faith. And open theologians understood that as well, though they are more sympathetic to process thought because of its perceived greater emphasis on divine-human relationality than expressed in classical theism.

While Oord (and openness theologians) has expressed his dissatisfaction with classical theology's Neoplatonist elements in its metaphysical

---

86. Augustine, *Confessions*, 7.9. Augustine lists a host of significant christological texts (e.g., John 1:1–14; Phil 2:6–11; Rom 5:6; 8:32) in his understanding of the Word, Incarnation, and redemptive work.

87. Carter, *Interpreting Scripture*, 70.

88. This illustration of taking gold that belonged to God from pagan religions is how Augustine justifies his newfound understanding in *Confessions*, 7.9.

language and concepts,[89] it would be a genetic fallacy to disregard classical metaphysics based on that alone. Rather, one needs to show the metaphysics are flawed and incoherent if they conflict with biblical teaching. One must engage not only in careful exegesis but also in careful metaphysics.[90]

---

89. Oord, *NOL*, 58; Pinnock, "Systematic Theology"; Hasker, "A Philosophical Perspective."

90. Mullins, *Timeless God*, xiii.

5: Essential Kenosis

Oord's Relational Account of Divine Providence

Introduction

THIS CHAPTER EXAMINES THE *apex* of Oord's Evangelical Process Theology: *Essential Kenosis*. Essential Kenosis is Oord's "biblical theology of love."[1] But it is more than that. It is a relational model of divine providence. It is also an ontological expression of God. For Oord, it defines the essential essence and being of God. Essential Kenosis "affirms involuntary divine self-limitation,"[2] which means that God is necessarily self-giving.[3] Furthermore, *Essential Kenosis* is Oord's solution to the problem of evil.

Examining and evaluating a doctrine of providence is an excursion. The previous chapters of this study covered key aspects of Oord's doctrine of God, as well as explicating his process metaphysic, as it functions in biblical interpretation and theological dialogue, from which I will draw material from throughout my evaluation. Points of specific interest to be examined within an Essential Kenosis theology are: the doctrine of kenosis, divine freedom, divine impassibility, divine action, coercion, miracles, doctrine of creation, theodicy, and eschatology. Obviously, such topics could be book-length treatments. Due to space limitations, my evaluation of these aspects will be brief. My method is cumulative. The aim of this chapter is to examine Oord's doctrine of providence to see if it is internally and scripturally consistent.

My claim throughout this study is that Oord's process metaphysic has primacy in his Evangelical process theology, which results in an *un*-Evangelical model. Granted, every interpreter of Scripture has an underlying

---

1. Oord, *NOL*, 122.
2. Oord, *NOL*, 125.
3. In contrast to Jürgen Moltmann, John Polkinghorne, Clark Pinnock, and John Sanders, who advocate a self-*limiting* model.

metaphysic that guides his reading and dogmatic formulations. And Oord is free to operate from a process construct. But Oord subjects himself to the authority of Scripture, which forms the foundation of the Christian faith. So then, can one observe Oord's model of relational providence and be able to deductively trace his propositions back to the "nuts and bolts" within the documents on which it is supposed to be grounded? A doctrine of providence must be transcendently and imminently comprehensive. And I will argue that Oord's model is inapt as a doctrine of providence. Constructively, my critique will further demonstrate that the general sense of Scripture agrees more with a classical view.

Essential Kenosis: A Biblical Theology of Love

In *The Uncontrolling Love of God*, Oord writes, "God's self-giving, uncontrolling love is a necessary, eternal, and logically primary aspect of his divine nature."[4] His understanding of *kenosis* as espoused in his Essential Kenosis model is the guiding presupposition behind his Evangelical process theology. Oord says the Essential Kenosis model of providence "allows us to say God is not culpable for failing to prevent the dastardly deeds free creatures sometimes do. Because of God's immutable nature of self-giving, others-empowering love, God cannot prevent genuine evil."[5] Oord's Essential Kenosis model is an attempt to demonstrate that Christ's self-emptying in the incarnation was a "self-giving, others-empowering love of God revealed in Jesus Christ."[6] And in this self-giving, which is grounded in the text "God is love" (1 John 4:8), God's "uncontrolling love" for all creatures, serves as his preeminent attribute.[7]

Essential Kenosis is also Oord's "full solution to the problem of evil."[8] The problem of evil Oord adopts has been explained in this general formula: If God is omnipotent then he can prevent evil; if he is omnibenevolent, then he must want to prevent evil; since evil occurs, God then is not omnipotent or omnibenevolent. Ultimately, Oord presents a view of God who does not permissively nor decretively ordain evil, which, on the surface, satisfies the *intellectual* problem of evil. But how it fares with the biblical data is the measure being sought after.

---

4. Oord, *ULG*, 165.
5. Oord, *ULG*, 170.
6. Oord, *ULG*, 160.
7. Oord, *ULG*, 163.
8. Oord, *ULG*, 169n41.

Oord's aim in his Essential Kenosis model is to pull back the mask of the monarchial God of the classical tradition, revealing the Deity who truly meets us where we are, "the fellow-sufferer who understands."[9] According to Oord, theological systems that place primacy on power and control portray a God who is untrustworthy in his motives for doing what he does *or* for *not* doing what he should do. For Oord, coercion is deleterious to Christian theism. A God who coercively saves some and damns others is not a loving God. Oord asserts that the arbitrary nature of predestination removes the necessary freedom needed in order for one to be truly responsible for what could be an eternally tortuous destination.[10] An essentially kenotic God does not exercise coercion or pre-determinative power because his nature does not allow it.

Oord's Doctrine of Kenosis

In developing Essential Kenosis, Oord takes his cue from the well-known *kenotic*[11] hymn of Philippians 2:4–13. Much theological speculation and debate over the years regarding *kenosis theory* pertains to the relinquishing of Christ's divine attributes in the incarnation.[12] However, in recent discussions, *kenosis* has functioned as a lens through which Christ's actions reveal the divine attributes of God.[13] This view stems from the ethical thrust of Paul's message in Philippians. Paul emphasizes a unity of mind with Christ, demonstrated in his condescension from his throne and servanthood to the Father. Paul was espousing an "other-oriented love" in the weakness and power of the cross.[14] Because God approved of Christ's humility, thus "highly exalting him and bestowing on him the name above all names" (Phil 2:9), Paul exhorts his readers to pursue such a salvation.[15]

Other discussions in the kenosis debate center on *how* to see kenosis. According to Oord, abstract "container-language" does not seem to

---

9. Whitehead, *PR*, 351.

10. Oord, *NOL*, 155.

11. The phrase from Philippians 2:7 is *heauton ekenōsen*, translated as "he emptied himself." "*kenoō*," in BDAG, 539. BDAG, 539, defines it as "a divesture of position or prestige: of Christ, who gave up the appearance of his divinity and took on the form of a slave."

12. For a current treatment on kenotic Christology, see the collaborative work, Evans, *Exploring Kenotic Christology*.

13. Feenstra, "Kenotic Christological Method," 139–64; Davis, "Kenotic Christology," 190–218.

14. Oord, *ULG*, 154.

15. Oord, *ULG*, 154.

rightly explain the context of what Christ had done; rather, a relational interpretation more aptly resonates with Paul's context. Interpretations of kenosis in the contemporary scheme range from "self-emptying" and "self-withdrawing," to that of "self-limiting," or "self-giving."[16] The latter two interpretations speak more to the humility of Christ, portraying his voluntary mission in not only giving himself up on the cross but translating the *nature* and *being* of God exegeted through the Word-image of God made flesh (John 1:18; Heb 1:3).

Open and relational theists[17] prefer a *self-limiting* interpretation, where God purposely limits his power for the sake of finite creatures. Oord sees problems with a *self-limiting* view because it "says God does not always use for good the power God essentially possesses."[18] And, therefore, because genuine evil exists in the world, God, from a self-limiting perspective, has chosen not to use his power to prevent it. God, then, *is* culpable for evil.

In the context of Philippians, Oord believes Paul is concerned with his readers' need to promote the common good. He writes,

> Self-giving kenosis promotes overall well-being. In addition, those who imitate Christ's actions ultimately glorify God. Jesus' kenotic life and death reveal that God engages in self-giving, other-empowering love. To put it differently, Jesus' kenosis reveals that God self-gives to promote overall well-being. The Philippians passage concludes by indicating that God's kenotic love empowers us to promote good as we live out our salvation.[19]

While Oord sees within the relational-kenotic camp an inconsistent divine-love paradigm due to adopting a *self-limiting* interpretation, he believes an interpretation of a "self-giving, others empowering love" better supports the Christian ethic Paul taught and Christ revealed.[20] Oord clarifies that self-giving does not mean God gives his divinity to creatures; God cannot "lose" himself to others.

After defining *kenosis*, Oord qualifies it as *essential*, in that it is "logically primary in God's eternal essence."[21] And because self-giving love is logically primary in God, everything God does is grounded in love. Love

---

16. Oord, *ULG*, 156.

17. Oord, *ULG*, 157. Advocates of this view Oord cites include, Pool, *Divine Vulnerability*; Brümmer, *What Are We Doing*; Polkinghorne, "Kenotic Creation and Divine Action."

18. Oord, *ULG*, 158.

19. Oord, *ULG*, 160.

20. Oord, *ULG*, 160.

21. Oord, *ULG*, 160.

precedes, substantiates, and governs God's decisions and actions. God is incapable of *not* loving; he is not free to not love; "to be unloving . . . would require God to be other than divine."[22]

Critical Evaluation

My concern is that Oord's metaphysic of Essential Kenosis, as he defines it, in the construction of a doctrine of providence will ultimately cause it to collapse. Due to the complexities a doctrine of providence has to consider and hold together, so that it is faithful to the text and to the practice of the faith, the test of biblical fidelity comes when one's philosophical pinch-points divert one away from the terminus of the text. Circumventing biblical texts due to philosophical disparity leads to a deformative *ad hoc* doctrine of providence. Oord's attempt at developing a model that fits into an Evangelical mold cannot hold its form because a process philosophy guides the shaping.

The first section of this chapter is intended to establish his doctrine of Essential Kenosis. As demonstrated in chapter 3, Oord's definition of love is arbitrary, in the contrived sense, lacking a *contextual* biblical basis that takes into consideration the many facets of love in the Bible. And because he believes that love should be the starting point of theology, his definition of love serves as the theological rudder, guiding the formulation of his system.

Oord's interpretation of 1 John 4:8, "God is love," as God is uncontrollingly loving is a leap. What does that even mean? Oord does not expound on how he derives this concept from this text or any other. Rather, he steeps all of God's actions in love. But he never explicates the various notions of love. If we follow the apostle through the context of his letter, starting in verse 7, we notice that he qualifies love in a manner different than Oord:

> Dear friends, let us love one another, because love is from God, and everyone who loves has been born of God and knows God.[8] The one who does not love does not know God, because God is love.[9] God's love was revealed among us in this way: God sent his one and only Son into the world so that we might live through him.[10] Love consists in this: not that we loved God, but that he loved us and sent his Son to be the atoning sacrifice for our sins.[11] Dear friends, if God loved us in this way, we also must love one another. (1 John 4:7–11)

Verse 7 locates love in God. But the apostle also makes the important point that such love is how one knows God. In the Greek, verse 7 says: *kai*

---

22. Oord, *ULG*, 161.

pas ho agapōn ek tou theou gegennētai kai ginōskei ton theon. John makes the distinction that those who are presently and actively loving God (*pas ho agapōn*), are those who have been born (*gegennētai*) of God. *Gegennētai* is the perfect passive form of the verb denoting what happened prior to *and* in order for one to know and love God.[23] And then the one who does not love (i.e., has not been born of God) does not know God because God is love. Knowing God and loving God *come* from God. And then in verses 9–11, John defines what this love looks like, in that God's action in sending Christ to atone for sin, so that those born of God would live through him. Deducing that God loves uncontrollingly from 1 John 4:8 is a misreading of the passage because we actually see God's love as anything but uncontrolling; rather, it is specific and intentional, so that it defines who are born of God and models love within the church.

In the Philippians 2 context, Paul's teaching regarding Christ's act of humiliation and exaltation are not about promoting overall well-being. Granted, Paul assures his readers that God will finish the good work he started in them (1:6), but the context and overall theme of the letter does not promote such an understanding. The Christians at Philippi were a persecuted church. Paul is writing from prison, using his current position as a platform to showcase the gospel. Paul writes to encourage them in their faith, in obedience to God, and love for each other because "it is God who works in you, both to will and to work for his good pleasure" (2:13). To claim the intention behind Paul's profound christological statement was to "promote overall well-being" is a rather mundane reading of the text. More importantly, "[Paul] is talking about how to work out what it means to live as a follower of Jesus Christ in a world where there are many things that are good and many things that are not."[24] Holding firm to the word of life (Phil 2:16), having the same attitude as Christ, who lived in humility unto death, being pure and faultless, so that his Father would be glorified in his actions, who then exalted his Son into glory, is the aim of Paul's mission and hope for all those in Christ. Promoting well-being, as Oord defines well-being, is absent from Paul's theology.[25]

---

23. There is a tendency to miss the order of the verbs, emphasizing the participial clause (everyone who loves) over the perfect passive action (has been born of God).

24. Wright, "Philippians," 136.

25. The closest understanding of "over all well-being" that could be construed from Paul's writings is 1 Corinthians 12:7, "A manifestation of the Spirit is given to each person for the common good [*stympherō*: to be advantageous, *help, confer a benefit, be profitable/useful*, BDAG, 960]." The context of the passage connotes a common good within the body of believers—who are given the Spirit so that they can live united as one.

The pressing issue for the Philippians was continuing on under the threat of persecution and dealings with sin, as those joyous in having been granted belief in Christ but nevertheless having been "*granted* . . . [*charizomai*: to give feely as a favor] to suffer for him" (Phil 1:29, emphasis added). Paul's allegiance to Christ results in his imprisonment, all for the glory of the Lord. In order to encourage the Philippians to persevere in a hostile world, Paul's emphasis in the "spectacular poem of 2:6–11" is *not* Jesus' "self-giving and empowering of others for overall well-being"; rather, the *poem* served to demonstrate his equality with God in doing only that which God can do: the incarnation and crucifixion, through which God gives the suffering Jesus, the Messiah, honor and glory.[26] And under the lordship of Christ, contrary to that which Caesar offers and demands (see Mark 10:42–45), believers must press on, working out their salvation in a world governed by darkness.[27]

The struggle of faith lies in the conflict between living in light of the revealed triumph of Christ over the dominant powers of the world, while at the same time seeing that Christ, Paul, and those who follow, appear to have been overtaken by it. The Philippians are called to remain steadfast servants of God, living united as one in Christ, doing everything out of humility for others, as Christ has done for us. And all of this for the glory of God the Father. Oord's view, I believe, misses the greater theological import of the text. He has smuggled in his definition of love and appropriated it with his *kenotic* theory.

Essential Kenosis: Essential Freedom

A libertarian account of human freedom[28] is another crucial, if not central, piece in Oord's theological model. It is an assumed—and needed—position in order for Oord's relational theology to be coherent. For Oord, "Libertarian

---

26. O'Brien, *Philippians*, 216, writes that "the hymn reveals not only what Jesus is truly like but also what it means to be God."

27. Wright, "Philippians," 137.

28. *Incompatibilists* (or *libertarians*), writes open theist David Basinger, "believe that given the conditions preceding any involuntary decision, more than one decision must be possible—the person making the decision must be in a position to choose differently." Basinger, *Freewill Theism*, 26. Interestingly, open theist Greg Boyd writes, "we are beings who have to *decide* what we will become. This is what it means to be *self*-determining." Yet on the next page, he adamantly affirms "that fallen humans would never choose to accept God's offer of salvation if it were not for the work of the Holy Spirit in our lives. . . . [O]ur 'natural' orientation is rebellion against God." Boyd, *God of the Possible*, 137–38.

free will says genuine freedom is irreconcilable with being fully determined to act in a particular way."[29] The "chooser" or agent making the choices "is the source of its actions rather than some other causes."[30] And libertarian free will is integral to all open/relational schemes. The assumption is that if one is to love, one must be genuinely free to do so. "How else can there be loving relationships?"[31] While God has provided salvation for all, "he will not restore the broken relationship without our free consent."[32] For Oord, it does not make "sense to say that creatures love if God irresistibly [unilaterally speaking] supplies all the love expressed by creatures."[33] If man is made in the image of God, then he must, *within his being*, have the freedom to love others for their sake, not *only* because God has given his creatures love to dispense. The relational-communal element is already existent; it just needs to be fully actualized by the Holy Spirit.

For Oord, freedom is "the notion that one's free choice originates in oneself and is not dependent upon conditions that make it the case that one cannot do otherwise."[34] His doctrine of free will, he terms "essential free-will theism,"[35] differs slightly from the other forms of libertarianism. His form, like the others, recognizes that man's personal freedom is limited because free creatures exert influence on each other. Freedom is limited to what is possible, given the set of circumstances one is faced with. In other libertarian models, God limits himself and "*could* withdraw or override creaturely powers."[36]

In essential free-will theism, no room is given nor is there the "metaphysical"[37] possibility for God to do such actions. God cannot "unilaterally determine others because all actual individuals are essentially free."[38] And since God does not have a localized, divine body, he cannot "exert bodily impact" on any *bodied* creature.[39] Ultimately, the grounding reason is because of the free, loving nature of God. "God could not decide

---

29. Oord, *ULG*, 59.
30. Oord, *ULG*, 59.
31. Pinnock, *Most Moved Mover*, 128.
32. Sanders, "Divine Providence," 206.
33. Oord, "MTP," 221.
34. Oord, "MTP," 225.
35. Oord, "Process Wesleyan Theodicy," 199.
36. Oord, "Process Wesleyan Theodicy," 199.
37. Oord, "Process Wesleyan Theodicy," 199.
38. Oord, "Process Wesleyan Theodicy," 200.
39. Oord, "Process Wesleyan Theodicy," 208.

not to give us freedom, because God's nature is freedom—giving love."[40] Because he is uncontrollingly loving, he cannot override or hinder any of his creatures free choices, and he is unable to prevent evil, thus bearing no culpability for the evil acts humans do.[41]

Essential Human Freedom: Doctrine of Prevenient Grace

As a Wesleyan, Oord holds to the doctrine of prevenient grace, which he defines, "as God lovingly acting first to make possible free creaturely responses."[42] For Wesley, *prevenient grace* is where salvation begins, where one feels "the first slight transient conviction of having sinned against [God]."[43] It is the beginning of deliverance, where the insensible heart has a "first wish to please God." And true salvation, then, is wrought about through "convincing grace, which Scripture terms repentance."[44] John 1:9, 12:32, and Titus 2:11 are key biblical texts Wesleyans use to support the doctrine of prevenient grace.

In Wesley's view of John 1:9, "The true light that gives light to everyone, was coming into the world," he understood that prevenient grace was a supernatural working of God, restoring the measure of free-will needed to every man, together with that "true light" that "enlightens every man that cometh into the world."[45] In the atonement passage of John 12:32, Jesus says, "As for me, if I am lifted up from the earth I will draw all people to myself." The universality of the atonement implies that Christ died for all; therefore, grace has gone out to all, though men still resist the call.[46] Grace, then, "is at work in our lives before we come to know Him. We seek Him because he sought us. The lifted-up Christ draws all people toward himself."[47]

---

40. Oord, personal email to author, March 15, 2019.

41. Oord, "Process Wesleyan Theodicy," 201.

42. Oord, *NOL*, 129. Interestingly, Oord believes it is possible for someone to be sinless, despite one's past or what happens in the present. Oord, personal email to author, December 20, 2018.

43. Wesley, *Works*, 6:509.

44. Wesley, *Works*, 6:509.

45. Wesley, *Works*, 6:229–30.

46. Reasoner, "Wesley's Doctrines," 99–102.

47. Woolsey, *1 & 2 Thessalonians*, 105.

However, Oord has a stricter view of grace than Wesley.[48] Oord says prevenient grace is actually "necessary grace."[49] In Oord's understanding of the being of God, grace is necessary due to the fact that God's eternal nature of love necessarily means he cannot *not* give love and grace for the well-being of his creation. For Wesley, grace is necessary in that it allows human beings to engage their God-enabled free will to accept the salvific offer of God. However, the grace conferred upon humans does not make their response inevitable.[50] Oord, likewise, does not believe God's grace imposes a necessity on creatures to choose the good. Wesley said that "since the fall, no child of man has a natural power to choose anything that is truly good."[51] A sinner's will, writes Wesley, is "free only to evil; free to 'drink in iniquity like water;' to wander farther and farther from the living God, and do more 'despite to the Spirit of grace!'"[52]

For Oord, however, when it comes to one's choosing to sin, Adam and Eve or the fall have nothing to do with it; one sins because one "freely chooses to do other than what God calls us to do."[53] Humans do not sin because they are sinners; "we are sinners because we sin." And thus, Oord believes that "prevenient grace makes it possible for us to be sinless, despite what anyone in the past or present has done."[54] Oord refers to salvation—God's "delivering creatures from sin"—as a miraculous gift. "God acts first when offering salvation, and creatures enjoy salvation when they respond appropriately to God's initiative." Salvation is miraculous due to "the ingrained habits of sin," which require "God's initiating special action."[55] God's divine enabling—prevenient grace—is necessary for creaturely action; it is God's "loving power" that "makes creaturely responses possible."[56]

Oord says experience best supports his view that "genuine freedom is irreconcilable with being fully determined to act in a particular way."[57]

---

48. Wesleyan theology has various forms of prevenient grace. Reasoner, "Theology of Grace," 100–101; Royster, "Missiological Perspective," 73–93. So, for Oord to advance a version that is not in complete conformity to Wesley does not violate Wesleyanism.

49. Oord, *NOL*, 129.

50. Reichard, "Causality to Relationality," 128–29.

51. Wesley, *Works*, 10:350.

52. Wesley, *Works*, 5:104.

53. Oord denies that there was a literal/historical Adam and Eve, but he does admit that the fall is a reality, but it is not tied directly to Adam and Eve. Oord, personal email to author, December 6, 2018.

54. Oord, personal email to author, December 7, 2018.

55. Oord, *ULG*, 205.

56. Oord, *ULG*, 190.

57. Oord, *ULG*, 59.

And the ability to address issues in life and the world are predicated on one's ability to exercise freedom, either rightly or wrongly. Life does not make sense if free will is an illusion.[58] If it is an illusion, writes Oord, then "[b]eing morally responsible is impossible."[59] We can only be morally responsible if we are "freely respons-able."[60]

Critical Evaluation

For Oord, prevenient grace acts as the divine enabler in order for humans to exercise free will, rightly or wrongly. Looking at the biblical text, particularly what Scripture has to say about human nature, leads me to question the validity of Oord's claim. Do humans have free will only by the gift of prevenient grace? Earlier we noted Wesley's comments regarding fallen man, in that since the fall, mankind lacks the *natural* power to choose the good. The fall, then, marked a pivotal turn when mankind lost the natural ability to choose that which is good, becoming free only to choose evil.

The biblical authors reveal that man's dilemma is his inherent evil (cf. Jer 13:23; 17:9), thus man is in need of divine enablement, or rather, a new, *holified* nature to choose what is good. Spiritually speaking, apart from the grace of God, all humanity chooses evil (Rom 3:10–12; cf. Eccl 7:20; 9:3). Man's orientation is toward sin, which means his sinful inclinations, arguably, are what determine his will to choose in the manner it does because "he is a slave of sin" (John 8:34). Therefore, humans do not have genuine freedom *from* their natural disposition to sin. Paul expounds on his own condition in Romans 7:18, observing that "nothing good dwells" in him. Ephesians 5:8 establishes the contrast between good and evil, pertaining to the regenerative work of God: "For once you were darkness, but now you are light in the Lord." Christ has come to purify a people, circumcising their hearts through the Spirit (Deut 30:6; Rom 2:29).

If man was given prevenient grace in order to exercise free will, then, importing Oord's view of prevenient grace into the biblical narrative, it seems that God's enabling man's will to be free manifested in a propensity toward evil. However, that understanding conflicts with Oord's view of salvation, the miraculous act of God delivering man from his ingrained habits of sin. Here is the inconsistency: If all of humanity has been given prevenient grace, which Oord says enables creatures to be sinless, then what entails in the process of God delivering creatures from their "ingrained

---

58. Oord, *ULG*, 61–62.
59. Oord, *ULG*, 60.
60. Oord, *ULG*, 60.

habits of sin," after responding—through prevenient grace—appropriately to God's call? If they have prevenient grace, then they should be able to deliver themselves from their own habits of sin.

Oord's doctrine of man and understanding of prevenient grace are inconsistent because he does not consider such texts as noted above in his anthropological framework. Furthermore, in Oord desiring to stress the complete freedom of man, his doctrine of prevenient grace stifles his argument: a divine act is still needed in order to enable human beings with the power to say "yes" or "no." Oord's view of prevenient grace is actually a stronger argument *against* libertarian freedom than even what a determinist would argue. Classical Reformed orthodoxy does not deny human free choice; rather, it affirms that God has given human creatures the freedom and power to act upon choice.[61] However, man only desires to sin, so he chooses what he wants, when he wants, according to what he desires. This accords with what Jesus says in John 3:19, "The light has come into the world and people loved (ēgapēsan) darkness rather than the light because their deeds were evil" (cf. Rom 8:7–9). So, apart from Oord's doctrine of *necessary* grace, it seems that the human will would be catatonic. Oord says that life is senseless if free will is an illusion. But if grace is necessary for humans to say "yes" *or* "no,"[62] then it appears that free will is still an illusion.

Essential Kenosis: God's Necessity to Love

Interestingly, when it comes to God, according to Oord, his essentially kenotic nature means that he is not free to *not* love. It is his "preeminent attribute."[63] Oord writes,

> Coherently conceiving of God's necessary love and genuine freedom requires an open future. If God necessarily loves creation but foreknows all occurrences in a closed and settled future, God would not be free. The God whose nature includes love for creation but foreknows future creaturely decisions could not freely choose from an array of possible actions. A God with exhaustive foreknowledge would know with certainty which single option is most loving. God's loving nature and a closed future would force God to choose the single option God knows is most loving. God could not do otherwise. In short, the God with exhaustive

---

61. Reeves, *1689 Baptist Confession*, 9.1
62. Oord, personal email to author, March 15, 2019.
63. Oord, *ULG*, 162.

foreknowledge and an eternal nature that includes love for creatures would not be free to decide *how* to love.⁶⁴

For Oord, because God is essentially kenotic, he expresses kenosis inevitably, which means "love is the necessary expression of God's timeless nature.... God loves necessarily."⁶⁵ While creatures can express love, they are not essentially loving; rather, "creaturely love is sporadic, occasional, and contingent." God's uncontrolling "love is the heart of God," which means his love will never stop.⁶⁶ Oord, importantly, makes the judgment that God's love is not something God chooses; otherwise, he could choose to not be loving. Rather, God, though free, cannot freely choose to not love; love in God "is a natural necessity."⁶⁷

Oord makes a distinction as it relates to God's love and his freedom. However, the distinction does not pertain to whether or not and to whom God chooses to love; rather, it pertains to God's freedom in *how* he expresses his love. Oord writes, "Creation differs from God in that free creatures are free both in deciding whether to love and in deciding how to express love. They do not have eternal natures in which love is preeminent and necessary."⁶⁸ Succinctly put, like creatures, God is free in how he decides to express love, but, unlike creatures, he is not free *from* expressing love. The "significant virtue of open and relational theology: God loves necessarily."⁶⁹ In contrast to classical theology that espouses an eternally decretive God, open and relational theology sees that the future is open, unsettled, which means God does not have knowledge of future events. God cannot know what will be until it actually occurs. And when the events come to pass, "God freely chooses how to love among various possibilities."⁷⁰

Oord's doctrine of creation contends that God necessarily creates because "God is ever Creator, because God's love is creative."⁷¹ And while he claims that "freedom [is] a necessary aspect of God's eternal nature, he *must* love creation."⁷² He believes this is a much stronger position to hold if we affirm that God is essentially loving. Oord rejects the doctrine of *creatio ex nihilo* because it implies that since God decided to create, thus denoting a

---

64. Oord, *NOL*, 140–41.
65. Oord, *ULG*, 161.
66. Oord, *ULG*, 161.
67. Oord quoting Arminius, "Summit of Blasphemy," 2:33–34, in Oord, *ULG*, 161.
68. Oord, *ULG*, 162.
69. Oord, *ULG*, 162.
70. Oord, *ULG*, 162.
71. Oord, personal email to author, December 20, 2018.
72. Oord, *NOL*, 138.

time when he started loving creation, then God could decide to stop loving creation. Oord says, "God creates necessarily." However, "that does not imply a specific creation; rather, some creation is necessary."[73] As God is essentially and necessarily love, he is also essentially and necessarily Creator.

Critical Evaluation

For Oord, holding to divine exhaustive foreknowledge (as held in classical theism) is incoherent. Oord's God must have the freedom to choose. If the future is settled, then God is *constrained* to choose the most loving option. If God knows the future with certainty, then he knows, with certainty, what the most loving action would be in any situation. It seems to me that Oord sees that a settled future limits God. God is not free if the future is settled. But how does it limit God? It would be limiting to God if he were subservient to another divine being's decree, leaving God unable to choose otherwise if he wanted. However, if God has decreed what is to come to pass, then any *decision* (in a logical manner) he has made that is part of his decree is done so by his free will.

Oord thinks it is incoherent because of his assumption that God must be in time, as creatures are in time. "Unloving options are 'off the table' for a God whose eternal nature is love."[74] But Oord has not demonstrated that an eternal God's choices are limited by an eternal, foreknown decree. An eternal God is not limited by divine exhaustive foreknowledge if it is his foreknowledge that has determined what will come to pass, since he determined what will come to pass. Oord says, "God freely chooses *how* to express love in each moment."[75] Oord's statement agrees with an eternal view of God, with the difference being that in an eternal view God decreed *how* he was going to express his love *before* the moment comes to pass.

For Oord, it is more rationally coherent to claim that God is free to act most lovingly in the moment in contrast to a God who is not free to decide how to love in the moment. But Oord's view creates inconsistency when handling specific biblical texts. Again, Oord is concerned with what is rational and coherent. In our Lord's instructions to his disciples on how to pray, Jesus commands them to not babble on like the Gentiles (Matt 6:7), who give long, wordy prayers hoping to effectively persuade their deities to act. On the contrary, Jesus makes an appeal to the Father, contrasting the true God from mere idols. In Matthew 5:8, he says, "Don't be

73. Oord, personal email to author, January 5, 2019.
74. Oord, *NOL*, 141.
75. Oord, *ULG*, 162.

like them, because your Father knows the things you need before you ask him." Jesus' statement makes prayer sound irrational because what is the purpose of prayer if God already knows what needs we have before asking him? John Calvin asked the same question. But he observes that the very design of prayer provides the simple answer:

> Believers do not pray, with the view of informing God about things unknown to him, or of exciting him to do his duty, or of urging him as though he were reluctant. On the contrary, they pray, in order that they may arouse themselves to seek him, that they may exercise their faith in meditating on his promises, that they may relieve themselves from their anxieties by pouring them into his bosom.[76]

Or, even more simply stated: prayer is worship. Oord discusses prayer as it pertains to people not getting the miracle they ask for from God. Oord seeks to establish the more practical nature of open theology compared to conventional theologies because the open view sees that God is unbound from a theology espousing a settled future (i.e., classical theology, which Oord states is irrational and incoherent) in that prayer can actually make a difference.[77] But, does not Jesus' words and the following instruction on prayer (Matt 6:9–13) conflict with Oord's view?

According to Jesus, the Father *already knows* the needs every individual believer has and gives the church a *prayer script* to follow, which is tailored for worship and reflection on God's will for his people. Jesus is not concerned with the Father having an array of possibilities so that he can choose *how* he can express love best. Rather, as we can infer from the text, the Father already knows what is best because Jesus says the Father *already* knows their needs and then Jesus gives them a model of prayer to follow. The model of prayer, then, is what is best for God's people, which ultimately is for them to worship and offer humble hearts, desiring for the Lord's will to be done. An eternal view of God, who has exhaustive foreknowledge, as affirmed in classical theism, offers a more consistent interpretation of this text (also, Ps 139:4, "Before a word is on my tongue, you know all about it."). While it is challenging for finite creatures to rationalize how God can know every need (and every word for that matter) his children have before asking him, coherency with the biblical text, rather than rationalizing a view of God that coheres within a finite framework, has greater importance.

Oord aimed to show that a God who is not bound to an eternal, decreed, and settled view of time, as is the God of classical theism, is truly

---

76. Calvin, *Evangelists*, 1:314.
77. Oord, *NOL*, 91.

free because he can choose *how* he wants to express love in each real-time moment. But, as mentioned earlier, an eternal view of God does not mean God is unable to choose *how* he wants to express love best. Rather, following Isaiah's theme, God declared from old what he wants and/or plans to do (according to his free will) and then he does it, and therefore, his decree comes to pass (Isa 48:3–5). It is perfectly coherent to hold that God freely determined how he would respond to his creatures' decisions *before* they occurred in time.

Oord's argument is not persuasive because he does not successfully demonstrate that an eternal God is less-free than a time-full God and, more importantly, he does not exegetically use Scripture to support his arguments; rather, he sparsely uses texts that speak about God's love and then philosophically defines and implies what those texts mean. And lastly, he does not engage with biblical texts that speak contrary to his view. Oord rejects a deterministic view of God because that means God cannot do other than what has been determined, according to divine exhaustive foreknowledge. Well, if God necessarily loves his creation (Oord's claim), no matter what, because his nature necessitates (i.e., it compels him to love) that he cannot do otherwise, then it seems that God cannot do other than what has been determined—he *must* love. Determinism, then, *is* part of Oord's theology, he just qualifies it in a different manner.

Another important point of his argument, which Oord fails to elaborate on, is that while he says there are multiple options for God to love, he does not go through what or how God chooses which actions to take. While Oord says, my point is "asking the impossible,"[78] Scripture identifies why God does do what he does: He makes decisions for the sake of his name or his glory. Psalm 19:1–4 says God created the heavens and the earth for his own glory. Isaiah 43:7 says God created man for his own glory. Psalm 106:8 says God parted the waters and rescued Israel "for his name's sake, to make his power known" (cf. Isa 63:12–14). Exodus 9:16 says that God left Pharaoh in power "for this purpose: to show you my power and to make my name known on the whole earth." And in Isaiah 48:9, in the face of Israel's rebellion and idolatry, God says "for his name's sake [not for love of Israel] I defer my anger, for the sake of my praise I restrain it for you" (ESV).

In the New Testament, God allows Lazarus to die so that God would be glorified in Jesus' raising him back to life (John 11:4). King Herod is struck down "because he did not give God glory" (Acts 12:23). God allows people to be sick so that he would be glorified in healing them (John 9:3). In the passion week, we see that Jesus' earthly mission and suffering is for God's glory (John

---

78. Oord, personal correspondence to author, July 27, 2019.

12:27–28; 17:4–5). And Jesus' aim is that those who belong to God see and enjoy his glory (John 17:24). And in Ephesians, Paul reveals that the purpose behind God's rich blessings in electing and redeeming sinners through Christ is "to bring praise to his glory" (1:12, 14). Lastly, everything that happens is for his glory: "From him and through him and to him are all things. To him be the glory forever. Amen" (Rom 11:36). More Scriptures could have been given to support the consistent, interwoven theme that God's main purpose in doing what he does is for his own glory.[79]

This question is important: Why does it matter if options were viewed from eternity past or at the moment requiring God to decide?[80] Oord claims that God choosing among options better supports the claim that God is loving. But how? Why would more options better support the claim that God is loving? Because, for Oord, it is only rational and coherent for a personal being to act and make decisions in time, as human creatures do. Therefore, what makes most sense is that God, as a personal being, is faced with possibilities to show love, as creatures are. And while creatures can choose not to love in response to various possibilities, God, cannot *not* love. His nature determines that he *has to* love. He, as the almighty and perfectly wise God, chooses *how* he will best demonstrate his love. While Oord's view has rationality, his position lacks scriptural support. Furthermore, his argument is unpersuasive, as already mentioned, in supporting his claim that a time-full God, faced with possibilities to choose from, better supports the claim that God is loving in contrast to an eternal God, who has decreed a closed future, with the single option that God knows is most loving. While Oord says, "it's impossible for God to be absolutely certain which possible divine action would be most loving in any

---

79. Cf. Ps. 79:2; 79:9; 96:3; 106:8; 115:1; Isa 48:11; Jer 13:11; 14:7; Ezek 20:44; 36:22. Paul speaks of the old and new ministries of God's plan, with the first ministry of condemnation in Moses and now the ministry of righteousness in Christ, as ministries of *glory* (2 Cor 3:7–18). One could construct a rival account of God doing what he does because of his love (cf. Ps 136; John 3:16); however, as noted by Vanhoozer, the challenge in contemporary discussions on love is that "the problem is not *that* God loves, but rather *what* God's love is." Vanhoozer, "Introduction," 7. In the two passages cited, both challenge *what* God's love is in that both follow up with aspects of God's activity of judgment tied up in his love. Contemporary theism struggles seeing how love and judgment cohere. *God's glory*, however, as his motivation for doing what he does, better accounts for the two, pointing to a grander purpose—than love—behind God's will. To answer Vanhoozer, the *what* of God's love, then, would be his own glory.

80. A classical Reformed view understands that God decrees what will happen in history, with his interactions with creation already determined in light of his foreknowledge of those events. He does not deliberate *because* he is perfect in knowledge and wisdom.

moment,"[81] a deterministic perspective—understanding the perfection of God, the fixed decree of all things, and the responses God decreed to give during various points of redemptive history—arguably presents a more consistent view of the loving God as portrayed Scripture.

Problems of Persuasion

Oord comments on the tragic bombing that took place at the Boston Marathon in 2013, stating that God could not have unilaterally prevented the brothers from carrying out this attack.[82] It would require taking away the freewill he has gifted to his creatures. Oord asserts that God does not have the ability to prevent evil because his divine, localized body "is an omnipresent spirit."[83] Because he does not have a physical body, his ability resides in the power of persuasion. God can call upon creatures to act heroically to prevent a bombing or save a person from a burning building, but creatures can ignore his commands.[84]

However, this understanding creates a problem regarding Jesus' arrest. How did God ensure that his Son would be delivered to the Romans for crucifixion at the time he planned from eternity past? In the Gospel of John, we see Christ side-stepping the mob and escaping capture because "his hour had not yet come" (8:20, cf. 8:30, 44; 10:39). When the Romans arrested Jesus, Peter tells us that *God* delivered Jesus into their hands. This was part of the plan, of which Christ was fully aware. So, did God persuade the Jews and the Romans to act evilly in the arrest and crucifixion of Christ? Or was it that Christ stepped into their trap at the planned time? One could easily avert the first question and state that God did not have to persuade the Jews and Romans to arrest and kill Jesus because they already hated him; rather, God just led Jesus into their hands. However, the next question presents a problem for Oord.

According to Oord's view of the future, God cannot guarantee a particular outcome; rather, it would be a divine guess at best. But the Scriptures do not suggest such a view, for John specifically indicates that Jesus' arrest did not happen because his hour had not come. And when it finally came,

---

81. Oord, *NOL*, 141.
82. Oord, *ULG*, 170.
83. Oord, *ULG*, 179.
84. Oord does not engage with passages such as Ps 138:8; Eph 2:8–10; Phil 1:6; 2:12–13; 1 Thess 3:12, which demonstrate God's working in believers to complete what he has planned for them. He refers to Phil 2:12–13, which he interprets as God "enabling" one to work out one's salvation, according to his doctrine of prevenient grace.

Scripture says that Herod and Pontius Pilate, along with the Gentiles and the Jews had done "whatever [the Lord's] hand and [his] plan had predestined to take place" (Acts 4:27–28). God had planned a specific date, time, and place to deliver his Son up for the sins of the world. However, his crucifixion was an evil act. So then, and here is the real problem, did God attempt to persuade others to save Jesus, but they ignored his commands? Or did he *not* call anyone to save him and just let his sinless Son go into the hands of evil men? If this were truly an evil act, would not God try to persuade the Jews and the Romans to let him go? But if God planned for it to happen, why would he try to persuade them to let him go? Scripture's testimony regarding Christ's crucifixion shows it was necessary; therefore, it follows that God would not have called upon nor have used persuasion to stay Jesus' death.

While Oord seeks to get God off the hook for evil, it seems that in this case, God would be responsible in some manner for the murder of his Son at the hands of evil men because he did not attempt to persuade others to save him.[85] Oord rejects this logic[86] because God loves perfectly; therefore, he does not cause evil nor is he culpable for failing to prevent it.[87] And he holds this position because God's perfect love "cannot control others or situations."[88] And therefore, God is not culpable for the murder of the Son because God cannot coerce others. Oord defines coercion, as we will evaluate later, as God having complete control of an agent or situation where the one being controlled "loses all capacity for causation, self-organization, agency, or free will."[89] However, that is not what I am challenging. I am asking if Oord's God tried to *persuade* those involved in the murder of Jesus from committing it, even though God ordained his crucifixion. Oord says a loving God persuades human agents from committing evil, but the agents have the power to reject God's call. But, in this case, I claim that God would not have tried to persuade an agent from the evil murder of the only sinless being to

---

85. In fact, Romans 3:25 says, "God presented him as an atoning sacrifice." And then in 3:26, Paul says, "God presented him to demonstrate his righteousness at the present time, so that he would be righteous and declare righteous the one who has faith in Jesus." So, in these passages, we see God's intentionality in sending his Son to the cross, whereby the death (murder) of Christ is vindicative for *God's* righteousness because in his patient mercy passed over former sins. In the most heinous and sinful act of crucifying Christ, *that very act* purposed to demonstrate God's righteousness, in order to be lawfully in the right to declare sinners righteous. God's infinite wisdom is astonishing. And this event was typified in the story of Joseph in Genesis 37–50.

86. Oord, personal correspondence to author, July 27, 2019.

87. Oord, *ULG*, 68.

88. Oord, *ULG*, 183.

89. Oord, *ULG*, 183.

ever walk the earth. It does not make sense that God would if he planned it. So, in some manner, God planned for an evil act to occur.

Oord rejects the view that Jesus' crucifixion was determined from eternity past, according to a timeless view. However, I am asking if God planned this event *at all*? I believe Oord, if he is committed to what the Scriptures say (e.g., Rev 13:8), would agree that God planned Jesus' death. My point is to demonstrate that God stands behind evil in some manner, though he is not culpable for evil. But Oord says "[a] God worthy of our worship cannot be Someone who causes, supports, or allows genuine evil."[90] However, if we take the biblical text for what it plainly says, that Jesus was delivered up to be crucified "according to God's determined plan and foreknowledge" (Acts 2:23),[91] then the inescapable conclusion is that God, to use Oord's words, "causes, supports, or allows"[92] evil in *some manner*.

The events that took place in Christ's earthly life established a pattern of life for the church. Altering the grounding hope of God's sustaining power for the believer through a life that *will* experience persecution unsettles the foundation of trust in God's promise of salvation. Peter says, "For what credit is there if when you do wrong and are beaten, you endure it? But when you do what is good and suffer, if you endure it, this brings favor with God. For you were called to this, because Christ also suffered for you, leaving you an example, that you should follow in his steps" (1 Pet 2:20-21). According to this text, suffering as Christ suffered is the Christian lot; Peter says, we are called to it. And those who endure suffering for good, God gives them favor (e.g., Joseph's narrative in Genesis 37-50).

If the Christian calling is to suffer as Christ suffered and those who endure it find favor with God, then it seems that God would not persuade others to refrain from persecuting Christians, even though such acts are evil. Peter makes the point that if one is beaten for doing wrong, then one deserves it. If God wants us to follow in the steps of Christ, which includes persecution, then I would argue that God would not attempt to persuade the persecutors to refrain; rather, he lets them carry out their wickedness, fulfilling Christ's words, "You will be hated by everyone because of my name. But the one who endures to the end will be saved" (Matt 10:22).[93]

---

90. Oord, *ULG*, 68.

91. Other translations of this passage: "This man was handed over to you by God's deliberate plan" (NIV); "who was handed over by the predetermined plan and foreknowledge of God" (NET); "delivered up according to the definite plan and foreknowledge of God" (ESV).

92. Oord, *ULG*, 68.

93. That is not to say that God does not persuade persecutors from slaughtering his sheep. Many are spared, and God delivers many from such trials.

Oord sees that creatures can cooperate by fulfilling necessary roles to carry out God's good plans. Furthermore, he says God's involvement in positive actions should be understood to mean that he "played the primary causal role in such events."[94] What about the death of his Son? Oord restricts his understanding of creaturely involvement and God's causal role only to his "good purposes." In the death of his Son, both parties are involved in an event that in and of itself (i.e., the murdering of an innocent person) cannot be classified as good. However, while the event was truly the only unjust death to occur, Scripture shows it was necessary for the salvation of the world (John 1:29; 1 John 3:5; 4:14). Therefore, Jesus' death must be "good." However, I do not think Oord recognizes the implications of it.

Oord says that the crucial question, which all other theologies fail to adequately answer, is: "Why doesn't a powerful and loving God prevent *all* evil that is genuinely evil, especially specific instances of horror in our personal lives?"[95] The previous paragraphs suggest that God chooses not to stop persecution—which could be instances of horror in one's personal life—because that is what Christians are called to endure, in following the example of Christ before us. Oord might respond, stating that Jesus' death was not a genuine evil because "*all* things considered," his death would *not* have made "the world worse than it might have been otherwise."[96] But since Oord does not believe God knows the future and man has libertarian free will, then how would God know the impact a particular event would have on the world?

A God, perfect in knowledge, righteousness, wisdom, and love who has perfectly predetermined and ordained all the events of redemptive history and how he would perfectly ensure they are carried out in love (Acts 2:23; 3:18; 4:28; 13:27; Rom 8:31–39; Eph 1:4; 1 Pet 1:19–21; Rev 13:8; 17:8), more accurately portrays *how* God demonstrates his love.[97]

---

94. Oord, *ULG*, 179.

95. Oord, *ULG*, 144.

96. Oord, *ULG*, 141.

97. With that said, all doctrinal systems (e.g., Calvinism, Trinitarianism, etc.) have "awkward" passages that challenge the integrity of each system (e.g., 1 John 2:2; Mark 13:32). So, Oord is not alone here.

Essential Kenosis: God's Providence

God's Gift of Agency

Coercion (as Oord understands it) is an offensive aspect of classical theism, which Oord seeks to detach from Christian theism. For Oord, a classical model that holds to divine determinism implies coercion on God's part (i.e., complete control over his creatures). According to Oord, God forcing his way on creatures to get what he wants does not demonstrate nor reflect what it means to love, particularly, if God is love.

Essential Kenosis affirms God is persuasive but cannot control anyone; therefore, he cannot be blamed for the evil actions free creatures do.[98] Oord (and the process tradition) posits that God cannot coerce any creature; rather, he "exclusively"[99] uses the power of persuasion, but persuasion and/or compelling does not guarantee that God's purposes will be fulfilled. Essential Kenosis explains why God does not "prevent evil that simple creatures with agency cause or even simpler entities with mere self-organizing capacities cause."[100] Agency is a gift, and God cannot take it back or fail to provide it. And God's essentially loving nature means he has to give freedom to creatures, even if they use it for evil. God cannot thwart such evil actions alone.[101]

Critical Evaluation

In the book of Job, Eliphaz's statements of how God does great and unsearchable things, giving rain to the earth and setting the lowly on high, includes God "frustrating" (Heb. *parar*, in the hifil, to hinder or prevent) "the devices of the crafty, so that their hands achieve no success" (5:12, 14).[102] Job proclaims to God that he knows "that [he] can do all things, and that no purpose of [his] can be thwarted" (42:2). Proverbs 10:3 says, "The LORD does not let the righteous go hungry, but he thwarts the craving of the wicked." And Paul, quoting Job 5:12, writes that God "will destroy the wisdom of the wise, and the discernment of the discerning [he] will thwart

---

98. Oord, *ULG*, 171.

99. Oord, "Divine Power," 1.

100. Oord, *ULG*, 171.

101. Oord, *ULG*, 170. Key passages Oord cites to support his views are: Lam 3:22–23; Phil 2:4–13; 1 Cor 1:18–25; 3:9; 2 Cor 6:1.

102. Job 5:12–14 shows a progression of God thwarting, capturing, and then punishing them. Alden, *Job*, 94. And the chapter continues ascribing God as the primary cause behind many other providential works.

(*athetēsō*)" (1 Cor 1:19).[103] Oord does not address these passages or others like them. Rather, he asserts that the measure of God's ability to respond to evil is determined through creaturely response to his loving influence to stop evil. But the thrust of these passages does not assume that is the case. Glory and praise are given to God *because* he does these things.

Divine Coercion

A key distinction between Oord's view of classical theism and the view I affirm is that of *coercion*, specifically, the working definition behind each one's view of it. For Oord, an essentially loving God cannot control others because love cannot control. A God who does so is fictional; he does not exist.[104] Oord does claim that "God exerts direct, indirect, top-down, lateral, and bottom up causal influence" upon all.[105] However, he assumes God's causal influence as efficient, not sufficient, causation because an efficient causal view does not "entail unilateral determination."[106] Those who adopt a unilateral determinist view, where God acts a sufficient cause, Oord refers to it as "ontological coercion" because God determines "absolutely and completely" every "creaturely outcome or entity."[107] Whereas, an efficient causal view accounts for the ordinary and extraordinary ways that people experience God working in their lives.[108] For Oord, because God's essential nature is love, divine love involves granting freedom/agency to others. And "because God steadfastly loves all creation, God is not able to present forms of existence that would be unloving."[109]

Recognizing the multiple meanings of the word *coerce*, Oord defines and applies *coerce* in a metaphysical sense, in that it means to control entirely. More specifically he believes one who is coerced, "loses all capacity for causation, self-organization, agency or free will."[110] And this view of coercion is what Oord synonymously associates with unilateral determination—i.e., classical theism. However, his assumption of a congruent relationship between the two is inaccurate. Unilateral determining power

---

103. "atheteō," in BDAG, 24, is primarily "to reject something as invalid; to *declare invalid, nullify, ignore*, but also to reject and/or disallow."
104. Oord, *ULG*, 180.
105. Oord, "The Divine Spirit," 470.
106. Oord, "The Divine Spirit," 471.
107. Oord, "The Divine Spirit," 472.
108. Oord, "The Divine Spirit," 469.
109. Oord, *ULG*, 200.
110. Oord, *ULG*, 183.

is not the same as coercive power. Oord conflates these two different categories, creating a straw man argument.

At this point, I want to address Oord's position that God does *not* exercise unilateral power *over* creaturely actions. While I argue that God does, I want to specifically show that God's exercise of unilateral power is not in the category of *over*, as in we can distinctively observe God strong-arming a situation, so that those involved are aware of his active "force" in the event, *over* their own freely chosen actions. The ontological framework of Holy Scripture depicts God's power working in and through his creatures, in a manner that does not violate their wills. It is the narrator's perspective, the divine author providing the commentary, *revealing* to the reader *why* certain events transpire in the manner that they do.

A classical view's understanding of the ontological nature of Scripture means that there are always two authors; therefore, we "must pay attention to what the divine author is saying through the human authors as well, which necessarily involves the interpreter in mystery."[111] In the story of Joseph (Gen 37–50), for example, apart from the narrator's reminder that God was with Joseph (Gen 39:1–4, 21, 23; 41:37–40; 45:9), a modern reader may chalk up such events to bad luck or misfortune.[112] Joseph's brothers' treachery against him, though sparing his life, resulted in him being taken into slavery. Sometime later he was given a place of authority, only to then be cast into prison for a crime he did not commit.

Many read misfortune into the context and then see God getting Joseph out of the situation.[113] A secular mindset, generally speaking, sees unfortunate circumstances as bad luck, unless the person had done something to deserve such an outcome (*Karma?*). But the narrator reveals the theological details, key inspired pieces to the story, so that the reader does not relegate the storyline to that of misfortune or fortuity. These events were not written

---

111. Carter, *Interpreting Scripture*, 25.

112. Though we read, for example, in Genesis 39:1–4 that Potiphar saw that the Lord was with Joseph, the implicit understanding from the context is that Potiphar *physically* observed the working of God in his life, as manifested in Joseph's success. That does not mean the characters in the story were not aware of God's presence; rather, divine action in and through human action was commonplace. Besides miraculous events in Scripture, the ontological nature of Scripture manifests itself in the situations that even the biblical characters do not always see (i.e., perceived random tragic events, e.g., 1 Kgs 22:34, 38.). The divine narrator enters into the storyline in situations where the reader might assume God is not involved in such events, making the reader aware that he is directly involved.

113. This is observable in the interpretive translations of Genesis 50:20, where God is said to turn the evil event into good, or he makes good come out of the evil. However, such translations detract the entire storyline.

as they played out—real time; rather, the story and the commentary came after the events, so that God's people could have a proper understanding of what, why, and how God has, is, and will be fulfilling his promise to Abraham and to Israel (cf. Rom 15:4; 1 Cor 10:11).

Understanding inscripturation in this manner enables us to *see* divine action (i.e., causation).[114] The eternal God is not strapped to a chronological timeline; rather, "for in him *we* live and move and have our being" (Acts 17:28, emphasis added). As Christians committed to the truth of divine revelation in Scripture, the ontological nature of the Word, which is Spirit produced, transcending the limits of the created order, should form the foundation of our hermeneutical metaphysic. As stated already, Oord, and the process tradition, posit that God cannot coerce any creature; rather, he "exclusively"[115] uses the power of persuasion, but persuasion and/or compelling does not guarantee that God's purposes will be fulfilled. Furthermore, the view of "ontological coercion"[116] that Oord attributes to classical theism, where "the one being controlled [by God] loses all capacity for causation, self-organization, agency, or free will,"[117] is *not* the type of power affirmed in classical theism.

In supporting his view of an uncontrolling God of love who does not coerce human agents, Oord attempts to bolster his position, saying, "I find no biblical passage that explicitly says God entirely controls others."[118] We are in agreement; I have not found a single verse in the Bible where God controls human agents in the manner *Oord* defines coercion/control.[119] Oord quotes leading theologians from the classical tradition, Warfield, Calvin, Bavinck, and others, insisting that they affirm his characterization of their position.

---

114. Seeing the ontological nature of Scripture in this manner provides a counter argument against Hume's (and others') claim of denying that we can have a knowledge of God through causation because we cannot observe it empirically. Divine inspiration provides the reader a behind-the-scenes detailing of the events that occurred. While empirically speaking, one can see the succession of events and interactions in the biblical story, the Spirit enables one to see the divine action/causality behind those events and within those interactions. And therefore, the events etched by the divine pen establishes this normative view of God's ongoing, divine activity in his creation, even if the canonical record is closed. John's final verse in his Gospel carries this sentiment, noting that the world could not contain the books that could be written of the myriad works Christ performed (John 21:25).

115. Oord, "Divine Power," 1.

116. Oord, "The Divine Spirit," 472.

117. Oord, *ULG*, 183.

118. Oord, "Essential Kenosis View," 95.

119. One might claim 1 Samuel 26:12 as a passage demonstrating God completely controlling someone, in that Saul and his soldiers do not wake up to David's presence "because a deep sleep from the Lord came over them."

However, while these theologians affirm that "God's will is the ultimate account of all that occurs,"[120] that "[t]he great works of the Lord are carefully crafted in respect of all that he wills,"[121] and "in some unfathomable way, God totally causes every event,"[122] none of these theologians claim that God coerces human creatures in the manner Oord has defined it. When it comes to God's sovereign working in his creation to fulfill his purposes, "God does not determine the actions of humans *against* their wills, but *through* their wills."[123] Coercion entails threats and physical force. God does not use threats or physical force; rather, "he providentially influences human hearts to willingly accomplish his purposes in all things."[124]

One might argue that God "threatened" Israel to obey, otherwise he would punish them; however, that is not a form of coercion; rather, God gave his people warnings, which would result in punishment and curses for disobedience (Deut 28). Coercion occurs in a context of deceitful intentions on the part of the one acting coercively. God is not man that he should act in such a manner. Rather, his holiness demands that he judge and punish sinners; however, his loving and merciful nature caused him to administer warnings to Israel of the judgment to come as a means to steer their hearts to his grace and love. Unfortunately, Oord ardently protests against a view that is non-existent in the historical classical tradition.

God Only Compels or Persuades—Critical Evaluation

My evaluation is two-fold. First, I will use specific sovereignty-responsibility texts[125] to test the cogency of Oord's claim that God *only* compels or uses persuasion to bring about events and to substantiate Oord's claim that coercion, as he defines it and ascribes to classical theology, is the kind

---

120. Oord quoting Warfield, "Predestination," 21, in Oord, *ULG*, 84.

121. Oord quoting Calvin, *Secret Providence*, 81, in Oord, *ULG*, 84.

122. Oord, *ULG*, 84. These are Oord's words, referencing Bavinck, *Reformed Dogmatics*, 2:614–15; and Turretin, *IET*, 1:500–17. However, his summarized sentence does not adequately represent the technical and careful treatment Bavinck and Turretin give on the doctrine of concurrence, while ensuring that it is Scripture that draws the line, where God's sovereignty and human freedom come together.

123. Bignon, *Excusing Sinners*, 23.

124. Bignon, *Excusing Sinners*, 23.

125. Other than Genesis 50:20, nowhere in his writings does he engage with key biblical texts that exhibit the asymmetrical nature of God's will behind man's will, which I call "breaking-point texts"—Exod 4:21; 7:2–3; 11:9; Deut 2:30; 29:4; 1 Sam 2:25; 2 Sam 17:14; 1 Kgs 12:15; 1 Chr 14:8–11; 2 Chr 25:16, 20; Isa 10; Jer 32:36–42; Ezek 11:16–20; Acts 2:23; 4:27–28.

of power classical theism attributes to God in its affirmation of unilateral determinism. Second, my intention is also constructive, in that I am going to demonstrate further[126] how the general sense of Scripture agrees more consistently with a classical view than Oord's process-relational view, pertaining to passages about divine power. Before moving forward, it is important to define *unilateral determinism* from a classical view, in distinction from Oord's view of it.

Defining Unilateral Determination

In classical theism, *unilateral determination*[127] is defined as God's divine activity to bring about a state of affairs according to his specific purposes.[128] The implication of this definition is that God can act in a manner that thwarts the free-willed choices/actions of human creatures (Job 42:2; Ps 33:10).[129] But God does not act in a manner that forces, compels, or overrides (i.e., completely controlling) one to decide or perform an act that goes

---

126. Chapter 2 of the thesis pertained more specifically to Oord's philosophical view of divine power. And chapter 4 delineated classical and process metaphysical hermeneutical approaches to Scripture.

127. Philosophically speaking, a classical view defines omnipotence, to which unilateral determination is synonymously connected, as God having "the power to bring about every state of affairs which it is logically possible for him to bring about." Brink, *Almighty God*, 223. But to avoid nominalism, a more biblically precise definition is that "God can do anything compatible with his attributes." Frame, *Systematic Theology*, 342; Kenny, *God of the Philosophers*, 98. Ancient writers employ similar language but emphasize God doing whatever he wills or wants to do. Cf. Augustine, *City of God*, 21.7; Aquinas, *ST*, 1.25.3; Turretin, *IET*, 1.21; Shedd, *Dogmatic Theology*, 289. Steven Charnock, following his discourse on God's power in Job 26:14, writes, "the power of God is that ability and strength whereby he can bring to pass whatsoever he please, whatsoever his infinite wisdom can direct, and whatsoever the infinite purity of his will can resolve." Charnock, *Works*, 2:106.

128. Cf. Ps 115:3. God does not lay out a plan, sit back, and watch it come to fruition. Rather, as God has said through the prophet Isaiah: "Remember what happened long ago, for I am God, and there is no other; I am God, and no one is like me. I declare the end from the beginning, and from long ago what is not yet done, saying: my plan will take place, and I will do all my will. I call a bird of prey from the east, a man for my purpose from a far country. Yes, I have spoken; so I will also bring it about. I have planned it; I will also do it" (46:9–11. Cf. Acts 4:27–28).

129. To use confessional language, a classical view affirms that "God has provided the human will by nature with liberty and power to act upon choice; it is neither forced, nor determined by any intrinsic necessity to do good or evil" (Matt 17:12; Jas 1:14; Deut 30:19). Reeves, *1689 Baptist Confession*, 9.1

against one's will or desire. However, the events that do come to pass, no less, do so because they are divinely determined.[130]

Oord defines *unilateral determination* as "the ability of one individual to control *entirely* an action of another."[131] Oord's meaning of the term does not align with a classical view of unilateral determinism. The problematic issue with Oord's version is in how he understands divine control. He assumes that the type of control affirmed in a classical view is one that coerces another being to the point that it "loses all capacity for causation, self-organization, agency, or free will."[132] This form is metaphysical or ontological coercion, where God acts as sufficient cause. But coercion, in that sense, is absent from a classical, unilateral determinative framework (see chapter 5 of this study).

However, in the present context, *unilateral* has a particular nuance to its meaning, in that the question at hand is: Can God directly (*unilaterally*) perform an act that affects/impacts physical bodies? Classical and open theologies affirm that God can and does directly and indirectly act on physical bodies. But the disparity between classical and open theology is whether or not God can act unilaterally *determinatively*. Can God unilaterally act in a manner that determines an outcome for a particular person or group? Classical theology claims Scripture affirms that God can and does act unilaterally to accomplish his purposes (i.e., determinatively). But Oord says God cannot act both directly *and* determinatively on any human creature, entity, or object within his creation. My claim is that the general sense of Scripture agrees more with a classical view—that God can and

---

130. As a Calvinist, I am committed to a view of divine causal determinism that posits: "For every event E, God decided that E should happen and that decision was the ultimate sufficient cause of E." Anderson, "Calvinism," 105. However, it would be a misunderstanding to say that God's foreknowledge (i.e., divine causal determinism) leads to fatalism. Rather, a proper view states that if God foreknew that John would sin, then John does not (rather than *cannot*, as fatalism would have it) refrain from sinning. A free, moral agent's actions are foreseen not because they are foreseen; rather, they are foreseen because the actions are certain *to* happen. And to express this understanding from a confessional manner, God is the primary cause of all that occurs, "yet by his providence he arranges them to occur according to the nature of secondary causes, either necessarily, freely, or contingently" (Gen 8:22; Jer 31:35; Exod 21:13; Deut 19:5; Isa 10:6–7). Reeves, *1689 Baptist Confession*, 5.2. For example, a fruit tree by necessity produces fruit (thus that would properly define *necessity*), but it does not necessarily produce fruit because the secondary (*contingent*) causes of weather and climate may prevent the tree from producing fruit. The natural effect of the tree is fruit, but there is not a natural necessity that it will do so without fail. Cf. Aquinas, *SCG*, 3.72.2, 8.

131. Oord, "Divine Power," 8. Oord further notes, "God cannot control others or situations." Oord, *ULG*, 183.

132. Oord, *ULG*, 183.

does act both directly *and* determinatively—of divine power than Oord's view. Another important aspect of my claim is that a classical view allows for Oord's reading of Scripture, in that it does not delimit God based on a particular conception of God's power, as Oord (and the process tradition) holds; rather, it accepts what the text predicates about God's divine activity and attempts to construct a theology around it, even if the conclusion situates God behind evil and/or human free-will choices in some manner that may leave the reader holding to a paradox.

Deuteronomy 2:30

"But King Sihon of Heshbon would not let us travel through his land, for the Lord your God had made his spirit stubborn and his heart obstinate in order to hand him over to you, as has now taken place." In the context of this passage, Israel just ended forty years of wandering the desert, and the new generation is making its way through the Transjordan, en route to its final destination: the land of Canaan. As they pass through the lands of Edom, Moab, and Ammon, in verse 25, the Lord commands Israel to cross the Arnon Valley and engage in battle with King Sihon of Heshbon and take possession of the land. The Lord will put the fear of Israel in all who are in their path; they will fear and tremble before them. In verses 26–29, the Lord sends a charitable message to Sihon, stipulating that Israel will march straight through his land, buying and exchanging goods and commodities along the way until they crossed the Jordan.

However, in verse 30, King Sihon "was not impressed"[133] and did not take the deal. He did not take the peace offering because, Moses says, the Lord "made [*qashah*][134] his spirit stubborn and his heart obstinate [*amets*][135] *in order to* hand him over to you." Some commentators merely acknowledge the tension in this passage between God's will and Sihon's actions.[136] Others, however, recognize the determinative aspect implied in the passage.[137] But

---

133. Merrill, *Deuteronomy*, 101.

134. The Hebrew verb *qashah* is a hiphil form, thus it is causative.

135. *amets* is in the piel, indicating that God put Sihon's heart in that state of obstinance.

136. Wright, *Deuteronomy*, 38; Thompson and Wiseman, *Deuteronomy*, 94; Cook, *Reading Deuteronomy*, does not even comment on it.

137. Merrill, *Deuteronomy*, 4:101; Brueggemann, *Deuteronomy*, 38–39, observes, "This was not a freely made human policy decision, by Sihon, but an act willed by YHWH before which Sihon could exercise no free will."

Chisholm, "Divine Hardening," 429–30; Beale, "Hardening of Pharaoh's Heart," 135. Interestingly, Joshua, in his recalling of the conquests and the kings that were struck down, writes, "For it was the Lord's intention to harden [*chazaq*] their hearts, so that

the question is, did God persuade and/or compel Sihon to refuse the peace offering and engage in battle, or did God attempt to persuade or compel him to accept it, but he was not persuasive enough, which resulted in a battle?

Interestingly, the author tells us in 2:24 that God had already handed[138] Sihon and his land over to Israel; therefore, Israel is to go, engage in war, and take the land. God, then, *already* determined Sihon's outcome. In verse 26, we see that the Lord sent a message of peace, which seems to be for the express purpose of avoiding war on Sihon's end and thus avoiding capture and/or death (a means of persuasion?). But then verse 30 says that Sihon would not let Israel pass through *because* the Lord hardened his spirit, *so that* he would be handed over to Israel. In following the logic of these passages, in God's decree, the defeat of Sihon and giving of his land to Israel were already completed events, they just had not been carried out yet. But it was through Sihon's rejection of the peace offering that the Lord brought about the fulfillment of his decree. Therefore, I conclude that Sihon's defeat, according to the text, was already determined, according to God's will, so whether God used persuasion or compelling power to achieve his purpose is irrelevant.[139] Rather, it makes sense to recognize God's will as the determinative factor in this situation. Oord understands that "God's compelling power is always based upon genuine love and the concern to achieve what is best given what is possible."[140] With that understanding in mind, God's purpose for Sihon, though unfortunate for him, was grounded in covenant love for Israel. One might object to God's determination of Sihon's death; however, the reality is that Sihon was a blasphemous sinner, deserving of death like the rest of mankind.

God fulfilled his intentions without completely controlling Sihon, according to Oord's definition. And this is where the divine narrator provides

---

they would engage Israel in battle, be completely destroyed without mercy, and be annihilated, just as the Lord had commanded Moses" (11:20); *chazaq*, is in the piel, meaning to make unchanging in will, opinion, and/or desire.

138. The NET, understanding the force of the verb *nathan* in the qatal form, which is a whole and complete action, "without respect to the time of the action," translates it as "already delivered over to you." See "qātal," in Heiser and Setterholm, *Glossary*.

139. Green, *Deuteronomy*, 53, writes, "How can Wesleyans interpret this concept of a callused heart? A Wesleyan might find a clue to the hardening of Sihon in his resistance to the peace negotiations. . . . This reflects the typology that is found in the hardening of Pharaoh's heart. Request is made to Pharaoh, and refusal ensues. A fundamental assumption of the OT is that human beings have a choice between good and evil. Is this text a breach of this principle, or is it pointing to a reality that resistance and refusal harden the perspective of a person?" Green, however, does not answer that question.

140. Oord, "Divine Power," 9.

the details to inform the reader *why* such events transpired. If we remove the second clause of verse 30, then the assumption might be that Sihon just did not want to let Israel pass through. But the divine narrator wanted the reader to know that Sihon's decision to not let Israel pass through was due to the Lord's *Spirit-to-spirit* efficacious hardening of Sihon's heart that did *not* violate his will, causing him to lose all capacity for causation, self-organization, agency, or free will, so that Israel could possess the land the Lord had given them. God did what he did out of *hesed* love for Israel.

1 SAMUEL 2:25

"If one person sins against another, God can intercede for him, but if a person sins against the Lord, who can intercede for him?" But they would not listen to their father, since the Lord intended to kill them." Eli, a priest of the Lord, his sons were wicked. As priests, they treated the Jews' offerings to the Lord with contempt, taking their portions of the offering before giving the Lord his (cf. Lev 3:3–5; 7:30). Furthermore, it was a known fact among the people that they were sleeping around with female servants (1 Sam 2:22–24). And though Eli warned his sons about the severity of their sins against God, the divine author tells us that they refused to listen to their father *because* the Lord intended to kill them.[141] According to Oord's understanding of divine power, did God attempt to persuade or compel Eli's sons to turn from their sin, but they did not turn and repent because the Lord was not compelling or persuasive enough? Now, I submit that Eli's father, in fear and admonition of the Lord, tried to compel his sons to turn from their sins. But, interestingly, Eli's compelling plea had no effect *because* of the Lord's divine prerogative to kill them. From 2:27–34, the Lord rebukes Eli, declaring that his sons' sins brought dishonor to God; therefore, every descendant to follow will die violently. In verse 34, God says, "This will be the sign that will come to you concerning your two sons Hophni and Phinehas: both of them will die on the same day." And in 3:11, we read that the Philistines slaughtered Eli's two sons on the same day.

Oord could argue that God was not persuasive enough; however, the text indicates that God did not intend to persuade them to turn from sin because it was his will to kill them. In other words, God's will did not *allow* it. While Scripture says God does not take pleasure in the death of the wicked (Ezek 18:23), 1 Samuel 2:25 could also be translated as "the LORD

---

141. Tsumura, *First Book of Samuel*, 161, writes, "Eli's words of warning had no effect on his 'worthless' sons who had no ears to listen. For God had decided the destiny of Eli's sons."

was pleased"[142] to kill them. However, Scripture tells us that God loves justice and hates the wicked (Isa 61:8; Ps 11:5), so acting upon the unjust is pleasing to God. Old Testament Commentators Keil and Delitzsch note that their [the sons] "father's reproof made no impression on them, because they were already given up to the judgment of hardening."[143] Divine hardening is a retributive act of God, which God *actively* uses to bring about his purposes (e.g., Exod 4:21; Deut 2:30; Rom 9:17–18).[144] Therefore, in looking at the context of this passage and the logic of the text, the decree and fulfillment of that decree demonstrates that God's will had primacy in the deaths of Eli's sons. Their inability to respond to Eli's reproof was not because God, through Eli, was not persuasive enough or compelling enough; rather, it was because God had already determined to kill them.[145] God fulfilled his plan without the use of metaphysical coercion, as Oord defines it.[146]

1 KINGS 12:15

"*The king did not listen to the people, because this turn of events came from the Lord to carry out his word, which the Lord had spoken through Ahijah the Shilonite to Jeroboam son of Nebat.*" This chapter marks the kingdom divide within Israel. Chapter 11 was the unraveling of Solomon's rule, after his heart strayed from God (11:9). Therefore, the Lord decreed, through the prophet Ahijah the Shilonite, that he was going to strip the kingdom away from Solomon. After Solomon's death, his son, Rehoboam, became king in his place (11:43). Upon taking up the throne, the people complained to Rehoboam of the heavy yoke Solomon placed on their backs, asking that he lighten their load (12:1–4). Rehoboam consulted two sets of advisors, one who advised for his father and those who had grown up with Rehoboam. Rehoboam rejected the elders' advice to lighten the load and went with his friends' advice to increase it along with harsher punishments for the non-compliant (12:6–14).

---

142. Bergen, *1, 2 Samuel*, 81. So also Auld, *I & II Samuel*, 50, but he does not comment on the deterministic implications of this passage.

143. Keil and Delitzsch, *Commentary*, 2:387.

144. On a grander scale, it is to demonstrate God's glory and for his name to be proclaimed in all the earth. See Piper, *Justification of God*, 159–71; Beale, "Hardening of Pharaoh's Heart"; Chisolm, "Divine Hardening."

145. Steussy, *Samuel*, 3, while in agreement with the determinative implications, nevertheless, she concludes that "this is a God who is not merely harsh, but one who shifts blame for divine actions onto humans."

146. Oord, *NOL*, 152.

In verse 15, the author tells us "the king did not listen to the people *because* this turn of events came from the LORD" (Emphasis added).[147] So, did this event take place because God failed to persuade Rehoboam to follow the elders? That is plausible; however, when we take a step back, we see that he did not listen to the people *because* of God's decree from 11:31 to split the kingdom. The kingdom divide was to take place according to God's decree; persuasion and/or compelling had no bearing on the outcome.

ISAIAH 10

Isaiah 10 is one of the strongest proof-text examples in Scripture, definitively expressing the mysterious paradox of divine sovereignty and human responsibility.[148] The context of this chapter is that of divine judgment against Israel. God makes it clear that Assyria is merely a tool in his hand. And while he will punish Israel with "his rod," Assyria, God will likewise punish Assyria for its pride and arrogance, thus also keeping his promise that a remnant will return from Assyria's captivity.[149] Isaiah 10:5–7 reveals God's purposes with Assyria;[150] however, Assyria does not see itself as carrying out Yahweh's aim and purpose in punishing Israel, to return them back to their covenant relationship with God. And that is why God will judge Assyria; it desired to destroy Israel and devour its wealth.

In Isaiah 10:12–13, God decrees to bring judgment upon the king of Assyria for arrogantly thinking that his victory over Israel was "done by [his] own strength and wisdom."[151] While God says he was "the rod of my

147. The Hebrew word, *sibbah*, a noun, translated as the phrase "turn of events" only appears once in the Old Testament, so a contextual study is difficult. ESV renders this passage as "a turn of affairs brought about by the Lord." And the NET says, "because the LORD was instigating this turn of events so that he might bring to pass the prophetic announcement he had made." Sweeney, *I & II Kings*, 170, concurs with the translation, noting that "Verse 15 explains the reason for Rehoboam's ill-considered response as divine intervention—that is, YHWH had caused a *sibbah*, literally a 'turning' (of events)." And House, *1 & 2 Kings*, 182, commenting on this passage, writes, "Nothing occurs here because of 'chance.' There is no 'chance.' God is sovereign. Still, Rehoboam's decision is his own. The text maintains the tension between God's sovereignty and human responsibility that pervades all of Scripture."

148. I would class three other texts in this category: Gen 50:20; Acts 2:23; 4:27–28. Romans 9 (also the wider context in chs. 10–11), no less profound and perplexing, provides a glimpse of an answer to such mysterious truths.

149. Oswalt, *Isaiah*, 262.

150. Schroeder, *Agency of God*, 50, to put it plainly, writes, "Assyria is the instrument of YHWH's judgment."

151. See also Daniel 4:34–37 and 5:18–24, which are also absent from Oord's writings and equally, if not more so, devastating to his position (esp., 5:23).

anger," thus punishing Israel *through* him, God attributes this activity to *himself*, done by his own power and wisdom. In verse 15, God, speaking through Isaiah, shows the folly of Assyria's arrogance, stating: "Does an ax exalt itself above the one who chops with it? Does a saw magnify itself above the one who saws with it? It would be like a rod waving the one who lifts it! It would be like a staff lifting one who isn't wood!" Assyria does not see that it was God who wielded it in power to conquer Israel.[152] Why should a saw get the glory and praise over the one who saws with it? And in verse 24, the Lord tells Israel not to "fear Assyria, though they strike you with a rod and raise their staff over you as the Egyptians did. In just a little while my wrath will be spent, and my anger will turn to their destruction."

So, what are we to make of this passage? How does Oord explain this text in light of his view of divine power? As stated, Oord does not offer an exegetical response or simply an explanation that can coherently account for his view of God's power in the sovereignty-responsibility texts, except Genesis 50:20, which I have addressed elsewhere (see chapter 5). A classical reading of this passage understands God's sovereign power to bring about judgment on his people *indirectly* through another group of people, which aligns with Oord's view of divine power. But it also understands that God brings about punishment, which includes death to whomever he wills, because he has the right and power to do so, without being culpable for any charge of evil (as the general sense of the text demonstrates. cf. Rom 9:14–24).

God can use the free-will *sinful* decisions of one person or group to achieve his divine purposes but also judge that person or group for their evil desires in carrying out what they did, though it fulfilled God's justice. Is that a mystery? It is; a classical view maintains the mystery because the text reveals it. Oord will not embrace such a view. He writes, "theologians pay a high price when claiming divine omnipotence means that God possesses absolute sovereignty . . . because it supports a conception of power inconsistent with the main thrust of the Biblical witness. Determinism further implies that an individual's sinful act is, at least indirectly, the work of God."[153]

---

152. Smith, *Isaiah*, 256, writes, "The prophet's divine perspective enables him to clarify God's role in using Assyria and to point out Assyria's perversion of God's plan. Initially the Assyrians are pictured as instruments used by God to accomplish his will. God is sovereign and he employs many nations to accomplish his plans on earth. But the Assyrians can only act according to God's directions." In agreement with my interpretation, John Goldingay, a highly regarded scholar in the open theism community, writes, "God doesn't see anything unjust in utilizing people's wrong instincts yet still evaluating them on the basis of those instincts. . . . They get no slack because God uses them." Goldingay, *Isaiah for Everyone*, 47–48.

153. Oord, "Divine Power," 3.

Oord's indictment of the God of determinism fails because his appropriation of "sinful act" and "the work of God" does not distinguish between guilt and responsibility. Causal responsibility does not imply moral guilt. A theological determinist sees that the moral evils that God does cause, do in fact come about because the God of the Bible, whose wisdom, knowledge, goodness, and holiness infinitely surpasses that of a fallen, sinful creature, deems that their occurrence is overall more preferable than for them not to come about.[154] Likewise, indeterminists that hold to classical doctrines, such as exhaustive foreknowledge and divine sovereignty, argue the same case of "preference," in that God as the cause of all that exists is responsible for the existence of sin and evil because he prefers that humans have freewill; therefore, God has "ordained" (according to his preference) that sin and evil exist. Because God cannot sin (applying *via negativa*), he cannot be guilty (as efficient cause) for bringing about sinful actions according to a *moral* scale.

The hurdle for Oord in his understanding of a determinist view of God is that he equates ordaining with performing. So, if God ordains a murder, then God is murderous. And that is the danger in stretching anthropomorphic categories. The pedagogical tactic of *via eminentiae* maintains the perfections of God in the involvement of evil, consistently pointing back to the dis-analogy (*via negativa*) between God and creatures in the bringing about of evil actions. Creatures carryout evil acts according to their sinful intentions. God cannot sin; therefore, his involvement behind evil (as cause) is not sinful.

But for Oord, a view of God that rests on mystery is nothing more than a "blank check" or "escape hatch" to wiggle out of an uncomfortable position.[155] For Oord, an appeal to mystery lacks explanatory consistency, which does not allow us to make sense of life.[156] However, Oord does not offer an interpretation of such difficult passages in order to make sense of them within a process construct. If Oord cannot formulate a theology that at least attempts to explain these types of difficult, yet extremely important, passages in a manner consistent with his theology, then what else can Oord appeal to other than mystery—or claim ignorance, maybe? Oord does not allow mystery to have a place in God's involvement with evil. Oord writes that his conception of divine power "meets the requirements demanded by process theologians that God's power be conceived in such a way as to prevent

---

154. Bignon, *Excusing Sinners*, 189.
155. Oord, *NOL*, 10.
156. Oord, *ULG*, 89.

indicting God as culpable for the world's evil."[157] Oord concludes that process theology determines the kind of power God must have, thus governing how he interprets passages that pertain to God's power.

General Sense Reading

For Oord, "Divine power involves God's persuasion and exercise of indirect bodily impact without unilateral determination."[158] That is a very attenuated claim. An important question to ask is: When one reads passages pertaining to God's action with/toward creation, is Oord's view of God's power a naturally derived assumption from the text? By *naturally*, I mean is that the "general sense" of the text? For example, 1 Samuel 25:38 says, "About ten days later, the LORD struck Nabal dead." In reading this text and the context, is it a more natural or a general sense reading to think that God directly acted and *struck Nabal dead*, or is it a more natural or a general sense reading of the text to think God used persuasive power to indirectly move another physical body to bring about Nabal's death? With that said, a general sense reading may determine that God struck down someone *indirectly* by means of another (e.g., Josh 10:10; Isa 10:1–24; Acts 2:23; 4:27–28). And that is where a classical reading provides greater consistency, in that it understands that God *directly* and *indirectly* acts in/within his creation. A process view delimits what God can do, regardless of a general sense reading of the text.

While the above portion focused on specific sovereignty-responsibility texts, this final portion seeks to answer the question, if the general sense of Scripture more coherently aligns with a classical view of divine power than Oord's process view. Again, Oord's claim is that God *cannot* unilaterally or directly impact another body. Though only one passage is needed to counter Oord's objection, the purpose is to demonstrate that a classical view of God's power is warranted from a general sense reading of Scripture. And to do so, I will examine a set of biblical passages (and referencing others) that show God unilaterally or directly carryout an action that has a direct, physical impact on another creature or group of individuals. And I will also engage with the passages Oord specifically uses to support his view.

---

157. Oord, "Divine Power," 16.
158. Oord, "MTP," 8.

Oord's Scriptural Support for an Indirect and Persuasive View of Divine Power

Before moving forward, in fairness to Oord, it is important to look at the texts that he does use to support his reading or what he calls the "main thrust of the biblical witness" pertaining to God's power. A basic assertion of Oord's view is that God exerts compelling power and cannot directly impact bodied creatures. Oord writes: "'God is Spirit' (John 4:24), not a football player, human mother, or embodied object. . . . The divine Spirit does not possess a wholly divine body with which to bump and bang. Bodily impact requires the agency of embodied creatures, and God does not have a body in the sense that creatures have bodies."[159]

Oord looks to the Spirit/wind analogy from John 3:8 to establish his fundamental understanding of God's activity in the world. In this text, Jesus compares the occurrence of spiritual rebirth by the Spirit with the movement of the wind; we do not know where it comes from or where it goes. Jesus' analogy, Oord writes, "offers clues to how we might best conceive of divine action in the universe."[160] And this makes sense in real life because "causation itself is, like the Spirit, imperceptible by our five senses."[161] And because the Spirit is God, and the Spirit is imperceptible, God "neither intervenes from the outside nor coerces by acting as sufficient cause."[162] God, therefore, influences and compels through a divine call, to influence all creatures to act for the common good. And God, as omnipresent Spirit, is always exerting "the greatest influence possible to persuade creatures to act in ways that promote overall well-being."[163] In explaining how God is personally and variously efficacious, Oord writes, "I propose that being personal for God means causally influencing others, in each moment, by calling them to actualize possible ways of being."[164] Oord looks to process metaphysics in order substantiate his account of God's activity through calling and influencing other creatures to respond in love.

What Scriptures does Oord use to support his view of God's indirect, persuasive and compelling power? God is Almighty, says Oord, quoting Deut 10:17, which means "God is the mightiest being that exists, and God exerts

---

159. Oord, *NOL*, 128.
160. Oord, "The Divine Spirit," 467.
161. Oord, "The Divine Spirit," 469.
162. Oord, "The Divine Spirit," 474.
163. Oord, "The Divine Spirit," 475.
164. Oord, "The Divine Spirit," 474.

might in various ways upon all others."¹⁶⁵ But his almightiness must be seen in light of his love, which means that when Jesus said to "his disciples, 'follow me' (Matt 4:19), . . . God's call awaits our free response."¹⁶⁶ This idea of prevenient grace (as described above) comes from passages such as Philippians 2:12b–13, where "[i]n freedom, says Paul, we 'work out [our] own salvation with fear and trembling.' Such work is only possible because God 'is at work in [us], enabling [us] both to will and to work for his good pleasure.'"¹⁶⁷

Another passage we observed earlier Oord references to support a compelling-view of power is 2 Chronicles 7:14–20, a form of God's activity grounded in covenant relations with Israel. In this passage, God uses compelling power to get Israel to humble themselves and turn from their wicked ways. Otherwise, God will pluck them out of the land he has given to them. Oord asks, rhetorically, does God's act of "plucking" mean that he is going to unilaterally "scoop up" Israel and "transport them to some far-off land?"¹⁶⁸ Other examples Oord uses to support a purely *indirect* view of divine action are 1 Corinthians 5:1–5 and Matthew 10:34 (cf. Matt 21:12–13). These passages refer to God acting through his people to minister to the church. For Oord, divine acting is divine calling. God calls individuals to exercise physical force upon others, such as a holy kiss, excluding someone from church, violent cleansing of the temple, oppositions to oppressive governments, and even use of the sword.

---

165. Oord, *NOL*, 128.

166. Oord, *NOL*, 129.

167. Oord, *NOL*, 129. Oord's view on this passage is a common interpretation in Evangelical circles. See Melick, *Philippians*, 111, who writes, "Human energy could never accomplish the work of God, yet God did not accomplish his purposes without it." And also Wilson et al., *Commentary*, 197. Oord also refers to 2 Corinthians 3:17, which says, "The Lord is the Spirit, and where the Spirit of the Lord is, there is freedom," to support a view of God's essential nature providing freedom/agency to all creatures. Oord, *NOL*, 126. However, he does not provide any commentaries to support his interpretation. And in surveying a handful of Evangelical commentators, none of them are in agreement with Oord, as it pertains to this passage implying God giving freedom to all creatures. Rather, they identify that Paul's context is in reference to believers being free from obedience to the law, since they are not under the veil of Moses, in that the Spirit enables all believers to turn from sin to freely serve Christ. See Garland, *2 Corinthians*, 198; Scott, *2 Corinthians*, 99; Barnett, *Second Epistle*, 203; Barrett, *Second Epistle*, 123–24.

168. Oord, "Divine Power," 9.

A Brief Response

I will offer a brief response to Oord's interpretation of the 2 Chronicles passage because it is a perfect example of Oord's view missing the wider interpretation and understanding of God's power as affirmed in classical theism, supported by a general sense reading. To answer Oord's question about God unilaterally "plucking up" Israel, a classical view *agrees* with him, saying, "No." But here lies the disparity. A wider reading of the context will notice that this passage is actually a prophetic statement, as part of the blessing and cursing that will come to Israel based upon their faithfulness or lack thereof (cf. Deut 28:37; Jer 24:4—25:14).

After reading the 2 Chronicles passage and the other related passages, when we get to Jeremiah 24, the Lord's pronouncement comes to fruition. The Lord, *through* Nebuchadnezzar, plucks Israel from their land, who then transports them to "the far-off land" of Babylon (cf. 2 Chr 36:15–20; Ezra 5:12). It is because God is omnipresent Spirit that the embodied creatures cannot hinder God from working in and through other human agents to fulfill his purposes. But, as will be observed below, God as omnipresent Spirit also means that embodied creatures cannot hinder God from directly impacting them as well.

On the one hand, Oord's understanding of the Spirit/wind analogy has merit. God's working to bring about salvation is mysterious, and we do not know exactly how God works, nor do we understand *how* God brings about miracles. However, the work of the Spirit in the hearts of his children is God's stamp of salvation, whereby the Spirit affirms and assures one's adoption as a child of God (cf. Rom 8). The context of this analogy in John 3 more directly speaks to God's work of rebirth by his willing, his calling, and not by human willing. The wider application of the Spirit/wind analogy purposed to show how the Spirit and the wind works/moves is analogous in that (1) we cannot know where they come from, God's working to bring about rebirth, and the winds ability to move, but (2) the Spirit works as he pleases to bring about rebirth and the wind blows as it pleases.[169] A sinner is born again by the work of the Spirit according to the Spirit's pleasure (cf. John 1:12–13). And that is why Nicodemus could not grasp what Jesus was saying—*because* he was not born from above by the Spirit. But Oord's view of divine power does not allow God to change sinful hearts according to God's will; rather, salvation is according to the free-will decision of man,

---

169. Oord's analogy falls apart, in that wind also has the power to *coerce* trees into falling over and can even blow people off cliffs against their will.

not according to predestination or election. To do so is arbitrary, which a steadfastly, loving God cannot do.[170]

God Strikes

Oord claims God *cannot* act directly toward/on another physical body. Rather, God calls on "individuals, groups, or nations to exercise physical force upon others."[171] In one sense, Oord's claim is true; however, it stops short of what Scripture *fully* articulates about God's activity. One of the clearest examples to demonstrate my point are passages that pertain to God striking individuals with sickness or death. In this section, I will review passages that express direct divine action and filter them through a classical and process (Oord's particular reading) reading to identify which view offers greater consistency with the general sense of Scripture.

We already observed the example in 1 Samuel 25:38, referring to God striking [Heb. *nagaph*] Nabal dead. But I want to elaborate further. The Hebrew word *nagaph* translated as *struck*, is an active verb form, with the sense of acting against another to kill or strike dead.[172] In the context of the passage, God brought judgment "back on [Nabal's] head" (25:39) for withholding payment for David's protective services over his goods.[173] But the passage has other important details pertinent to the discussion. In this passage, David offered praise to God because David *wanted* to strike Nabal down, but God "restrained [him] from doing evil." And a few passages earlier, David praised the Lord for preventing him from hurting Nabal's wife, Abigail, who ran to confront David and plea with him not to kill Nabal for his stupidity (25:23–26). And then David also praised the Lord for sending Abigail because her gracious words calmed his anger. So, while we have a clear case of God *unilaterally*—God acting directly on a physical body—striking down Nabal, we have a clear case of God acting *indirectly*

---

170. Oord, *NOL*, 155.

171. Oord, "Divine Power," 11.

172. Walter Brueggemann, a widely accepted and cited scholar in the open theist community, comments about possible explanations for the cause of death; however, he concludes that "the narrator is quite explicit about the cause of death. Yahweh smote him (v. 38). What David refrained from doing, Yahweh did." Brueggemann, *First and Second Samuel*, 180.

173. Bergen, *1, 2 Samuel*, 252, writes, "But the writer was careful to note that the ultimate cause of Nabal's death was not an unfortunate medical problem: 'The Lord struck Nabal.' His death came as the direct result of personally administered divine judgment."

to restrain David from bloodshed and avenging, through means of sending Abigail to calm David's angry heart.

But the indirect aspect elicits a question: Why did Abigail decide to go and persuade David from killing Nabal? While we read that one of Nabal's men notified her of what was going to happen, in the final details of the event, David says *God* sent Abigail to meet him, which would ultimately prevent David from carrying out an evil act. And that is what David praised God for doing. From the context, there is agreement with Oord's position that God indirectly persuades/compels human creatures to act, but also *disagreement* with Oord that God's power is not strictly limited to only that form of divine action.

But there is another element to this story. The words from Abigail are prophetic, revealing David's destiny before his very eyes: "Please forgive your servant's offense, for the LORD is certain to make a lasting dynasty for my lord because he fights the LORD's battles. Throughout your life, may evil not be found in you" (25:28). The Lord determined to give David a great dynasty. And Abigail, as Robert Bergen notes, "encouraged David to put the recent events in perspective; David could tarnish or destroy God's future plans for him if he acted foolishly in the present." Bergen continues; however, "David had no need to defend himself in such matters because the LORD would watch over him: [Abigail says] 'My lord's life is tucked safely in the place where the LORD your God protects the living, but he is flinging away your enemies' lives like stones from a sling.'" The Lord would not only protect David, but he would also fling his enemies away from his anointed one.[174] And that is what he did in striking down Nabal. Oord's reading of the text does not allow God the ability to determine David's future, protect David from making choices that could disqualify him for his role, nor fling David's enemies away, as observed in God directly striking down Nabal. A general sense reading better coheres with a classical view.

In 2 Samuel 6:7, we read: "Then the LORD's anger burned against Uzzah, and God struck [Heb. *nakah*] him dead on the spot for his irreverence, and he died there next to the ark of God." The Hebrew word *nakah* means *to smite* and is in the hifil verb form, which expresses that the subject of the verb causes the object of the verb to participate in the action of the verb.[175] The context of the passage shows God punishing Uzzah because he profaned God's holiness by placing his "unholy" hand on the ark. Nowhere in the context do we see that another person or creature acted on behalf of God, nor do we see that God

---

174. Bergen, *1, 2 Samuel*, 250.

175. Heiser and Setterholm, *Glossary*. For example, in the sentence, "Steve caused the plane to crash," the plane, as the direct object, participates in the action that the subject, Steve, caused.

indirectly persuaded another physical body to strike down Uzzah. A general sense reading coheres with a classical view that God—"not some impersonal force"[176]—as Creator and Lord ended Uzzah's life.[177]

In 2 Samuel 12:15, we read: "Then Nathan went home. The Lord struck [*nagaph*] the baby that Uriah's wife had borne to David, and he became deathly ill." The well-known situation with David is tragic. David's sins are horrendous, resulting in the death of his son conceived with Bathsheba. Most standard translations[178] employ the word *struck*. A general sense reading of the text places God as the subject of the direct action of bringing about the child's death. He did not persuade or compel another body to indirectly end the child's life. God unilaterally determined that David's son would die; and God brought it about.

2 Kings 15:5 says, "The Lord afflicted [*naga*] the king, and he had a serious skin disease until the day of his death." The king spoken of here is Azariah of Judah. *Naga* is in the piel verb form, which expresses the object of the verb suffering the effect of the action, i.e., it is put into a state by the action. In this context, the Lord directly acts to afflict Azaria, who, as the object of the action, suffers the effect. The context is similar to the other retributive accounts, where God brings judgment as punishment for sin, which in this case the Lord afflicts/strikes the guilty party with a disease.

In 2 Chronicles 13:20, we read: "Jeroboam no longer retained his power during Abijah's reign; ultimately, the Lord struck [*nagaph*] him and he died." While the context does not expound further regarding the end of Jeroboam, since we know he lived a few years after Abijah, we should be inclined to see his death in light of 1 Kings 14, where God decreed to destroy Jeroboam's house for his wicked idolatry.

In 2 Chronicles 21:18, we read: "After all these things, the Lord afflicted him in his intestines with an incurable disease." King Jehoram did what was evil in the Lord's eyes; therefore, God, like the previous accounts following a retributive theme—"you have sinned, so you will suffer,"[179] "smote him in his bowels to (with) disease, for which there was no healing."[180] Though the translation uses *afflicted*, the Hebrew verb is *nagaph*. The Lord decreed in 21:15 that Jehoram would be struck with many illnesses, including disease of the intestines, and it was the Lord who directly brought it about.

---

176. Bergen, *1, 2 Samuel*, 330.

177. Campbell, *2 Samuel*, 69, places "Uzzah's death at God's hand." Later, he writes, "it was the action of YHWH striking Uzzah dead that prevented the ark from being brought by David to Jerusalem." Campbell, *2 Samuel*, 211.

178. CSB, NKJV, KJV, NASB, NRSV, and NIV.

179. "Retribution," in Dillard, *2 Chronicles*, 76–81.

180. Keil and Delitzsch, *Old Testament*, 3:646.

A few other uses of the Hebrew word *naga* is translated into English as *touch*. Psalm 104:32 says, "He looks at the earth, and it trembles; he touches [*naga*] the mountains and they poor out smoke." And Psalm 144:5 says, "LORD, part your heavens and come down. Touch [*naga*] the mountains and they will smoke." These occurrences in the Psalms, though poetic, reveal that the author understood God's activity as directly acting on/with his creation to bring about certain events/outcomes. While the discussion can move into, *how* God brings about such activities, ultimately, *how* is where the mystery looms.[181] Nevertheless, in a general sense reading of the text (which also seems to be what the immediate author had in mind when writing the text), it is apparent that God acts directly *and* indirectly with his creation, which a classical view affirms as well. Oord's process framework only allows indirect divine activity.

Two last examples to review are from the New Testament, the death of Ananias and Sapphira in Acts 5:1–10 and Paul's warning to the church about God's judgment on those taking communion in an unworthy manner in 1 Corinthians 11:27–31.[182] Both situations are about divine (albeit temporal) judgment, as in the examples from the Old Testament. A general sense reading of the account in Acts implies that Ananias' and Sapphira's "dropping dead" were a result of God acting directly to end their lives.[183] We do not see God persuading or compelling indirectly through another physical body to carry out their deaths. God knows the heart and determines to judge according to his will. And in 1 Corinthians 11, Paul gives warning about God's judgment (temporal) for taking communion in an unworthy manner, resulting in illness and sometimes death. The basic principle is that if the Corinthians had judged themselves appropriately, they would not have experienced judgment. It is another situation of God knowing one's heart and inflicting judgment for sin.[184]

---

181. And Oord agrees that we cannot explain how God acts, particularly in performing miracles. Oord, "Miracles," 207.

182. Jesus raising Lazarus (John 11:40–44) is one of the strongest proof-text examples, supportive of God *directly* acting on a physical body. Oord, as noted, is silent on the matter.

183. Bock, *Acts*, 224–25, observes, "The instant nature of the judgment is shocking, but that is the point. Attempts to explain this on natural terms (a heart attack or something similar) fail to honor the linkage to Sapphira's death. . . . This is an exceptional case of instant judgment, but it also indicates that God, as the one who knows and makes assessments, acts in judgment within God's community (cf. 1 Cor 11:30; Jas 5:20; 1 John 5:16–17; 1 Cor 5:5; 1 Tim 1:20).

184. Oord, *NOL*, 151–52.

There are many more passages that I could have included in this section.[185] Other types of direct action in the biblical text are those instances of God closing and opening women's wombs.[186] We also see passages of God causing an agent(s) to fall asleep, as in the opening account of Genesis, where God "caused a deep sleep to come over the man" so that God could take out one of his ribs to fashion Eve (2:21). A general sense reading also tells us that God *took a rib out of Adam*—truly a direct, physical action on an embodied being.[187] And God kept Saul's soldiers asleep so David could pass by undetected (1 Sam 26:12).

In getting back to the main point of this study, what is a more general sense understanding of the nature of God's power as articulated in Scripture? A classical view sees God acting directly and indirectly as the omnipresent and omnipotent Lord of his creation, according to his specific purposes. Oord's view of divine power cannot be adequately accounted for in a general sense reading of Scripture, rendering classical theology greater explanatory ability in articulating a coherent doctrine of God.

Conclusion

Oord's position is difficult to maintain in light of the four sovereignty-responsibility passages above. Nowhere do we see that a certain event took place based on God's persuasive ability. In my examination of the texts, God's divine will *alone* surfaced as the determinative catalyst. Exegetical evidence to support Oord's presuppositions is wanting. The second aspect of my approach offered a constructive account, which aimed to demonstrate that the general sense of Scripture more consistently agrees with a classical view. And it demonstrated that Oord's delimitation on God's power, due to what a process construct allows, failed to meet a general sense reading of the biblical text.

On one hand, Oord is correct when claiming that God does use persuasion and compelling power with his creation, but on the other hand, he greatly weakened his claim that a process view of power has greater agreement with the general thrust of the biblical witness, than a classical

---

185. Gen 20:6–7; 38:7; Exod 9:23; 12:29; 32:35; Num 11:33; Josh 10:10; 1 Sam 6:19; 2 Kgs 6:18; 2 Chr 13:20; Isa 27:7; Amos 4:9; Hag 2:17.

186. Gen 16:2; 20:18; 29:31; 30:22; 1 Sam 5–6. The Hebrew verb is *atsar*, which is a causative act of God making women barren. And the text explains that God had done so based upon his will because of the circumstances within the context, according to his own purposes. And *pathach* is a causative verb in God's decision to open a woman's womb to conceive.

187. Oord denies that there was a literal/historical Adam and Eve.

view. His thesis failed because he did not offer an explanation on biblical texts that (1) cannot be interpreted in an either/or fashion (e.g., Isa 10; Acts 2:23; 4:27–28) and (2) a general sense reading demonstrates a view of power (i.e., that God can and does act unilaterally and determinatively, directly on bodied creatures within his creation) that conflicts with Oord's view (i.e., God *can only* influence *indirectly* and cannot directly impact bodied creatures within his creation).

What are the challenges that a unilateral view of determinism has to face? It has to discern the mystery between conflicting *true* statements, where the temporal and the divine order come together. A classical view of divine power attempts to hold all the strings together, maintaining the tension within the text to ensure balance and fair handling, in order to do justice to the general biblical-theological view of Scripture. Oord claims that "an omnicausal view [classical view] goes against our commonsense understanding of the world. . . . [I]t makes no sense to say that God totally causes something and that creatures also cause it."[188] But to make such claims is to flatten out such texts (e.g., Gen 50:20; Isa 10; Acts 2:23; 4:26–27) and claim that they are an either-or interpretation.

John Calvin acknowledges this tension when he writes, "God rules not only the whole fabric of the world and its several parts, but also the hearts and even the actions of men."[189] Yet, he also observes,

> We do not make the minds of men to be impelled by force external to them so that they rage furiously; nor do we transfer to God the cause of hardening, in such a way that they did not voluntarily and by their own wickedness and hardness of heart spur themselves on to obstinacy. What we say is that men act perversely not without God's ordination that it be done, as Scripture teaches.[190]

There is a causal order within these passages, which the Spirit enables us to see. While recognizing them is helpful and important, the tension does not dissipate. Rather, to avoid collapsing one side into the other (i.e., fatalism or utter arbitrariness), the divine sovereignty-responsibility tension must

---

188. Oord, *ULG*, 85. Oord's equating omnicausal with classical theology is misrepresentative of classical theism.

189. Calvin, *Predestination*, 162. See Prov 16:1, 9; 19:21; 20:24; 21:1; 21:30; Ps 37:23; Isa 46:10; Jer 10:23; Eph 1:11. It is interesting that the majority of these passages, which speak of man planning his ways while God determines his steps or ends, are found in the Wisdom literature.

190. Calvin, *Predestination*, 174–75. See Rom 3:10–18; Eph 2:3; Eccl 7:20; Isa 64:6; Job 14:4; 15:14, 16; Jer 17:9.

remain, even at the expense of it being intellectually unsatisfying. And that is what Oord, and the process tradition, finds unsettling.

There are many more *texts of tension* that I could have used to demonstrate God's unilaterally fulfilling his purposes through coercion contrary to Oord's definition of it. God achieves his purposes through human beings without violating their wills. And God can act directly on physical bodied creatures, apart from their wills, to achieve his purposes. In Oord's preference for process philosophy and a misinformed understanding of the classical view of divine coercion, his view of divine power (i.e., God exclusively indirectly, persuades or compels) does not shape the tension in a manner that better conforms to the biblical data, as a classical view does.[191]

Miracles—Critical Evaluation

The previous chapter in this study addressed the differences between Oord's view and a classical view of metaphysics and Scripture, using miracles as the platform to identify those differences (see chapter 4). This section further elaborates on those difficulties, in contrasting Oord's explanation and a classical approach to one of the most memorable accounts in all of Scripture—the parting of the Red Sea. A traditional approach to explaining how this event occurred says that God used his unilateral power—his omnipotent will—to separate the waters and bring them back down. Oord provides an alternative view of this historic event, through the lens of his understanding of God's power, which he claims offers better explanatory power than the traditional (i.e., classical) view.

In the last chapter of this study, we saw that Oord opts for a naturalistic explanation of the Red Sea event, where violent winds blew apart the water, so the Israelites could pass. God was involved as a coordinator of the event, in that he can coordinate random and/or spontaneous events within various levels of existences, simple to complex, creaturely and noncreaturely, "in ways that bring about unexpected and good results." Oord says, "this coordination is possible because of God's omnipresence and complete knowledge of what has occurred and is occurring."[192] However, according to Oord, such events can take place only if the elements of creation decide to respond to God's call.

Oord's explanation exposes inconsistencies in his view, based on his understanding of God's knowledge. In the parting of the Red Sea, God could not have known when the random winds would be drying up parts of it if

---

191. Carson, *Divine Sovereignty*, 221.
192. Oord, *ULG*, 209.

he is unable to know the future, given the assumption of randomness and chance of such events. How could God have known the right time to command Moses to raise his arms up (Exod 14:15, 21), to part the sea, and bring it back down upon the Egyptians while they were crossing (14:26)? Oord writes, "God may foreknow with high probability that the winds would push back the water leaving the ground dry enough for passage," and "Moses may intuit God's 'still small voice' that calls him to lead the Israelites to the water at the opportune time."[193] Oord sees that this miracle occurred because God called for special creaturely cooperation. And because he was aware of the developing conditions and processes of the natural world, he was able to bring about such events in nature. But such an account of the parting of the Red Sea does not sufficiently provide explanatory power. While Oord speaks of the requirement of creation to respond to God's invitation in order for a miracle to occur, such as the parting of the Red Sea, Scripture tells us, the Red Sea parted because God rebuked the water and "it fled" (Ps 104:7; cf. Ps 18:15); he rebuked it, "and it dried up" (Ps 106:5).

The parting and bringing down of the waters of the Red Sea required precise timing. Two options seem most plausible and sufficient to explain what happened: Either God exerted his divine power over his creation, parting the Red Sea and bringing it back down on the Egyptians according to *his* timing, or he had future knowledge of the precise timing of the winds that were to part the sea and future knowledge of the precise timing when the winds would stop (and of the Egyptians attempting to pass through), thus bringing the sea back down on top of the Egyptians at the time of their crossing.

Oord argues that God's love of creation means he cannot supersede, intervene, or coerce the law-like regularities observed in nature. God calls upon "intentional agents" to "respond in ways that subsequently affect inanimate objects and natural systems."[194] So when God, through Moses, parted the Red Sea, God "acted in a special way" with the random, spontaneous conditions of the turbulent and violent winds, offering forms of possibilities to create the miracle of passing through the Red Sea.[195] Oord says God

---

193. Oord, *ULG*, 210.

194. Oord, *ULG*, 209.

195. Oord, *ULG*, 209. Interestingly, in Exodus 14:27 the text says, "While the Egyptians were trying to escape from [the sea], the Lord threw [*naar*] them back into [it]." It seems God the Spirit localized some sort of power to exert physical impact on the Egyptians *against their wills*. *Naar*, literally means "to shake, shake out or off," and in this passage it is in the piel, denoting that the object of the verb, in this case the Egyptians, suffer the effect of the action (i.e., it is put into a state by the action). "Naar" in Heiser and Setterholm, *Glossary*.

can coordinate random, spontaneous actions of various elements within his creation because he has complete knowledge of the past and current events. But elsewhere Oord says, randomness is "indiscriminate, unplanned and unforeseen. . . . To control randomness, God would need to foreknow random events were about to occur and then interrupt the lawlike regularities of existence that make them possible."[196] Does Oord's logic hold up here? On one hand, he says that God can organize random and spontaneous events because of his omniscient knowledge of past and present reality, yet "God does not know which possibilities for randomness will become actual."[197] To do so, God would have to "deny himself."[198]

The explanations Oord gives regarding miracles actually do the opposite of what he set out to accomplish: provide explanatory power for the divine workings of God in Scripture. What benefit does one get in accepting such an explanation of God's activity if he is contingent on nature to act? With the unsurety of God's involvement in the seemingly miraculous, why should one accept such claims?

Essential Kenosis: A Solution to the Problem of Evil

In providing a full solution to the problem of evil, Oord believes that the problem requires reconceiving traditional views of God. Oord rephrases the question, asking, "Why doesn't our loving and almighty God prevent genuine evil?"[199] His answer: A perfectly loving God cannot prevent genuine evil. Oord believes his approach better addresses the issue. In qualifying evil with *genuine*, Oord defines it as an evil act or event that makes "the world, all things considered, worse than it might have been."[200] He does not, however, dismiss the existence of necessary evils—the painful trials believers go through to make their lives better—for a greater good. Oord's solution consists of five dimensions: empathetic, didactic, therapeutic, strategic, and sovereignty.[201]

---

196. Oord, *ULG*, 173.
197. Oord, *ULG*, 173.
198. Oord, *ULG*, 173.
199. Oord, "Essential Kenosis View," 78.
200. Oord, "Essential Kenosis View," 78–79.
201. Oord, "Essential Kenosis View," 80. The five dimensions contain elements that I have already addressed throughout this study.

Empathetic Dimension

In the empathetic dimension, contrary to the "ancient doctrine of impassibility,"[202] which says God remains unaffected by his creatures' joy and sorrows, God, in an analogous manner, is the greatest empathizer that could be conceived. Oord affirms a "strong" passibility view of God, which means "God influences creatures and creatures influence God."[203] God feels emotions when influenced, as Scripture overwhelmingly depicts.[204] He believes God rejoices and mourns with his creatures, and his creatures' rejoicing and mourning affect him as well.[205] Oord notes, the mistake of prior generations of theologians was in thinking that "God's love involves only outgoing benevolence with no receptive relationality."[206] The biblical examples of God having compassion and offering forgiveness for sin plainly demonstrate a giving-and-receiving divine-human relationality.

Oord looks to Jesus as a supportive argument for a passibilist position, observing in the Bible that "Jesus relates to others, expresses emotions, feels compassion, and suffers on the cross," as he acts like God.[207] Relations assume moment-by-moment *change*, which is where Oord makes the distinction in his view about God, who is *impassible* in nature but is *passible* in his experiences with creation.[208] Affirming God as such allows one to hold to a doctrine of divine transcendence and immanence. The troubling concern Oord has with holding to a doctrine of impassibility is that it fails to affirm how God is similar to his creatures, how he is affected by others, and how his experience changes in relationship. Oord writes, "I find it impossible to make sense of basic Christian claims about God as Creator, redeemer, Savior, forgiver, and so on, if God's experience does not change."[209] Three reasons why a strong passibilist position is important is because (1) it is important to everyday living in that Christians offer petitionary prayers to God, asking him to do something. An impassible God would be unaffected by such prayers. (2) Scripture shows God empathetically responding to creatures (2 Cor 1:3–5). An impassible God is unaffected and cannot empathetically relate. And 3)

---

202. Oord, "Essential Kenosis View," 80.
203. Oord, "Strong Passibility," 129.
204. Oord lists a sample of passages: Gen 1; 2; 6:6; Exod 3:7; 6:5; 32:9–14; Deut 4:31; 2 Kgs 20:1–7; Ps 106:45; Isa 54:10; Jer 41:10; Joel 2:18; Hos 11:8–9; Zeph 3:17. Oord, "Strong Passibility," 131.
205. Oord, "Strong Passibility," 131.
206. Oord, "Strong Passibility," 134.
207. Oord, "Strong Passibility," 133.
208. Oord, "Strong Passibility," 142.
209. Oord, "Strong Passibility," 136.

the Bible commands us to act like God—to love, be kind, tenderhearted, forgiving, holy, and compassionate (Luke 6:36; Eph 4:32; 5:1–2; 1 Pet 1:14–16). How can one imitate an impassible God that requires passibility to imitate?[210] Therefore, for Oord, a strong passibilist approach offers the most consistent position in that it maintains the similarities and dissimilarities between God and creatures, as Scripture portrays.[211]

Human relationality is important. And God understood that as well (Gen 2:18). However, Oord's assertion regarding impassibility is misguided. The "ancient doctrine of impassibility" predicates that God's nature and character cannot undergo emotional change; *change* is different from *affected*.[212] A proper view of the doctrine is that God is not ruled by emotions, as man can and is. Impassibility (*apatheia*) never intended to say that God was indifferent.[213] Rather, it was originally used *apophatically* to safeguard the biblical God from being lumped together with the prideful, power-hungry, lust-filled pagan gods of Stoicism.[214] Oord attempts to answer this objection, stating that "God's unchanging nature makes it possible for God to feel and express emotions in accordance with God's wise and good nature."[215] But the problem remains in Oord's terminology of God *feeling* and having *emotions*.

Classical theism does not deny that creatures can affect God. Psalm 147:11 says, "The LORD values those who fear him, those who put their hope in his faithful love." And Psalm 149:4 says, "For the LORD takes pleasure in his people; he adorns the humble with salvation." And those who are evil are detestable to God (Prov 11:20). Creaturely actions are either pleasing or repulsive to God. Divine impassibility affirms that God cannot be swayed to act in a manner contrary to how his holy, good, and loving nature should act. And Oord argues for his position based on that observation as well. But the difference is a *causal* one. The change that does occur is not due to a creature's ability to cause a change in God; rather, God expresses the perfections of his love and kindness because he possesses them in "the superabundance of his purely actual being,"[216] not through experience as creatures do. In creatures, perfections are not intrinsic to them; rather, they are added to them. And creatures gain such perfections through experience. Experience

---

210. Oord, "Strong Possibility," 138–39.
211. Oord, "Strong Possibility," 143.
212. For a survey of the discussion between impassibility and passibility, see Scrutton, "Divine Passibility," 866–74.
213. Helm, "Impassionedness," 145.
214. Hart, "No Shadow," 185.
215. Oord, "Strong Possibility," 141.
216. Dolezal, "A Strong Impassibility Response," 152–53.

entails gaining new knowledge in time; God has perfect knowledge; therefore, he does not undergo experience as creatures do. Rather, God's love and kindness is maximal toward those he loves. God does not grow or increase in love, as human creatures do as experience entails.

Thomist language is helpful in explaining impassibility. God is perfectly in act, meaning he perfectly expresses (actualizes) joy and sorrow according to his will, but his ability to execute his holy and righteous purposes are not subject to "emotive" expressions. Thomas Weinandy is helpful on this: God is passionless,

> not in the sense that he does not love, but because, being pure act, there is no need for an arousal of his will to love the good and so to come to desire the good as loved, and so rejoicing and delighting in it, is eternally and perfectly in act. If there were changeable and passible passions within God, as these are found in human beings, it would mean that he is not fully loving for he would have to actualize further 'loving' potential.... Being fully in act his love is fully in act and therefore his passion is fully in act.... God is impassible precisely because he is supremely passionate and cannot become anymore passionate.[217]

Humans can and do make sinful choices in anger and even in joy. Augustine writes, "if [*apatheia*] be taken to mean an impassibility of spirit and not of body, or, in other words, a freedom from those emotions which are contrary to reason and disturb the mind, then it is obviously a good and most desirable quality, it is not one which is attainable in this life."[218] God has accommodated himself to his creatures; however, creatures, unlike God, can be "derailed" due to the "ebb and flow" of human passions.[219] In the Christian life, one of the fruits of the Spirit is that of self-control, *enkrateia*, the *restraint* of one's emotions, impulses, or desires[220] (Gal 5:22–23; cf. 2 Tim 1:7; Titus 2:6, 12; 1 Pet 4:7; 2 Pet 1:6). Furthermore, Christian exercise of self-control is a definitional mark for the people of God, in contrast to the Gentiles, who are governed by their passions (1 Thess 4:3–8).

To sum up my response, I simply repeat James Dolezal's response to Oord on this matter, which points to the univocism that has plagued modern Christian theism. He writes,

---

217. Weinandy, *Does God Suffer?*, 126–27.
218. Augustine, *City of God*, 14.9.4.
219. Helm, "Impassionedness," 147.
220. "enkrateia," in BDAG, 274.

How do we know that the Bible, though it freely depicts God's providential dealings with creatures in passibilist language, assumes God literally engages in give-and-take relationship with creatures? We don't conclude that the Bible assumes divine materiality simply because it deploys corporealist language in relating God's providential dealings toward us. So why conclude it assumes modality of passion in God simply because it deploys passibilist imagery to speak of him?[221]

In the Christian life, passions or emotions, then, are something that should not have causative dominion over humans; rather, the indwelling Spirit of God causes creatures to manifest perfections in a manner like him, as one is being conformed into the image of Christ. One of the prominent differences is that *emotion* (i.e., passions) does not retain its original seat in modern theological discussion. God, as primary cause and perfect in all that he is *from* himself, cannot be acted upon and *caused* to manifest emotions, as humans are.

Oord's argumentation aimed at dispelling a view that he claims is proper to classical theism. One of my intentions in this study is to identify misconceptions Oord has of classical theism. And in doing so, I demonstrated that Oord's failure to properly articulate the doctrine of divine impassibility, as held in classical theism, hindered his case because he based his argument on a faulty premise.

Didactic Dimension

In his didactic dimension, God uses the evil in the world to better his creatures. He "squeezes whatever good can be squeezed from evil events that God did not want in the first place."[222] To illustrate this dimension, Oord refers to the story of Joseph in Genesis 37–50, with the key text being 50:20. The text says, "You planned evil against me, but God planned it for good, to bring about the present result—the survival of many people."

Oord objects to the traditional understanding that this action is predetermined because it implies that evil is part of God's master plan. If that were so, says Oord, then rape, genocide, and murder are according to God's will.[223] In his treatment of this passage, in his latest book, *God Can't*,[224] he writes,

---

221. Dolezal, "A Strong Impassibility Response," 152.
222. Oord, "Essential Kenosis View," 81.
223. Oord, "Essential Kenosis View," 81.
224. Oord, *GC*, 126–28.

> Scholars often translate the Hebrew word in Joseph's statement "intended," but it has other meanings. Unfortunately, "intended" can give the false impression Joseph's life was pre-orchestrated. It can lead to thinking God caused or permitted slavery and mass starvation with a foreordained good in mind.[225]

Oord continues,

> A better translation of this passage overcomes this misunderstanding. That translation supports the view that Joseph's brothers wanted him to suffer, but it does not imply his suffering was God's will. This translation says God *uses* evil to bring about good. "You wanted to harm me, but God *used* it for good," said Joseph to his brothers. God took what God didn't want in the first place and squeezed good from it.[226]

Oord's reasoning in opting for a translation that says God *used* the evil actions of Joseph's brothers for good is to put an end to thinking that God caused slavery and starvation for good. While Oord's book is intended for a popular level, he does not even offer a footnote to any linguistic or lexical sources or evidence to support his "better translation." Oord's choice for this translation seems better suited to his philosophical presuppositions.

I believe that Oord's preference creates theological issues that he either overlooks or he is not aware. Opting for a different meaning of the word has drastic implications for the rest of the story. First, the text itself, grammatically, the two first clauses in question: "you planned evil against me; God planned it for good," are parallel constructions.[227] The brothers' evil (*ra*) plot, intentions, plan (*chasab*), is mirrored with God's *chasab* with the pronoun (*hu*), "it," identified as the antecedent evil behavior of Joseph's brothers; therefore, changing the word "meant" to "turned" is not warranted.[228] It actually violates the grammar of the text, and the change in meaning alters the thrust of the passage. "Meant" is intentional; "turned" is reactive. I do not have the space to work through the entire Joseph narrative, but if one follows Oord's translation preference, a close examination of the text will see that it alters the

---

225. Oord, *GC*, 127.
226. Oord, *GC*, 127.
227. Gaiser, "'You Meant Evil,'" 35–36; Mandolfo, "'You Meant Evil,'" 463–64.
228. Mathews, *Genesis*, 927, identifies the parallelism between good and evil, "which heightens the contrast between the human and divine intentions," nevertheless, his interpretation is that "God transformed [the brothers'] evil intention into good." Rad, *Genesis*, 432, writes, "Even where no man could imagine it, God had all the strings in his hand. But the guidance of God is only asserted; nothing more explicit is said about the way in which God incorporated man's evil into his saving activity."

theological moral of the story.[229] And, lastly, I do not see how Oord's God can *proactively* "squeeze" any situation when God is unable to coerce. God must wait on creatures to decide if they want to be squeezed.

Therapeutic Dimension

In the therapeutic dimension, writes Oord, "God heals, to whatever extent possible, those who experience injury, destruction, and death.... We who endure pain and injury can trust that God works to bring healing."[230] Unfortunately, the therapeutic dimension only guarantees that God cannot heal. Trusting that God is *working* to bring healing does not comfort the afflicted. If God's ability to act is subject to creaturely freedom, in that God cannot override creaturely choices, then God cannot guarantee healing to a little girl who is chained to a bed in a basement and tortured daily. If God's power of persuasion is not strong enough to influence the torturer or others to free her and bring healing, then all God can do is say he tried. But how do we know that God tried hard enough? The ultimate reason for his failing to bring healing is because his uncontrollably loving nature places freedom above saving a little girl. Oord's aim is to remove culpability from God because, in this scenario, the God of classical theism has the power to save the girl but may choose not to do it. To be fair, a classical view has to struggle with the same issue of why God does not intervene to free a young girl from such a horrendous situation. As terrible as it is, a classical view rests on the complete goodness of God, in that such horrible situations, we trust that God has a greater purpose that justifies his decree of such events. For Oord and the process tradition, a classical view does not suffice.

Interestingly, concluding his therapeutic dimension, Oord speaks of healing that could occur in the "present reality" or the "afterlife."[231] But how can Oord's God guarantee healing in the afterlife? He cannot. What makes the afterlife different to where God can actually bring about healing? Oord says God always works to heal, but "[s]ometimes creatures don't cooperate, or conditions aren't accommodating."[232] Is it because sin is eradicated, and the physical elements and aggregates *will* all now agree with God's call for them to bring healing to creatures? I do not know how

229. Wenham, *Genesis 16–50*, 490, writes, "In these two passages [50:20-21] we have expressed the key idea that informs the whole Joseph story, that through sinful men God works out his saving purposes."
230. Oord, "Essential Kenosis View," 82.
231. Oord, "Essential Kenosis View," 82.
232. Oord, *GC*, 124.

that could happen, considering God cannot unilaterally stop someone from sinning. How is the afterlife different?

In speaking of healing in the manner he has, Oord provided himself an escape hatch in the face of unanswered prayers to healing. The hope of enduring the Christian life of suffering, following in the path of Christ, is that promise of a glorified existence devoid of pain, despair, hunger, and sadness. Oord's God is unable to offer that hope because the afterlife would only be bliss once all creatures decide to stop sinning.

Strategic Dimension

The fourth component in Oord's solution is his strategic dimension. It is one of the most important because solving the problem of evil requires human cooperation. God's means for bringing about good in the world is through the roles creatures have and in their responses to God's call in their lives to carry out his purposes.[233] Oord refers to the *Revised Standard Version*'s translation of Romans 8:28, showing the "cooperative nature of the strategic dimension,"[234] emphasizing "*in* everything God works for good *with* those who love him." In response, I refer to my comments in chapter 4. They address the same concerns.

Sovereignty Dimension

Oord's fifth dimension is the sovereignty dimension. Before getting into his treatment, Oord gives a brief account of a nine-year-old girl named Amy, who was kidnapped, taken into the woods, raped, and strangled to death. Such a horrible case, Oord says, is hard to believe could be anything other than genuine evil, and I agree.[235] In Oord's sovereignty dimension, God is unable to unilaterally prevent the evil done to Amy because God cannot deny himself. His argument flows from his interpretation of 2 Timothy 2:13, "If we are faithless, he remains faithful—for he cannot deny himself" (NRSV). Oord interprets this passage to mean that God cannot deny his nature, which "is self-giving, others-empowering love, and this love is necessarily uncontrolling."[236] He arrives at this conclusion because in light of all the passages that say what God cannot do, holding to a doctrine of

---

233. Oord, "Essential Kenosis View," 82–83.
234. Oord, "Essential Kenosis View," 82.
235. Oord, "Essential Kenosis View," 83.
236. Oord, "Essential Kenosis View," 84.

"limitless divine sovereignty is preposterous."[237] God's power has limits, and his nature of love means God cannot act in any manner that impacts the existence of any of his creations, even non-living, soul-less objects such as rocks. Therefore, his loving nature prevents him "from unilaterally preventing Amy's kidnapping, rape, and murder."[238]

As already observed in his Essential Kenosis model, God's logically primary attribute is self-giving love; therefore, his giving of "freedom, agency, and law-like regularities to creation" are gifts that God cannot revoke. If he did, "God would deny the divine nature of love."[239] Oord's model places a higher value on creatures having autonomous freedom than God overriding man's freedom to save a person from an evil perpetrator. But, again, Oord's understanding of God's overriding freedom is that of God completely controlling an agent, which he claims the classical tradition affirms in its view of divine sovereignty. He writes,

> God alone could not have averted this tragedy. To prevent Amy's rape and murder by causing a tree to fall on her perpetrator or suspending the law of gravity momentarily, God would need to forgo loving interaction with some portion of creation. Because God loves *all* creation and God "cannot deny himself," God could not have prevented Amy's suffering.[240]

A few of his critics respond, observing that his model smacks of process theism that "plays by the rules of naturalism—which is reason enough . . . to find it questionable,"[241] and that "we should call it for what it is: deism."[242] William Lane Craig, in his scathing response to Oord's view, writes that his "deity values the laws of nature above the interests of people, [which] is proof positive that such a being is not, despite [his] asseverations, really loving, for he values things above people, which is perverse."[243] Ultimately, Oord's deity is responsible for "choosing laws that would issue in creatures so vulnerable to natural evil, rather than choosing other laws or refraining altogether from creation."[244]

237. Oord, "Essential Kenosis View," 85.
238. Oord, "Essential Kenosis View," 85.
239. Oord, "Essential Kenosis View," 89.
240. Oord, "Essential Kenosis View," 92.
241. Cary, "Classic Response," 132.
242. Craig, "Molinist Response," 145. Craig further criticizes Oord's theodicy, stating it "is useless to the Christian because the view it entails is not Christianity. . . . [It] is manifestly unbiblical."
243. Craig, "Molinist Response," 147.
244. Craig, "Molinist Response," 147.

Conclusion

While I give Oord credit for his boldness, which I know stems from his deep concern to magnify God's goodness and love, my critiques above reveal the inadequacies of his solution. In the end, he does not engage the problem head on; his solution does not account for biblical passages that show God working in and through evil.[245] Furthermore, none of his dimensions are well-grounded in the biblical text. Rather, he imports a process view of divine power, based on the assumption that God does not stand behind evil in *any* manner, and therefore he side-steps and/or overlooks the theme of evil that flows through the story of redemption in the formulation of his solution. His solution, summed up, is that *God can't* prevent or stop evil. He may try to persuade or lure or compel another creature to abide by his commands, but even then, Oord does not explain *how* God does that. What does God persuading a creature look like?

Oord says his views have brought encouragement to many who have suffered tragedy and loss. Telling someone struggling with the loss of a child that God did not know it would happen nor did he allow nor want the child's death to occur, may offer temporary relief. But Scripture tells us that "The LORD gives, and the LORD takes away" (Job 1:21). David understood that fact in that God struck dead his newborn son as a consequence for his sin (2 Sam 12:12–13). Now, merely reciting these passages to someone to defend God's actions is not the most pastoral route to take. Rather, the pastoral aim is to minister to those in grief, working through the implications of these passages, pointing the mourning parents to the merciful outcomes of both situations,[246] with the hopes of bringing to light the bigger picture of God's promise of redemption to those who hold firm to the Word of the Lord, trusting his judgments and precepts.

Following Oord's view of God, I think, has devastating implications down the road. If God was unable to prevent the events/actions that lead to the child's death, then God is unable to guarantee that the mourning parents will be able to see him in the life to come. These parents cannot take comfort in Revelation 21:4, where we see that God "will wipe away every tear from their eyes. Death will be no more; grief, crying, and pain will be no more, because the previous things have passed away." According

---

245. For example, see Orr, "Easter through Evil," 99–113.

246. Job's faithful endurance resulted in his restoration with the Lord, "blessing the last part of Job's life more than the first" (42:12), providing him a new family and an abundant fortune. And David knew that in God taking away his sin, though the LORD took his son because of his actions, he would eventually go to be with him (2 Sam 12:23).

to Oord's view of God's power, it seems that this reality can only be fulfilled when the physical properties of the created order and free-willed creatures agree with God's calling and desires.

While Oord says God has "immeasurable resources and authority,"[247] what good is his authority if human free will is the determinative factor? Evil will come to an end when . . . all *creatures* decide to stop choosing evil? Oord's participatory eschatology means that creaturely participation is essential to fulfilling God's desired end.[248] And while he says creatures may be hell-bound because of their choice to refuse to listen to God,[249] he believes that "God will eventually woo all creation into eternal bliss of love."[250] But, if that is the case, how then should the Thessalonians interpret Paul's letter, in his offering of comfort because of their persecution for the gospel, when he writes:

> It is clear evidence of God's righteous judgment that you will be counted worthy of God's kingdom, for which you also are suffering, since it is just for God to repay with affliction those who afflict you and to give relief to you who are afflicted, along with us. This will take place at the revelation of the Lord Jesus from heaven with his powerful angels, when he takes vengeance with flaming fire on those who don't know God and on those who don't obey the gospel of our Lord Jesus. They will pay the penalty of eternal destruction from the Lord's presence and from his glorious strength? (2 Thess 1:5–9)

Oord's view of God removes the comforting effect Paul intended to provide, in assuring them of God's love for them in that he *will* take vengeance on those who have afflicted his people.

Concluding Remarks

While my evaluation did not take into consideration every aspect of Oord's relational model of providence, my findings in what I did evaluate sufficiently substantiated my claims. Oord's primary aim in constructing his theological system was to express that God's nature is uncontrollingly loving, and he therefore, shaped every element of his model around that presupposition, circumventing biblical texts and thematic elements in Scripture because

247. Oord, *NOL*, 157.
248. Oord, "BYU Presentation."
249. Oord, *NOL*, 156.
250. Oord, "BYU Presentation." Oord says this is what he hopes will happen; there is no guarantee.

his theology of love and a process metaphysic of divine power could not adequately account for them. In the end, Oord's philosophical disparity led to a deformative *ad hoc* doctrine of providence, inconsistent with the broad biblical witness and the historic Christian tradition.

6: Conclusion

THE PURSUIT OF TRUTH is the noblest of endeavors. And the beginning of that journey begins with the fear of the Lord (Prov 1:7). General views of the Bible have been inching further and further away off that path. The theological *un*orthodox views of the attributes of God (some have termed "theological mutabilism")[1] accepted by notably *orthodox* theologians reflect that issue as well (see chapter 4). Recent publications of dissertations, books, and articles[2] clarifying and reestablishing the doctrine of divine simplicity, for example, in orthodox Christianity have functioned as a clarion call to classical theology as a whole.[3] Long-held teachings of the faith, such as the doctrine of the Trinity, doctrine of creation (necessitating the Creator-creature distinction), and divine simplicity, as examples, are not appendages to traditional, classical theology. Every piece is connected and *essentially* linked together. So, when one piece is removed, it affects the entire framework.

The intention of my study was not to evaluate or involve work in an intramural discussion of these issues within classical theology nor use classical theology as a filter to screen or test Oord's theology. Rather, my aim was to evaluate a system of doctrine that epitomized a framework of a proposed model of Christian theism that substitutes classical metaphysics with another, *while* attempting to retain foundational doctrines that the now *cast out* philosophy aided to develop.[4] As stated, the issue is consistency.

---

1. Jones, "Reviewing Frame's Review of Dolezal," points this out, which he got from James Dolezal's book, *All That Is in God*.

2. Goad, "Simplicity"; Dolezal, *God without Parts*; Ortlund, "Divine Simplicity"; Duby, "Divine Simplicity"; Baines et al., *Confessing the Impossible God*; Dolezal, *All That Is in God*; Sanlon, *Simply God*; Barrett, *Divine Simplicity*; Muller, "Calvin on Divine Attributes," 199–218; Littlejohn, *God of Our Fathers*; Barrett, *None Greater*; Barret, *Simply Trinity*.

3. A recent article from Carl Trueman identifies this need. Trueman, "The Reformation."

4. This is similar to Craig Carter's observation when he writes, "When certain writers make a big show of rejecting metaphysics, what they are really doing is rejecting certain widely held metaphysical doctrines, usually without specifying what doctrines they themselves propose to replace them." Carter, *Interpreting Scripture*, 64. Although, Oord is clear on his choice of metaphysic.

Theological frameworks erected on philosophical foundations are akin to building a house and then placing the concrete foundation on top, assuming it will hold up. Contemporary theology is working to build entire tracts of houses following that kind of blueprint.

The primary difference between our (Oord and myself) theologies is that we have different commitments that we are unwilling to let go. For example, a classical view cannot let go of God's immanent and transcendent sovereignty, observed page-after-page, in Scripture (even statements such as God closing a woman's womb in Genesis 20:18). Oord's reading of the text sees a relational view of God, where God's essential immanent love of creation and man's ability to affect God, working *together with him* shines forth. In a classical view, God's sovereign rule as Lord over his creation is a pillar that it cannot take down. Whereas Oord is willing to knock down such pillars for the sake of expressing a loving view of God that, he believes, has been held back or "controlled" by a classical or traditional view of God. He wants to, in a sense, release God so that he is *uncontrolled* in his love. And he is to be commended for it.

I disagree, however, not in his desire to express God's love in that manner; rather, it is in how he has gone about doing it, in that he is willing to give up certain foundational doctrines of the Christian tradition. He is willing to give up these pillars, on which a classical view of God rests, because of his philosophical commitment to process metaphysics. Granted, I, as a classical theist, have a philosophical commitment to classical metaphysics (I also acknowledge that there are passages in Scripture that do not fit well within a classical framework, e.g., Gen 6:6; Jer 32:35; 1 Tim 2:4). While we both attempt to ground our philosophy in the biblical text, my study demonstrated that Oord's process view cannot support the doctrines of the Christian faith—that identify us as Christians—as the classical or traditional view has consistently done in almost the entirety of the Christian tradition.

My evaluation determined that Oord's doctrinal propositions were inconsistent because: (1) His process metaphysic, as applied to the doctrines of creation, the Trinity, and divine simplicity was proven internally inconsistent in maintaining the same *orthodox* form of these doctrines as established in classical theology. (2) His philosophically derived axiom of love, as the rector of his theological model, failed to account for the complexities of love expressed in Scripture. (3) His misguided assumptions of a classical view of divine action (i.e., coercion) undermined his entire position in that he created a straw man opponent, thus also placing strictures on God that were exegetically unjustifiable. (4) His doctrine of Essential Kenosis, his relational model of providence and doctrine of God, was incapable of withstanding biblical scrutiny, exposing its lack of depth, consistency, and harmony with the many interlocking facets of Scripture, as well as the historic doctrines of the faith, many of which he sought to preserve.

Oord's aim was to offer a theologically Christian alternative to that of "conventional" or "classical theology" that greatly minimizes or removes any ascriptions to divine mystery that situates God in some manner behind evil. For Oord, *because* God is love and that genuine evil exists, God must *not* be able to unilaterally put a stop to it because a God who is love would not allow such evil to occur *if* he had the power to prevent it. While Oord desires for the world to see the love of God, which is admirable, his theology absolutized what *he* believes the love of God is like. In the end, process philosophy was the "handler" instead of the "handmaiden" to his theology.

Bibliography

Agan, C. D. "Jimmy," II. "How Does God's Love Shape the Christian Walk." In *The Love of God*, edited by Christopher W. Morgan, 185–204. Wheaton, IL: Crossway, 2016.

Akin, Daniel L. *1, 2, 3 John: An Exegetical and Theological Exposition of Holy Scripture*. New American Commentary 38. Nashville: Broadman & Holman, 2001.

Alden, Robert. *Job: An Exegetical and Theological Exposition of Holy Scripture*. Nashville: Holman Reference, 1994.

Anderson, James N. "Calvinism and the First Sin." In *Calvinism & the Problem of Evil*, edited by David E. Alexander and Daniel M. Johnson, 104–20. Eugene, OR: Pickwick, 2016.

Aquinas, St. Thomas. *The Power of God*. Translated by Richard J. Regan. New York: Oxford University Press, 2012.

———. *Summa Contra Gentiles: Book Three: Providence: Part I*. Translated by Vernon J. Bourke. Notre Dame: University of Notre Dame Press, 1975.

———. *Summa Theologica of St. Thomas Aquinas*. Translated by Fathers of the English Dominican Province. 5 vols. New York: Christian Classics, 1981.

Arminius, Jacobus. *The Works of James Arminius*. 3 vols. Grand Rapids: Baker, 1991.

Augustine, St. *City of God*. London: Penguin Classics, 1984.

———. *Confessions*. Translated by R. S. Pine-Coffin. London: Penguin Classics, 1961.

———. *Homilies on the Gospel of John, Homilies on the First Epistle of John, Soliloquies*. In vol. 7 of *A Select Library of the Nicene and Post-Nicene Fathers of the Christian Church, First Series*, edited by Philip Schaff. New York: Christian Literature, 1888.

———. *The Trinity*. Translated by John E. Rotelle. Brooklyn: New City, 1991.

Auld, A. Graeme. *I & II Samuel: A Commentary*. Louisville: Presbyterian, 2011.

Ayres, Lewis. *Nicaea and Its Legacy: An Approach to Fourth-Century Trinitarian Theology*. New York: Oxford University Press, 2006.

Ayres, Lewis, and Michael R. Barnes. "God." In *Augustine through the Ages: An Encyclopedia*, edited by Allan Fitzgerald, 384–90. Grand Rapids: Eerdmans, 1999.

Badcock, Gary D. "The Concept of Love Divine and Human." In *Nothing Greater, Nothing Better: Theological Essays on the Love of God*, edited by Kevin J. Vanhoozer, 30–46. Grand Rapids: Eerdmans, 2001.

Baines, Ronald S., et al., eds. *Confessing the Impassible God: The Biblical, Classical, & Confessional Doctrine of Divine Impassibility*. Palmdale, CA: RBAP, 2015.

Baker, J. P. "Love." In *New Dictionary of Theology*, edited by Sinclair B. Ferguson and J. I. Packer, 398–400. Downers Grove, IL: InterVarsity, 2000.

Barnett, Paul. *The Second Epistle to the Corinthians*. New International Greek Testament Commentary. Grand Rapids: Eerdmans, 1997.

Barrett, Charles K. *The Second Epistle to the Corinthians*. Black's New Testament Commentary. Peabody, MA: Hendrickson, 1993.
Barrett, Jordan P. *Divine Simplicity: A Biblical and Trinitarian Account*. Philadelphia: Fortress, 2017.
Barrett, Matthew. *None Greater: The Undomesticated Attributes of God*. Grand Rapids: Baker, 2019.
———. *Simply Trinity: The Unmanipulated Father, Son, and Spirit*. Grand Rapids: Baker, 2021.
Barth, Karl. *Church Dogmatics*. Translated by G. T. Thomson et al. Edinburgh: T. & T. Clark, 1936–77.
Basinger, David. *The Case for Freewill Theism: A Philosophical Assessment*. Downers Grove, IL: InterVarsity, 1996.
———. "Divine Persuasion: Could the Process God Do More?" *The Journal of Religion* 64.3 (1984) 332–47.
Basinger, David, and Randall Basinger, eds. *Predestination & Free Will: Four Views of Divine Sovereignty & Human Freedom*. Downers Grove, IL: InterVarsity, 1986.
Bates, Matthew W. *The Birth of the Trinity: Jesus, God, and Spirit in New Testament and Early Christian Interpretations of the Old Testament*. Oxford: Oxford University Press, 2016.
Bauckham, Richard. "'Only the Suffering God Can Help': Divine Passibility in Modern Theology." *Themelios* 9.3 (1984) 6–12.
Bauer, Walter, et al. *A Greek-English Lexicon of the New Testament and Other Early Christian Literature*. Edited by Frederick William Danker. 3rd ed. Chicago: University of Chicago Press, 2001.
Bavinck, Herman. *Reformed Dogmatics*. 4 vols. Grand Rapids: Baker, 2008.
Beale, G. K. "An Exegetical and Theological Consideration of the Hardening of Pharaoh's Heart in Exodus 4–14 and Romans 9." *Trinity Journal* 5.2 (1984) 129–54.
Beilby, James K., and Paul R. Eddy, eds. *Divine Foreknowledge: Four Views*. Downers Grove, IL: InterVarsity, 2001.
Bergen, Robert D. *1, 2 Samuel: An Exegetical and Theological Exposition of Holy Scripture*. Nashville: Holman Reference, 1996.
Bignon, Guillaume. *Excusing Sinners and Blaming God: A Calvinist Assessment of Determinism, Moral Responsibility, and Divine Involvement in Evil*. Eugene, OR: Wipf & Stock, 2017.
Bock, Darrell L. *Acts*. Grand Rapids: Baker, 2007.
Boyd, Gregory A. *God of the Possible: A Biblical Introduction to the Open View of God*. Grand Rapids: Baker, 2000.
Bracken, Joseph, et al. "Trinity and World Process." *Proceedings of the Annual Convention of the Catholic Theological Society of America* 33 (1978) 203–28.
Bray, Gerald. "The Love of God (Romans 8:18–39)." *Evangel* 20.1 (2002) 3–8.
Brink, Gijsbert van den. *Almighty God: A Study of the Doctrine of Divine Omnipotence*. Kampen: Pharos, 1993.
Brown, Delvin. "The Love of an Open God." In *Semper Reformandum: Studies in Honor of Clark H. Pinnock*, edited by Stanley F. Porter and Anthony R. Cross, 59–72. Cumbria: Paternoster, 2004.
Brown, Robert F. "Schelling and Dorner on Divine Immutability." *Journal of the American Academy of Religion* 53.2 (1985) 237–49.

Brueggemann, Walter. *Deuteronomy*. Abingdon Old Testament Commentaries. Nashville: Abingdon, 2001.

———. *First and Second Samuel*. Interpretation. Louisville: Westminster John Knox, 1990.

Brümmer, Vincent. *The Model of Love: A Study in Philosophical Theology*. New York: Cambridge University Press, 1993.

———. *What Are We Doing When We Pray?: On Prayer and the Nature of Faith*. Burlington, VT: Ashgate, 2008.

Brunner, Emil. *The Christian Doctrine of God*. Philadelphia: Westminster, 1990.

Burrell, David B. "Distinguishing God from the World." In *Language, Meaning, and God: Essays in Honor of Herbert McCabe, with a New Introduction*, edited by Brian Davies, 75-91. Eugene, OR: Wipf & Stock, 2010.

———. *Knowing the Unknowable God: Ibn-Sina, Maimonides, Aquinas*. Notre Dame: University of Notre Dame Press, 1992.

Calvin, John. *Commentaries on the Catholic Epistles: 1 Peter, 1 John, James, 2 Peter, Jude*. Edited and translated by John Owen. Bellingham: Logos Research Systems, 2010.

———. *Commentary on a Harmony of the Evangelists Matthew, Mark, and Luke*. Edited and translated by John Owen. Bellingham, WA: Logos Research Systems, 2010.

———. *Concerning the Eternal Predestination of God*. Louisville: Westminster John Knox, 1997.

———. *Institutes of the Christian Religion*. Edited by John T. McNeill. Translated by Ford Lewis Battles. 2 vols. Louisville: Westminster John Knox, 1960.

———. *The Secret Providence of God*. Edited by Paul Helm. Wheaton, IL: Crossway, 2010.

Campbell, Antony F. *2 Samuel*. Grand Rapids: Eerdmans, 2005.

Carson, D. A. *The Difficult Doctrine of the Love of God*. Wheaton, IL: Crossway, 2000.

———. *Divine Sovereignty and Human Responsibility: Biblical Perspective in Tension*. Eugene, OR: Wipf & Stock, 2002.

———, ed. *The Enduring Authority of the Christian Scriptures*. Grand Rapids: Eerdmans, 2016.

———. *The Gospel according to John*. Grand Rapids: Eerdmans, 1990.

———. "Love." In *New Dictionary of Biblical Theology: Exploring the Unity & Diversity of Scripture*, edited by Brian S. Rosner et al., 646-50. Downers Grove, IL: InterVarsity, 2000.

Carter, Craig A. *Interpreting Scripture with the Great Tradition: Recovering the Genius of Premodern Exegesis*. Grand Rapids: Baker, 2018.

Cary, William. "The Classic Response." In *God and the Problem of Evil: Five Views*, edited by Chad Meister and James K. Dew Jr., 131-42. Downers Grove, IL: InterVarsity, 2017.

Castelo, Daniel. "Moltmann's Dismissal of Divine Impassibility: Warranted?" *Scottish Journal of Theology* 61.4 (2008) 396-407.

Charnock, Stephen. *The Complete Works of Stephen Charnock*. Vols. 1-5. Logos ed. Edinburgh: Nisbet, 1864.

Childs, Brevard S. *The Book of Exodus: A Critical, Theological Commentary*. Philadelphia: Westminster, 1974.

Chisholm, Robert B., Jr. "Divine Hardening in the Old Testament." *Bibliotheca Sacra* 153.612 (1996) 410-34.

Coakley, Sara. "'Persons' in the 'Social' Doctrine of the Trinity: A Critique of Current Analytic Discussion." In *The Trinity: An Interdisciplinary Symposium on the Trinity*, edited by Stephen T. Davis et al., 23–44. Oxford: Oxford University Press, 2002.

Cobb, John B., Jr. *A Christian Natural Theology: Based on the Thought of Alfred North Whitehead*. 2nd ed. Louisville: Westminster John Knox, 2007.

Cobb, John B., Jr., and Clark H. Pinnock. *Searching for an Adequate God: A Dialogue between Process and Free Will Theists*. Grand Rapids: Eerdmans, 2000.

Coleman, Monica A. "The World at Its Best: A Process Construction of a Wesleyan Understanding of Entire Sanctification." *Wesleyan Theological Journal* 37.2 (2002) 130–52.

Cook, Stephen L. *Reading Deuteronomy: A Literary and Theological Commentary*. Macon, GA: Smyth & Helwys, 2014.

Cooper, John W. *Panentheism: The Other God of the Philosophers: From Plato to the Present*. Downers Grove, IL: InterVarsity, 2007.

Craig, William Lane. "The Molinist Response." In *God and the Problem of Evil: Five Views*, edited by Chad Meister and James K. Dew Jr., 143–50. Downers Grove, IL: InterVarsity, 2017.

Culp, John. "Is Mutual Transformation Possible?: The Dialogue between Process and Evangelical Theologies." *Process Studies* 30.1 (2001) 132–46.

Daeley, Justin J. "Creatio Ex Nihilo: A Solution to the Problem of the Necessity of Creation and Divine Aseity." *Philosophia Christi* 19.2 (2017) 291–313.

Danaher, James P. "Human and Divine Love." *Modern Believing* 48.2 (2007) 33–43.

Davies, Brian. "A Modern Defence of Divine Simplicity." In *Philosophy of Religion: A Guide and Anthology*, edited by Brian Davies, 549–64. Oxford: Oxford University Press, 2000.

Davis, Stephen T. "Kenotic Christology and the Nature of God." In *Exploring Kenotic Christology: The Self-Emptying of God*, edited by C. Stephen Evans, 190–217. Oxford: Oxford University Press, 2006.

Davis, William C. "Why Open Theism Is Flourishing Now?" In *Beyond the Bounds: Open Theism and the Undermining of Biblical Christianity*, edited by John Piper et al., 111–45. Wheaton, IL: Crossway, 2003.

DeYoung, Kevin. "Divine Impassibility and the Passion of Christ in the Book of Hebrews." *Westminster Theological Journal* 68.1 (2006) 41–50.

Dillard, Raymond B. *2 Chronicles*. Word Biblical Commentary 15. Waco, TX: Word, 1988.

Dodds, Michael J. *The Unchanging God of Love: Thomas Aquinas and Contemporary Theology on Divine Immutability*. 2nd ed. Washington, DC: Catholic University of America Press, 2008.

Dolezal, James E. *All That Is in God: Evangelical Theology and the Challenge of Classical Christian Theism*. Grand Rapids: Reformation Heritage, 2017.

———. *God without Parts: Divine Simplicity and the Metaphysics of God's Absoluteness*. Eugene, OR: Wipf & Stock, 2011.

———. "Still Impassible: Confessing God without Passions." *Journal of the Institute of Reformed Baptist Studies* 1 (2013) 125–51.

———. "Strong Impassibility." In *Divine Impassibility: Four Views of God's Emotions and Suffering*, edited by Robert J. Matz and A. Chadwick Thornhill, 13–37. Downers Grove, IL: InterVarsity, 2019.

———. "A Strong Impassibility Response." In *Divine Impassibility: Four Views of God's Emotions and Suffering*, edited by Robert J. Matz and A. Chadwick Thornhill, 152–54. Downers Grove, IL: InterVarsity, 2019.

———. "Trinity, Simplicity and the Status of God's Personal Relations." *International Journal of Systematic Theology* 16.1 (2014) 79–98.

Dongell, Joseph. *John: A Bible Commentary in the Wesleyan Tradition*. Logos ed. Indianapolis: Wesleyan, 1997.

Duby, Steven J. "Divine Action and the Meaning of Eternity." *Journal of Reformed Theology* 11.4 (2018) 353–76.

———. "Divine Immutability, Divine Action, and the God–World Relation." *International Journal of Systematic Theology* 19.2 (2017) 144–62.

———. "Divine Simplicity: A Dogmatic Account." PhD diss., University of St. Andrews, 2014.

Edwards, James R. *The Gospel according to Mark*. Grand Rapids: Eerdmans, 2001.

Emery, Gilles. "The Immutability of the God of Love and the Problem of Language Concerning the 'Suffering of God.'" In *Divine Impassibility and the Mystery of Human Suffering*, edited by James F. Keating and Thomas Joseph White, 27–76. Grand Rapids: Eerdmans, 2009.

———. *The Trinitarian Theology of St. Thomas Aquinas*. Oxford: Oxford University Press, 2007.

———. *The Trinity: An Introduction to Catholic Doctrine on the Triune God*. Thomistic Ressourcement Series. Washington, DC: Catholic University of America Press, 2012.

Erickson, Millard J. "God and Change." *The Southern Baptist Journal of Theology* 1.2 (1997) 38–51.

Evans, C. Stephen, ed. *Exploring Kenotic Christology: The Self-Emptying of God*. Oxford: Oxford University Press, 2006.

Feenstra, Ronald J. "A Kenotic Christological Method for Understanding the Divine Attributes." In *Exploring Kenotic Christology: The Self-Emptying of God*, edited by C. Stephen Evans, 139–64. Oxford: Oxford University Press, 2006.

Feinberg, John S. *No One Like Him*. Wheaton, IL: Crossway, 2006.

Ferguson, Sinclair B., and J. I. Packer, eds. *New Dictionary of Theology*. Electronic ed. Downers Grove, IL: InterVarsity, 2000.

Fiddes, Paul S. *The Creative Suffering of God*. Oxford: Clarendon, 1992.

Frame, John M. *The Doctrine of God*. Phillipsburg, NJ: P&R, 2002.

———. *No Other God: A Response to Open Theism*. Phillipsburg, NJ: P&R, 2001.

———. *Systematic Theology: An Introduction to Christian Belief*. Phillipsburg, NJ: P&R, 2013.

Fretheim, Terence E. *Exodus*. Interpretation. Louisville: Westminster John Knox, 2010.

———. *The Suffering of God: An Old Testament Perspective*. Philadelphia: Fortress, 1984.

Gaiser, Frederick J. "'You Meant Evil against Me; but God Meant It for Good': Thinking Genesis 50:20." *Word & World Supplement Series* 4 (2000) 33–47.

Ganssle, Gregory E. "God and Time." In *Internet Encyclopedia of Philosophy*. https://www.iep.utm.edu/god-time/.

Garland, David E. *2 Corinthians*. New American Commentary. Nashville: Broadman & Holman, 1999.

Gavrilyuk, Paul L. *The Suffering of the Impassible God: The Dialectics of Patristic Thought.* Oxford: Oxford University Press, 2006.

Geisler, Norman L., and William D. Watkins. "Process Theology: A Survey and an Appraisal." *Themelios* 12.1 (1986) 15–22.

Goad, Keith. "Simplicity and Trinity in Harmony." *Eusebeia* 8 (2007) 97–118.

Gockel, Matthias, and John Daniel Holloway III. "God's Essential Will to Love: A Response to Thomas J. Oord's Criticism of Karl Barth's Theology of Divine Reason." *Wesleyan Theological Journal* 52.1 (2017) 184–99.

Goetz, Ronald G. "The Suffering God: The Rise of a New Orthodoxy." *The Christian Century* 103.13 (1986) 385–89.

Goldingay, John. *Isaiah for Everyone.* Old Testament for Everyone. Louisville: Westminster John Knox, 2015.

Gowan, Donald E. *Theology in Exodus: Biblical Theology in the Form of a Commentary.* Louisville: Westminster John Knox, 1994.

Grant, Colin. "For the Love of God: Agape." *Journal of Religious Ethics* 24.1 (1996) 3–21.

Green, Stephen G. *Deuteronomy: A Commentary in the Wesleyan Tradition.* Kansas City, MO: Nazarene, 2015.

Gregory of Nazianzus. *On God and Christ: The Five Theological Orations and Two Letters to Cledonius.* Translated by Frederick Williams and Lionel R. Wickham. Crestwood, NY: St. Vladimir's Seminary Press, 2002.

Gregory of Nyssa. *Dogmatic Treatises, Etc.* In vol. 5 of *A Select Library of the Nicene and Post-Nicene Fathers of the Christian Church, Second Series,* edited by Philip Schaff and Henry Wace. New York: Christian Literature, 1893.

Grenz, Stanley J., and Roger E. Olson. *20th-Century Theology: God and the World in a Transitional Age.* Downers Grove, IL: InterVarsity, 1993.

Griffin, David Ray. *Evil Revisited: Responses and Reconsiderations.* Albany, NY: State University of New York Press, 1991.

———. *God, Power, and Evil: A Process Theodicy.* Louisville: Westminster John Knox Press, 2004.

———. *A Process Christology.* Philadelphia: Westminster, 1990.

———. "Process Philosophy of Religion." *International Journal for Philosophy of Religion* 50.1/3 (2001) 131–51.

———. "A Process Theology and the Christian Good News: A Response to Classical Free Will Theism." In *Searching for an Adequate God: A Dialogue between Process and Free Will Theists,* edited by John B. Cobb Jr. and Clark H. Pinnock, 1–38. Grand Rapids: Eerdmans, 2000.

———. *Reenchantment without Supernaturalism: A Process Philosophy of Religion.* Ithaca, NY: Cornell University Press, 2001.

Grogan, Geoffrey. "A Biblical Theology of the Love of God." In *Nothing Greater, Nothing Better: Theological Essays on the Love of God,* edited by Kevin J. Vanhoozer, 47–66. Grand Rapids: Eerdmans, 2001.

Grudem, Wayne. *Systematic Theology: An Introduction to Biblical Doctrine.* 1st ed. Grand Rapids: Zondervan, 1994.

———. *Systematic Theology: An Introduction to Biblical Doctrine.* 2nd ed. Grand Rapids: Zondervan, 2020.

Haines, David. "Natural Theology and Protestant Orthodoxy." In *God of Our Fathers: Classical Theism for the Contemporary Church,* edited by Bradford Littlejohn, 53–85. Moscow: Davenant Institute, 2018.

Hanson, R. P. C. *The Search for the Christian Doctrine of God: The Arian Controversy, 318–381*. Grand Rapids: Baker, 2006.

Harnack, Adolf Von. *What Is Christianity?* Translated by Thomas Bailey Saunders. New York: Harper, 1957.

Hart, David Bentley. "No Shadow of Turning: On Divine Impassibility." *Pro Ecclesia* 11.2 (2002) 184–206.

Hartshorne, Charles. "The Dipolar Conception of Deity." *The Review of Metaphysics* 21.2 (1967) 273–89.

———. *The Divine Relativity: A Social Conception of God*. New Haven: Yale University Press, 1948.

———. *Man's Vision of God and the Logic of Theism*. Hamden, CT: Archon, 1964.

———. *Omnipotence and Other Theological Mistakes*. Albany, NY: State University of New York Press, 1984.

———. *Reality as Social Process: Studies in Metaphysics and Religion*. Glencoe, IL: Free, 1953.

Hasker, William. "A Philosophical Perspective." In *The Openness of God: A Biblical Challenge to the Traditional Understanding of God*, by Clark H. Pinnock et al., 126–54. Downers Grove, IL: InterVarsity, 1994.

———. "A Reply to David Ray Griffin." In *Searching for an Adequate God: A Dialogue between Process and Free Will Theists*, edited by John B. Cobb Jr. and Clark H. Pinnock, 39–52. Grand Rapids: Eerdmans, 2000.

Heath, E. A. "Grace." In *Dictionary of the Old Testament: Pentateuch*, edited by T. Desmond Alexander and David W. Baker, 371–75. Downers Grove, IL: InterVarsity, 2003.

Heiser, Michael S., and Vincent M. Setterholm. *Glossary of Morpho-Syntactic Database Terminology*. Bellingham, WA: Lexham, 2013.

Helm, Paul. "Eternal Creation." *Tyndale Bulletin* 45.2 (1994) 321–38.

———. "Impassionedness and 'So-Called Classical Theism.'" In *Within the Love of God: Essays on the Doctrine of God in Honour of Paul S. Fiddes*, 144–54. Oxford: Oxford University Press, 2014.

———. "The Impossibility of Divine Passibility." In *Power and Weakness of God: Impassibility and Orthodoxy*, 119–40. Edinburgh: Rutherford, 1990.

———. *The Providence of God*. Downers Grove, IL: InterVarsity, 1994.

Hendriksen, William. *Mark*. Grand Rapids: Baker, 1983.

Henry, Carl F. H. *God, Revelation, and Authority*. 6 vols. Logos ed. Wheaton, IL: Crossway, 1999.

Heschel, Abraham. *The Prophets*. Peabody, MA: Prince, 2000.

Hess, Elijah. Review of *The Uncontrolling Love of God: An Open and Relational Account of Providence*, by Thomas Jay Oord. *Journal of Analytic Theology* 4.1 (2016) 473–79.

Highfield, Ron. Review of *The Uncontrolling Love of God: An Open and Relational Account of Providence*, by Thomas Jay Oord. Annual Meeting of the Christian Theology Research Fellowship, San Antonio, TX, 2016.

Hilary of Poitiers, St. *St. Hilary of Poitiers*. In vol. 9 of *A Select Library of the Nicene and Post-Nicene Fathers of the Christian Church, Second Series*, edited by Philip Schaff and Henry Wace. New York: Christian Literature, 1899.

Holmes, Stephen R. *The Quest for the Trinity: The Doctrine of God in Scripture, History, and Modernity*. Downers Grover, IL: InterVarsity, 2012.

———. "'Something Much Too Plain to Say': Towards a Defence of the Doctrine of Divine Simplicity." *Neue Zeitschrift Für Systematische Theologie Und Religionsphilosophie* 43.1 (2008) 137–54.

House, Francis. "The Barrier of Impassibility." *Theology* 83.696 (1980) 409–15.

House, Paul R. *1 & 2 Kings*. New American Commentary 8. Nashville: Holman, 1995.

Howell, Nancy R. "Openness and Process Theism: Respecting the Integrity of Two Views." In *Searching for an Adequate God: A Dialogue between Process and Free Will Theists*, edited by John B. Cobb Jr. and Clark H. Pinnock, 53–79. Grand Rapids: Eerdmans, 2000.

Huffman, Douglas S., et al. *God under Fire: Modern Scholarship Reinvents God*. Grand Rapids: Zondervan, 2009.

Jenson, Robert W. *Systematic Theology: Volume 1: The Triune God*. New York: Oxford University Press, 1997.

John of Damascus. *John of Damascus*. In vol. 9 of *A Select Library of the Nicene and Post-Nicene Fathers of the Christian Church, Second Series*, edited by Philip Schaff and Henry Waco. New York: Christian Literature, 1899.

Jones, Marc. "Reviewing Frame's Review of Dolezal." https://calvinistinternational.com/2017/11/27/reviewing-frames-review-of-dolezal/.

Kallhovd, Stian André Sunde. "Developing a Rigorous Theology of Love: A Case Study of Thomas Jay Oord's Love Theory." Master's Thesis, University of Agder, 2013.

Keil, Carl Friedrich, and Franz Delitzsch. *Commentary on the Old Testament*. 10 vols. Peabody, MA: Hendrickson, 1996.

Keller, Catherine. *The Face of the Deep: A Theology of Becoming*. London: Routledge, 2003.

Kelly, Anthony J. "God: How Near a Relation?" *The Thomist: A Speculative Quarterly Review* 34.2 (1970) 191–229.

———. "Trinity and Process: Relevance of the Basic Christian Confession of God." *Theological Studies* 31.3 (1970) 393–414.

Kenny, Anthony. *The God of the Philosophers*. Oxford: Oxford University Press, 1987.

Kondoleon, Theodore J. "The Immutability of God: Some Recent Challenges." *The New Scholasticism* 58.3 (1984) 293–315.

Koop, Doug. "Closing the Door on Open Theists? ETS to Examine Whether Clark Pinnock and John Sanders Can Remain Members. (North American Report)." *Christianity Today*, January 1, 2003.

Köstenberger, Andreas J. *John*. Grand Rapids: Baker, 2004.

———. *A Theology of John's Gospel and Letters: The Word, the Christ, the Son of God*. Grand Rapids: Zondervan, 2009.

Kruse, Colin G. *The Letters of John*. Grand Rapids: Eerdmans, 2000.

Lane, Tony. "The Wrath of God as an Aspect of the Love of God." In *Nothing Greater, Nothing Better: Theological Essays on the Love of God*, edited by Kevin J. Vanhoozer, 138–67. Grand Rapids: Eerdmans, 2001.

Lane, William L. *The Gospel according to Mark: The English Text with Introduction, Exposition, and Notes*. Grand Rapids: Eerdmans, 1974.

Letham, Robert. *The Holy Trinity: In Scripture, History, Theology, and Worship*. Phillipsburg, NJ: P&R, 2004.

Levering, Matthew. *Scripture and Metaphysics: Aquinas and the Renewal of Trinitarian Theology*. Malden, MA: Wiley & Sons, 2008.

Lister, Rob. *God Is Impassible and Impassioned: Toward a Theology of Divine Emotion.* Wheaton, IL: Crossway, 2012.

Lodahl, Michael E. "Creation out of Nothing? Or Is Next to Nothing Enough?" In *Thy Nature and Thy Name Is Love: Wesleyan and Process Theologies in Dialogue*, edited by Bryan P. Stone and Thomas Jay Oord, 217–38. Nashville: Kingswood, 2001.

Lofthouse, William Frederick. "Ḥen and Ḥesed in the Old Testament." *Zeitschrift Für Die Alttestamentliche Wissenschaft* 51 (1933) 29–35.

MacArthur, John F., Jr. *Worship: The Ultimate Priority.* Chicago: Moody, 2012.

Mandolfo, Carleen. "'You Meant Evil against Me': Dialogic Truth and the Character of Jacob in Joseph's Story." *Journal for the Study of the Old Testament* 4 (2004) 449–65.

Mastricht, Petrus Van. *Theoretical-Practical Theology, Vol. 2: Faith in the Triune God.* Edited by Joel R. Beeke. Translated by Todd M. Rester. Grand Rapids: Reformation Heritage, 2019.

Mathews, Kenneth. *Genesis 11:27—50:26: An Exegetical and Theological Exposition of Holy Scripture.* Nashville: Broadman & Holman, 2005.

Matz, Robert J., and A. Chadwick Thornhill. *Divine Impassibility: Four Views of God's Emotions and Suffering.* Downers Grove, IL: InterVarsity, 2019.

McLaughlin, Ryan Patrick. "Unreasonable Hope: A Critical Evaluation of Thomas Oord's Eschatology." *Modern Theology* 33.2 (2017) 259–74.

Meister, Chad, and James K. Dew Jr., eds. *God and the Problem of Evil: Five Views.* Downers Grove, IL: InterVarsity, 2017.

Melick, Richard R. *Philippians, Colossians, Philemon.* Nashville: Broadman, 1991.

Merrill, Eugene H. *Deuteronomy: An Exegetical and Theological Exposition of Holy Scripture.* New American Commentary 4. Nashville: Broadman & Holman, 1994.

Moltmann, Jürgen. "The Passibility or Impassibility of God: Answers to J. K. Mozley's 'Six Necessary Questions.'" In *Within the Love of God: Essays on the Doctrine of God in Honour of Paul S. Fiddes*, 108–19. Oxford: Oxford University Press, 2014.

———. *The Trinity and the Kingdom: The Doctrine of God.* Minneapolis: Fortress, 1981.

Moo, Douglas J. *The Epistle to the Romans.* Grand Rapids: Eerdmans, 1996.

Morris, Leon. *The Biblical Doctrine of Judgment.* Grand Rapids: Eerdmans, 1960.

———. *The Gospel according to Matthew.* Grand Rapids: Eerdmans, 1992.

———. *Testaments of Love: A Study of Love in the Bible.* Grand Rapids: Eerdmans, 1981.

Mounce, William. *Pastoral Epistles.* Word Biblical Commentary 46. Nashville: Nelson, 2000.

Muller, Earl C. "Real Relations and the Divine: Issues in Thomas's Understanding of God's Relation to the World." *Theological Studies* 56.4 (1995) 673–95.

Muller, Richard A. "Calvin on Divine Attributes: A Question of Terminology and Method." *Westminster Theological Journal* 80.2 (2018) 199–218.

———. *Dictionary of Latin and Greek Theological Terms.* Grand Rapids: Baker, 1985.

———. "Incarnation, Immutability, and the Case for Classical Theism." *Westminster Theological Journal* 45.1 (1983) 22–40.

———. *Post-Reformation Reformed Dogmatics: The Rise and Development of Reformed Orthodoxy, ca. 1520 to ca. 1725.* 4 vols. 2nd ed. Grand Rapids: Baker, 2003.

Mullins, R. T. *The End of the Timeless God.* Oxford: Oxford University Press, 2016.

———. "Simply Impossible: A Case against Divine Simplicity." *Journal of Reformed Theology* 7.2 (2013) 181–203.

Nash, Ronald H. *The Concept of God.* Grand Rapids: Zondervan, 1983.

Neff, David. "Open to Healing: Anxieties and Attack Turn to Grace and Truth at ETS Meeting." *Christianity Today*, 2004.
Newlands, George. *Theology of the Love of God*. Atlanta: John Knox, 1982.
Nygren, Anders. *Agape and Eros*. Philadelphia: Westminster, 1953.
O'Brien, Peter T. *The Epistle to the Philippians: A Commentary on the Greek Text*. Grand Rapids: Eerdmans, 1991.
O'Keefe, John J. "Impassible Suffering? Divine Passion and Fifth-Century Christology." *Theological Studies* 58.1 (1997) 39–60.
Olson, Roger E. "Postconservative Evangelicals Greet the Postmodern Age." *The Christian Century* 112.15 (1995) 480–83.
———. *The Story of Christian Theology: Twenty Centuries of Tradition & Reform*. Downers Grove, IL: InterVarsity, 1999.
Oord, Thomas Jay. "Bio/Contact." http://thomasjayoord.com/index.php/biography.
———. "BYU Presentation.Pptx." https://drive.google.com/file/d/1RTi8bFyi2AQYqVpVpPCrlPkJh2cMQnKt/view?usp=drive_web&usp=embed_facebook.
———. "Can God Be Essentially Loving without Being Essentially Social?: An Affirmation of and Alternative for Keith Ward." *Philosophia Christi* 18.2 (2016) 353–61.
———. *Defining Love: A Philosophical, Scientific, and Theological Engagement*. Grand Rapids: Brazos, 2010.
———. "Divine Power and Love: An Evangelical Process Proposal." *Koinonia* 10.1 (1998) 1–18.
———. "The Divine Spirit as Causal and Personal." *Zygon: Journal of Religion & Science* 48.2 (2013) 466–77.
———. "An Essential Kenosis View." In *God and the Problem of Evil: Five Views*, edited by Chad Meister and James K. Dew Jr., 77–97. Downers Grove, IL: InterVarsity, 2017.
———. "Evangelical Theologies." In *Handbook of Process Theology*, edited by Donna Bowman and Jay B. McDaniel, 251–61. St. Louis: Chalice, 2006.
———. "God Always Creates out of Creation in Love: Creatio Ex Creatione a Natura Amoris." In *Theologies of Creation: Creatio Ex Nihilo and Its New Rivals*, edited by Thomas Jay Oord, 109–22. New York: Routledge, 2015.
———. *God Can't: How to Believe in God and Love after Tragedy, Abuse, and Other Evils*. Nampa, ID: SacraSage, 2019.
———. "Love as a Methodological and Metaphysical Source for Science and Theology." *Wesleyan Theological Journal* 45.1 (2010) 81–107.
———. "The Love Racket: Defining Love and Agape for the Love-and-Science Research Program." *Zygon* 40.4 (2005) 919–38.
———. "Matching Theology and Piety: An Evangelical Process Theology of Love." PhD diss., Claremont Graduate University, 1999.
———. "Miracles, Theodicy, and Essential Kenosis: A Response to John Sanders." *Wesleyan Theological Journal* 53.2 (2018) 194–215.
———. "Morals, Love, and Relations in Evolutionary Theory." In *Evolution and Ethics: Human Morality in Biological and Religious Perspective*, edited by Phillip Clayton and Jeffery Schloss, 287–301. Grand Rapids: Eerdmans, 2004.
———. *The Nature of Love: A Theology*. St. Louis: Chalice, 2010.

———. "An Open Theology Doctrine of Creation and Solution to the Problem of Evil." In *Creation Made Free: Open Theology Engaging Science*, edited by Thomas Jay Oord, 28–52. Eugene, OR: Wipf & Stock, 2010.

———. "A Perfect Theology Never Existed: A Rejoinder." In *God Reconsidered: The Promise and Peril of Process Theology*, edited by Al Truesdale, 151–60. Kansas City, MO: Beacon Hill, 2010.

———, ed. *Philosophy of Religion*. Kansas City, MO: Beacon Hill, 2003.

———. "A Process Wesleyan Theodicy: Freedom, Embodiment, and the Almighty God." In *Thy Nature and Thy Name Is Love: Wesleyan and Process Theologies in Dialogue*, edited by Bryan P. Stone and Thomas Jay Oord, 193–216. Nashville: Kingswood, 2001.

———. "Strong Passibility." In *Divine Impassibility: Four Views of God's Emotions and Suffering*, edited by Robert J. Matz and A. Chadwick Thornhill, 129–65. Spectrum Multiview Books. Downers Grove, IL: InterVarsity, 2019.

———, ed. *Theologies of Creation: Creatio Ex Nihilo and Its New Rivals*. New York: Routledge, 2015.

———. "Types of Wesleyan Philosophy: The General Landscape and My Own Research Agenda." *Wesleyan Theological Journal* 39.1 (2004) 154–62.

———. *The Uncontrolling Love of God: An Open and Relational Account of Providence*. Downers Grove, IL: InterVarsity, 2015.

Oord, Thomas Jay, and Michael E. Lodahl. *Relational Holiness: Responding to the Call of Love*. Kansas City, MO: Nazarene, 2005.

Orr, Brian J. "Easter through Evil: God's Pleasing Purposes in the Path to Glory." *Evangelical Quarterly* 91.2 (2020) 99–113.

Ortlund, Gavin. "Divine Simplicity in Historical Perspective: Resourcing a Contemporary Discussion." *International Journal of Systematic Theology* 16.4 (2014) 436–53.

Osborn, Eric. *The Emergence of Christian Theology*. Cambridge: Cambridge University Press, 1993.

Oswalt, John N. *The Book of Isaiah, Chapters 1–39*. Grand Rapids: Eerdmans, 1986.

Pannenberg, Wolfhart. *Basic Questions in Theology, Vol. 2*. Minneapolis: Fortress, 1971.

Peck, A. L. "Agape and Eros." *The Classical Review* 47.4 (1933) 137–39.

Peckham, John C. "The Concept of Divine Love in the Context of the God-World Relationship." PhD diss., Andrews University, 2014.

———. *The Love of God: A Canonical Model*. Downers Grove, IL: InterVarsity, 2015.

Pelikan, Jaroslav. *The Christian Tradition: A History of the Development of Doctrine, Vol. 1: The Emergence of the Catholic Tradition*. Chicago: University of Chicago Press, 1975.

Pinnock, Clark H., ed. *The Grace of God and the Will of Man*. Minneapolis: Bethany, 1995.

———. *Most Moved Mover: A Theology of God's Openness*. Cumbria: Paternoster, 2001.

———. "Systematic Theology." In *The Openness of God: A Biblical Challenge to the Traditional Understanding of God*, by Clark H. Pinnock et al., 101–25. Downers Grove, IL: InterVarsity, 1994.

Pinnock, Clark H., et al. *The Openness of God: A Biblical Challenge to the Traditional Understanding of God*. Downers Grove, IL: InterVarsity, 1994.

Piper, John. *God's Passion for His Glory*. Wheaton, IL: Crossway, 2006.

———. *The Justification of God: An Exegetical and Theological Study of Romans 9:1–23.* 2nd ed. Grand Rapids: Baker, 1993.

Piper, John, et al. *Beyond the Bounds: Open Theism and the Undermining of Biblical Christianity.* Wheaton, IL: Crossway, 2003.

Placher, William C. *The Domestication of Transcendence: How Modern Thinking about God Went Wrong.* Louisville: Westminster John Knox, 1996.

Plantinga, Alvin. *Does God Have a Nature?* Marquette: Marquette University Press, 1980.

Plummer, Robert L. "What Do the Apostles Teach about the Love of God?" In *The Love of God*, edited by Christopher W. Morgan, 75–94. Wheaton, IL: Crossway, 2016.

Pool, Jeff B. *God's Wounds: Hermeneutic of the Christian Symbol of Divine Suffering, Volume 1: Divine Vulnerability and Creation.* London: Lutterworth, 2011.

Prestige, G. L. *God in Patristic Thought.* Eugene, OR: Wipf & Stock, 2008.

Pugliese, Marc A. *The One, the Many, and the Trinity: Joseph A. Bracken and the Challenge of Process Metaphysics.* Washington, DC: Catholic University of America Press, 2011.

Purvis, Zachary. "The New Ethicist and the Old Bookkeeper: Isaak Dorner, Johann Quenstedt, and Modern Appropriations of Classical Protestantism." *Journal for the History of Modern Theology/Zeitschrift Für Neuere Theologiegeschichte* 19.1 (2012) 14–33.

Rad, Gerhard Von. *Genesis: A Commentary.* Louisville: Westminster John Knox, 1973.

Reasoner, Vic. "John Welsey's Doctrines on the Theology of Grace." In *Grace for All: The Arminian Dynamics of Salvation*, edited by Clark H. Pinnock and John D. Wagner, 177–96. Eugene, OR: Resource, 2015.

Reeves, Stan. *The 1689 Baptist Confession of Faith: In Modern English.* Cape Coral, FL: Founders, 2017.

Reichard, Joshua D. "From Causality to Relationality: Toward a Wesleyan Theology of Concursus." *Wesleyan Theological Journal* 49.1 (2014) 122–38.

———. "Of Miracles and Metaphysics: A Pentecostal-Charismatic and Process-Relational Dialogue." *Zygon: Journal of Religion & Science* 48.2 (2013) 274–93.

Rennie, Charles J. "A Theology of the Doctrine of Divine Passibility: Impassibility and the Essence and Attributes of God." In *Confessing the Impassible God: The Biblical, Classical, & Confessional Doctrine of Divine Impassibility*, edited by Ronald S. Baines et al., 279–304. Palmdale, CA: RBAP, 2015.

Rice, Richard. "Biblical Support for a New Perspective." In *The Openness of God: A Biblical Challenge to the Traditional Understanding of God*, by Clark H. Pinnock et al., 11–58. Downers Grove, IL: InterVarsity, 1994.

———. "Creatio Ex Nihilo: It's Not All about Nothing." *Wesleyan Theological Journal* 47.2 (2012) 110–23.

———. *God's Foreknowledge & Man's Free Will.* Minneapolis: Bethany, 1985.

———. "In Response to Nancy Howell." In *Searching for an Adequate God: A Dialogue between Process and Free Will Theists*, edited by John B. Cobb Jr. and Clark H. Pinnock, 86–95. Grand Rapids: Eerdmans, 2000.

———. "Process Theism and the Open View of God: The Crucial Difference." In *Searching for an Adequate God: A Dialogue between Process and Free Will Theists*, edited by John B. Cobb Jr. and Clark H. Pinnock, 163–200. Grand Rapids: Eerdmans, 2000.

Richards, Jay Wesley. "Divine Simplicity: The Good, the Bad, and the Ugly." In *For Faith and Clarity: Philosophical Contributions to Christian Theology*, edited by James K. Beilby, 157–77. Grand Rapids: Baker, 2006.

———. *The Untamed God: A Philosophical Exploration of Divine Perfection, Simplicity, and Immutability*. Downers Grove, IL: InterVarsity, 2003.

Riches, Aaron. *Ecce Homo: On the Divine Unity of Christ*. Grand Rapids: Eerdmans, 2016.

Roberts, Kyle. "What If God Doesn't Prevent Evil Because God Can't? On Thomas Oord's Loving and Limited God." *Unsystematic Theology* (blog), March 8, 2016. http://www.patheos.com/blogs/unsystematictheology/2016/03/can-god-prevent-evil-on-thomas-oords-loving-and-limited-god/.

Robertson, A. T. *Word Pictures in the New Testament*. Logos ed. Nashville: Broadman, 1933.

Rowe, Christopher Kavin. "Biblical Pressure and Trinitarian Hermeneutics." *Pro Ecclesia* 11.3 (2002) 295–312.

Royster, Mark. "John Wesley's Doctrine of Prevenient Grace in Missiological Perspective." DMiss., Asbury Theological Seminary, 1989.

Sanders, John. "Divine Providence and the Openness of God." In *Perspectives on the Doctrine of God: Four Views*, edited by Bruce A. Ware, 196–240. Nashville: B&H Academic, 2008.

———. *The God Who Risks: A Theology of Divine Providence*. Rev. ed. Downers Grove, IL: InterVarsity, 2007.

———. "Why Oord's Essential Kenosis Model Fails to Solve the Problem of Evil While Retaining Miracles." *Wesleyan Theological Journal* 51.2 (2016) 174–87.

Sanlon, Peter. *Simply God: Recovering the Classical Trinity*. Downers Grove, IL: InterVarsity, 2017.

Santiago Sia. "The Doctrine of God's Immutability: Introducing the Modern Debate." *New Blackfriars* 805 (1987) 220–32.

Sarot, Marcel. "Suffering of Christ, Suffering of God?" *Theology* 95.764 (1992) 113–19.

Savoy Declaration (1658). https://www.creeds.net/congregational/savoy/.

Schilpp, Paul Arthur. *The Philosophy of Alfred North Whitehead*. The Library of Living Philosophers. New York: Tudor, 1951.

Schreiner, Thomas R. "Does Scripture Teach Prevenient Grace in the Wesleyan Sense." In *Still Sovereign: Contemporary Perspectives on Election, Foreknowledge, and Grace*, edited by Thomas R. Schreiner and Bruce A. Ware, 229–46. Grand Rapids: Baker, 2000.

Schreiner, Thomas R., and Bruce A. Ware. *Still Sovereign: Contemporary Perspectives on Election, Foreknowledge, and Grace*. Grand Rapids: Baker, 2000.

Schroeder, Christoph O. *History, Justice, and the Agency of God: A Hermeneutical and Exegetical Investigation on Isaiah and Psalms*. Leiden: Brill, 2001.

Scott, James M. *2 Corinthians*. New International Biblical Commentary. Peabody, MA: Hendrickson, 2003.

Scrutton, Anastasia Philippa. "Divine Passibility: God and Emotion." *Philosophy Compass* 8.9 (2013) 866–74.

———. "God, Emotion, and Impassibility." PhD diss., Durham University, 2008.

Shanley, Brian J. *The Thomist Tradition*. London: Springer, 2011.

Shedd, William Greenough Thayer. *Dogmatic Theology*. Edited by Alan W. Gomes. 3rd ed. Phillipsburg, NJ: P&R, 2003.

Silva, Moisés, ed. "agapaō." In *New International Dictionary of New Testament Theology and Exegesis*. Grand Rapids: Zondervan, 2014.

Simoni, Henry. "Divine Passibility and the Problem of Radical Particularity: Does God Feel Your Pain?" *Religious Studies* 33.3 (1997) 327–47.

Smith, Gary V. *Isaiah 1–39*. New American Commentary 15A. Nashville: B&H, 2007.

Stead, Christopher. *Philosophy in Christian Antiquity*. Cambridge: Cambridge University Press, 1994.

Steussy, Marti J. *Samuel and His God*. Columbia: University of South Carolina Press, 2013.

Stoebe, H. J. "hesed." In *Theological Lexicon of the Old Testament*, edited by Ernst Jenni and Claus Westerman. Peabody, MA: Hendrickson, 1997.

Strange, Daniel. "Does the Love of God Require Universalism?" In *The Love of God*, edited by Christopher W. Morgan, 143–60. Wheaton, IL: Crossway, 2016.

Suchocki, Marjorie Hewitt. *God, Christ, Church: A Practical Guide to Process Theology*. Revised ed. New York: Crossroad, 1992.

Sunshine, Glenn S. "Accommodation Historically Considered." In *The Enduring Authority of the Christian Scriptures*, edited by D. A. Carson, 238–65. Grand Rapids: Eerdmans, 2016.

Surin, Kenneth. "The Impassibility of God and the Problem of Evil." *Scottish Journal of Theology* 35.2 (1982) 97–115.

Swanson, James. *Dictionary of Biblical Languages with Semantic Domains: Hebrew (Old Testament)*. Logos. Oak Harbor, WA: Logos Research Systems, 1997.

Sweeney, Marvin Alan. *I & II Kings: A Commentary*. Louisville: Westminster John Knox, 2007.

The Thirty-Nine Articles of Religion. http://anglicansonline.org/basics/thirty-nine_articles.html.

Thompson, John. *Modern Trinitarian Perspectives*. Oxford: Oxford University Press, USA, 1994.

Thompson, John Arthur, and D. J. Wiseman. *Deuteronomy: An Introduction and Commentary*. Downers Grove, IL: InterVarsity, 1981.

Thorsen, Don. *Calvin vs. Wesley: Bringing Belief in Line with Practice*. Nashville: Abingdon, 2013.

Tomkinson, J. L. "Divine Sempiternity and Atemporality." *Religious Studies* 18.2 (1982) 177–89.

Torrance, Alan J. "Is Love the Essence of God?" In *Nothing Greater, Nothing Better: Theological Essays on the Love of God*, edited by Kevin J. Vanhoozer, 114–37. Grand Rapids: Eerdmans, 2001.

Tsumura, David Toshio. *The First Book of Samuel*. New International Commentary on the Old Testament. Grand Rapids: Eerdmans, 2007.

Trueman, Carl R. "The Reformation We Need." https://www.firstthings.com/web-exclusives/2018/10/the-reformation-we-need.

Truesdale, Al. *God Reconsidered: The Promise and Peril of Process Theology*. Kansas City, MO: Beacon Hill, 2010.

Turretin, Francis. *Institutes of Elenctic Theology*. Edited by James T. Dennison. Translated by George Musgrave Giger. 3 vols. Phillipsburg, NJ: P&R, 1997.

Vanhoozer, Kevin J. "Introduction: The Love of God." In *Nothing Greater, Nothing Better: Theological Essays on the Love of God*, edited by Kevin J. Vanhoozer, 1–29. Grand Rapids: Eerdmans, 2001.

———. "Love without Measure?: John Webster's Unfinished Dogmatic Account of the Love of God, in Dialogue with Thomas Jay Oord's Interdisciplinary Theological Account." *International Journal of Systematic Theology* 19.4 (2017) 505–76.

———. *Remythologizing Theology: Divine Action, Passion, and Authorship*. Cambridge: Cambridge University Press, 2010.

———, ed. *Theological Interpretation of the New Testament: A Book-by-Book Survey*. Grand Rapids: Baker, 2008.

Vanstone, William Hubert. *Love's Endeavour, Love's Expense: The Response of Being to the Love of God*. London: Darton, Longman & Todd, 2007.

Vicens, Leigh C. "On the Possibility of Special Divine Action in a Deterministic World." *Religious Studies* 48.3 (2012) 315–36.

Volf, Miroslav. "Being as God Is: Trinity and Generosity." In *God's Life in Trinity*, edited by Michael Welker, 3–12. Minneapolis: Fortress, 2006.

Vos, Geerhardus. *Biblical Theology: Old and New Testaments*. Edinburgh: Banner of Truth, 1975.

Waltke, Bruce K., and Charles Yu. *An Old Testament Theology: An Exegetical, Canonical, and Thematic Approach*. Grand Rapids: Zondervan, 2007.

Ware, Bruce A. "An Evangelical Reformulation of the Doctrine of the Immutability of God." *Journal of the Evangelical Theological Society* 29.4 (1986) 431–46.

———. *God's Lesser Glory: The Diminished God of Open Theism*. Wheaton, IL: Crossway, 2000.

———. "A Modified Calvinist Doctrine of God." In *Perspectives on the Doctrine of God: Four Views*, edited by Bruce A. Ware, 76–120. Nashville: B&H Academic, 2008.

Warfield, Benjamin Breckinridge. *The Works of Benjamin B. Warfield*. Vol. 2. Grand Rapids: Baker, 1991.

Webster, John. *God without Measure: Working Papers in Christian Theology, Volume 1: God and the Works of God*. Philadelphia: T. & T. Clark, 2015.

———. *Holy Scripture: A Dogmatic Sketch*. Current Issues in Theology. Cambridge: Cambridge University Press, 2003.

Weinandy, Thomas. *Does God Change?* Still River, MA: St. Bede's, 2002.

———. *Does God Suffer?* Notre Dame: University of Notre Dame Press, 2000.

———. "Impassibility of God." In vol. 7 of *New Catholic Encyclopedia*. Washington, DC: Catholic University of America Press, 2003.

Wells, David F. *God in the Whirlwind: How the Holy-Love of God Reorients Our World*. Wheaton, IL: Crossway, 2014.

Wenham, Gordon J. *Genesis 1–15*. Word Biblical Commentary 1. Waco, TX: Word, 1986.

———. *Genesis 16–50*. Word Biblical Commentary 2. Waco, TX: Word, 1994.

Wesley, John. *The Works of John Wesley*. 14 vols. 3rd ed. Grand Rapids: Baker, 1996.

Westminster Confession of Faith. http://www.reformed.org/documents/wcf_with_proofs/index.html.

Westphal, Merold. "Temporality and Finitism in Hartshorne's Theism." *The Review of Metaphysics* 19.3 (1966) 550–64.

Wheeler, David L. "In Response to Nancy Howell." In *Searching for an Adequate God: A Dialogue between Process and Free Will Theists*, edited by John B. Cobb Jr. and Clark H. Pinnock, 80–85. Grand Rapids: Eerdmans, 2000.

Whitehead, Alfred North. *Adventures of Ideas*. London: Free, 1967.

———. *Process and Reality*. London: Free, 1978.

Whitehead, Alfred North, and Randall Auxier. *Religion in the Making: Lowell Lectures 1926.* New York: Fordham University Press, 1926.

Williams, Thaddeus J. *Love, Freedom, and Evil: Does Authentic Love Require Free Will?* Amsterdam: Rodopi, 2011.

Wilson, Earle L., et al. *Galatians, Philippians, Colossians: A Commentary for Bible Students.* Indianapolis: Wesleyan, 2007.

Witham, Larry. *The God Biographers: Our Changing Image of God from Job to the Present.* Lanham, MD: Lexington, 2010.

Wolterstorff, Nicholas. "Divine Simplicity." In *Inquiring about God, Volume 1: Selected Essays,* edited by Terence Cuneo, 91–113. Cambridge: Cambridge University Press, 2010.

Woolsey, Warren. *1 & 2 Thessalonians: A Bible Commentary in the Wesleyan Tradition.* Indianapolis: Wesleyan, 1997.

Wright, Christopher. *Deuteronomy.* New International Biblical Commentary. Peabody, MA: Hendrickson, 1996.

Wright, John H. "The Method of Process Theology: An Evaluation." *Communio* 6 (1979) 38–55.

Wright, N. T. "Philippians." In *Theological Interpretation of the New Testament: A Book-by-Book Survey,* edited by Kevin J. Vanhoozer, 134–39. Grand Rapids: Baker, 2009.

Yong, Amos. "Divine Omniscience and Future Contingents: Weighing the Presuppositional Issues in the Contemporary Debate." *Evangelical Review of Theology* 26.3 (2002) 240–64.

Zbaraschuk, Michael. "Process Theology Resources for an Open and Relational Christology." *Wesleyan Theological Journal* 44.2 (2009) 154–67.

Index

actual entity, defined, 10n69
agapao, 103–5
agape
    biblical understanding of, 81, 103–4n187, 103–5, 104n193
    as creative, 100
    as indifferent to value, 98–100
    as initiator of fellowship with God, 101–2
    Nygren on, 81, 95
    Oord's exposition of Nygren on, 96, 103–9
    as spontaneous and unmotivated, 97
Agape and Eros (Nygren), 96
agency, God's gift, 145
Akin, Daniel L., 77n23
Anselm, 47n106, 48, 49
Aquinas. *See* Thomas Aquinas
Arminian theology, 20n141, 106n199
Augustine of Hippo
    on impassibility, 174
    on love, 77n23
    on metaphysis of divine revelation, 121–22, 122n86
    Neoplatonism, 32n15
    on simplicity doctrine, 47n106, 48, 49
Ayres, Lewis, 48n113

Badcock, Gary D., 96n138
Barth, Karl, 50n125, 75, 79
Basinger, David, 71, 72, 73, 130n28
Bavinck, Herman, 79n36, 120n76
Bergen, Robert D., 163n173, 164
bible. *See* Scripture
"big-bang" theory, 41–42

bodily redemption, 70
Boston Marathon bombing (2013), 141
Boyd, Greg, 6, 130n28
Bray, Gerald, 90
Brueggemann, Walter, 163n172
Brümmer, Vincent, 81, 91
Brunner, Emil, 104
Burrell, David, 56

Calvin, John, 27–28, 72, 77n23, 138, 168
Calvinism, 26, 53
Campbell, Antony F., 165n177
Carson, D. A., 76, 77, 80–81, 96n138
causal influence, 117, 146
causality, defined, 9–10
Charnock, Steven, 150n127
Christian theism
    divine sovereignty, 21–22
    Hartshorne on, 11
    Oord on, 24–25
    presuppositions, 26–28
Church of the Nazarene, 10–11, 30
classical metaphysics, 31, 113–16, 184
classical theism, 3, 3n12, 27, 113–16, 120, 184
Cobb, John B., Jr., 32, 32n15, 33
coercion
    divine coercion, 146–49
    divine-human relationality and, 2
    misconception of, 71–73
    term usage, 71
    unilateral determination and, 37, 146–47, 150–52
compelling power, 37–39, 72, 153, 160–61, 167
composite beings, 58n155

contemporary metaphysic, 7
contemporary theology, 1–7
controlled intervention, 117
convincing grace, 132
cosmic dualism, 121
Craig, William Lane, 179, 179n242, 183n4
creatio ex nihilo, 26, 26n180
creation, Oord on, 40–42, 66–70, 136–37
creatures, God and, 70
cyclic theory, 42

Daeley, Justin J., 45n95
Davies, Brian, 48, 49
Davis, William C., 2n11
Delitzsch, Franz, 155
determinism
    definition of, 120n75
    divine causal determinism, 151n130
    Oord's theology, 139–41, 157–58
    self-determination, 36–39, 71
    unilateral, 22, 33, 36–37, 146–47, 150–52, 150n127, 159
Deuteronomy 2:30, God's purpose in, 152–54
didactic dimension of evil, 175–77
The Difficult Doctrine of the Love of God (Carson), 76
dipolar nature of God, 11
direct view, of divine action, 163–67, 166n182
divine accommodation, 27–28
divine aseity, 53
divine causal determinism, 151n130
divine coercion, 146–49
divine efficient causation, 118n61
divine foreknowledge, 2, 26–27, 27n185, 135–39
divine hardening, 155
divine impassibility, 3n17, 4, 4n19
divine inspiration, 148n114
divine love theology
    concluding thoughts, 108–9
    definition of love, 82–95
    God's necessary love for the world, 105–8
    Hartshorne on, 12

    Oord on, 106
    primacy of love, 74–82
    theology of love, 95–105
    See also Essential Kenosis
divine omnipotence, 37
divine perfection, Hartshorne on, 12–13
divine power
    Oord on, 22, 154, 159–61
    open view of, 5–7
divine self-limitation, 124, 124n3, 127
divine simplicity, 43–46, 97n143
divine sovereignty, 21, 114n32
divine-human relationality, 2, 25, 51, 122, 172
doctrine of divine simplicity (DDS). *See* simplicity
Dolezal, James, 47, 48n116, 174–75
doubtful presupposition, 81

the elect and election, 64, 81, 95, 106, 106n199, 121n78. *See also* predestination
empathetic dimension of evil, 172–75
empathy, love and, 83
Erickson, Millard, 75, 79
eros, term usage, 102n180
essential freedom, 130–41
Essential Kenosis
    agency, God's gift of, 145
    concluding thoughts, 167–69, 180–82
    Deuteronomy 2:30, 152–54
    didactic dimension, 175–77
    divine coercion, 146–50
    divine love theology, 95–105
    divine power and, 160–63
    empathetic dimension, 172–75
    essential freedom, 130–41
    evil, solution to problem of, 171–81
    general sense reading, 159
    God's necessity to love, 135–41
    God's providence, 145–50
    God's striking (activity of), 163–67
    Isaiah 10, 156–59
    1 Kings 12:15, 155–56
    miracles and, 169–71
    Oord's doctrine of, 126–28
    overview, 124–25

persuasion, problems of, 141–44
prevenient grace doctrine, 132–35
1 Samuel 2:25, 154–55
sovereignty dimension, 178–79
strategic dimension, 178
theology of love, 95, 125–30
therapeutic dimension, 177–78
unilateral determination, 150–52
Evangelical theology
    key doctrine distinctions, 19–20
    Oord on, 32
    relational turn in, 6
    term usage, 2n5
    theology of love, 19–24
Evangelical Theology Society (ETS), 1–2n4
evil
    didactic dimension, 175–77
    divine sovereignty, 21
    empathetic dimension, 172–75
    existence of, 3, 3n12, 20, 21–24
    Oord's definition of, 21–22, 21n146, 125
    a solution to, 171–81
    sovereignty dimension, 178–79
    strategic dimension, 178
    therapeutic dimension, 177–78
evolutionary theory, 67–68, 69
experient, defined, 10n69

fatalism, 151n130
Feinberg, John S., 54n137
Ford, Lewis, 71n220
forgiveness, of sins, 92, 100, 101, 172
Frame, John, 54n137, 120n72
freedom
    compatibilist understanding of, 72
    essential freedom, 130–41
    humans and, 14–15, 70, 130–34, 161, 161n167
    self-determination, 36–39, 71
free-will theism, 70, 131–32
Fretheim, Terrence, 115n37

glory, God and, 139–40
Glueck, N., 87n96
Goad, Keith, 58n159

God
    almightiness of, 5, 111, 160–61
    attributes of, 77n23
    creatures and, 70
    dipolar nature of, 11
    expressions of, 114
    glory and, 139–40
    love of, 4, 4n20, 16, 71
    power of, 150n127
    relationship to the world, 15–16, 16n114, 44, 105–8
    striking (activity of), 163–67
    suffering of God, 4
    super-relative aspect of, 11–12
    triune nature of, 16–17
    wrath of, 78, 81, 88, 88n100, 89n105
God Can't: How to Believe in God and Love after Tragedy, Abuse, and Other Evils (Oord), 20–21, 21n142
God in Patristic Thought (Prestige), 50
Goldingay, John, 157n152
grace
    convincing grace, 132
    irresistible grace, 92n120
    necessary grace, 133
    prevenient grace, 74, 84, 90, 101, 132–35
Grant, Colin, 96n138
Gregory of Nazianzus, 66n193
Griffin, David Ray, 21n146, 33, 67
Grogan, Geoffrey, 80
Grudem, Wayne, 53n137

Harnack, Adolf von, 100
Hartshorne, Charles
    on classical paradox, 60–64, 61n169
    on divine love, 12
    on divine perfection, 12–13
    God, relationship to the world, 15
    A Natural Theology for Our Time, 31
    on process theism philosophy, 11–14
    test of deity, 12n87
    on Trinity doctrine, 18
    on use of force, 37
    Westphal, response to, 63n182

Hasker, William, 17
healings, 118–19
Hegel, G. W. F., 8, 8n52
Heiser, Michael S., 164n175
hell, 89–90, 94–95, 94n130
Helm, 66n193
Henry, Carl, 104
hesed language tradition, 82, 87–88, 87n96
hesed love, 82
Hess, Elijah, 68
Hitler, Adolph, 38
holiness, love and, 83
Holmes, Stephen, 120n77
Holy Spirit, Oord on, 76
Howell, Nancy, 13–14, 15, 15n102
human freedom, 14–15, 70, 130–34, 161, 161n167

immutability
    objectors of, 53–54
    pastoral observation, 57
    Scriptural basis for, 50
    term usage, 50, 50n125
    theological priority, 54–57
impassibility
    doctrine of, 172–73
    objectors of, 53–54
    pastoral observation, 57
    Scriptural basis for, 52–53
    term usage, 49–51
    theological priority, 54–57
indirect view, of divine action, 161, 163–67, 168
intentional, facets of, 92
intentional actions, 84–85
irresistible grace, 92n120
Isaiah 10, God's power, 156–59, 157n152

John of Damascus, Saint, 47n106, 48n114
judgement, 70, 88–90, 94

Keil, Carl Friedrich, 155
kenosis doctrine
    doctrine of, 126–28
    "kenotic-relational rubric, 4n20

Oord's theology of love (*See* Essential Kenosis)
    reapplication of, 4
    Trinity and, 4
1 Kings 12:15, God's decree, 155–56
Kruse, Colin, 77n23

Lane, Tony, 88n100
Lazarus, resurrection of, 119n68
Levering, Matthew, 113n31, 115
libertarian free will, 130–31
Lofthouse, William Frederick, 87n96
love
    creation through, 66, 68, 136–37
    critical evaluation, 77–82, 86–95
    definitions of, 82–95
    Father-Son relationship, 68–69
    forms of, 104n193
    of God, 4, 4n20, 16, 71
    God's gift of, 68–69
    God's necessary love, 105–8, 135–41
    meanings of, 82–83
    non-human organisms and, 68
    primacy of, 74–82
    theology of love, 95–105
    See also agape; Essential Kenosis

Manichaeism, 121, 122
Mastricht, Petrus Van, 56
"Matching Theology and Piety: An Evangelical Process Theology of Love," (Oord), 31
Melick, Richard R., 161n167
metaphysics
    classical, 31, 113–16
    contemporary, 7
    critical response, 118–20
    miracles and, 40, 116–18
    of narrative, 7n47
    process approach, 110–13
    in process thought, 16
    process/classical contradistinctions, 120–23
    relational, 6, 6n43
    substance, 6, 31
mind-body analogy, 43–44
miracles, 40, 116–18, 166n181, 169–71
morally responsibilities, 68

Morris, Leon, 89n105, 90n107, 104
Mounce, William, 91n118
Muller, Richard, 55–56, 56n149
mutuality tradition, 91
mystery, Oord on, 76, 79–80, 157–58

natural theology, 32n15
Natural Theology for Our Time, A (Hartshorne), 31
naturalistic theism, 112
nature miracles, 118
Nature of Love, The (Oord), 74, 82
necessary grace, 133
necessary love, 105–8, 135–41
"Neoplatonic philosophy, 32, 32n15
Newlands, George, 81–82n53
Nicole, Roger, 1–2n4
Nygren, Anders
    agape (see *agape*)
    Agape and Eros, 96
    concluding thoughts, 103–5
    error of thesis, 102–3
    Oord's exposition of, 96, 103–8

O'Brien, Peter T., 130n26
omnipotence, 12, 37, 111, 150n127, 157
omnipresence, 40, 56, 113, 117, 169
omniscience, open theists definition of, 2n6
ontological dependence, term usage, 41
ontological differences, 51
Oord, Thomas Jay
    aim of work, 24–25
    background, 30–32
    on Classical theology, 27
    on creation, 40–42, 66–70, 136–37
    current research on, 25–26
    on divine love, 86n88
    on divine omnipotence, 37
    on divine power, 22
    on divine simplicity, 43–46, 73
    essential relatedness of all existence, 34–36
    Evangelical Process Theology, 19–24n193
    on evil, 21–24, 21n142, 125
    on hell, 94
    on judgement, 70, 88–90, 94, 95n134
    on love, 22–23, 30–32
    love, primacy of, 74–82
    "Matching Theology and Piety: An Evangelical Process Theology of Love," 31
    methodology, 28–29
    on miracles, 40, 116–18, 166n181
    on mystery, 76, 79–80
    Nature of Love, The 74, 82
    necessary love of God, 105–8
    on Nygren (see Nygren, Anders)
    process philosophy and, 32–34
    on Scripture, 24
    on sin, 132–35
    on Trinity, 60, 64–65
    triune nature of, 74–82
    Uncontrolling Love of God: An Open and Relational Account of Providence, The, 20, 94, 125
    on Whitehead, 32–33
open theism
    agreement with process theism, 14–15
    almightiness of God, 5
    departure from process theism, 15–18
    divine power and, 5–7
    ETS resolution on, 1–2n4
    on God's love, 75
    Oord on, 21–22
    philosophy of, 1–3
    on power, 20n141
Openness of God, The (Pinnock et al.), 1–2, 2n5
open/relational theology, 2n5

panentheism, 8, 8n50, 8n52, 36, 45n95
panexperientalist hypothesis, 39
pantheism, 8
participatory eschatology, 94, 94n128, 181
Peck, A. L., 96n138
Peckham, John C., 77n23, 80, 81n53, 87n96, 104n193
Pelikan, Jaroslav, 51n128
personalism, 10–11
persuasion, problems of, 141–44
persuasive power, 37–39, 95, 153, 159

phileo, 104n193
philia, 102–3, 102n180
physical pole, defined, 9
Pinnock, Clark H.
   on classical theism, 55n143
   on divine power, 5
   on dynamic relational categories, 6
   Evangelical Theology Society and, 1–2n4
   on evil, 23
   on open theologies, 21–22
   Openness of God, The, 1–2
   open/process theology impasse, 18–19
   philosophy of process, 7
Piper, John, 77n31
Plummer, Robert L., 86–87, 86n91, 107
prayer and praying, 137–38
predestination, 75, 101, 121n78, 126. *See also* the elect and election
prehensions, defined, 9, 10
Prestige, G. L., 50–51
prevenient grace, 74, 84, 90, 101, 132–35
"probabilistic prophecy," 2n4
process philosophy
   critical response, 118–20
   Hartshorne on, 11–14
   miracles and, 116–18
   Oord on, 32–34, 42–43, 110–13, 184–85
   Pinnock on, 7
   process/classical contradistinctions, 120–23
   relations and essentially related God, 34–36
   Whitehead on, 8–11
process theology
   agreement with open theism, 14–15
   compressed expression of, 13–14
   on creation, 40–42, 66–70, 136–37
   departure from open theism, 15–18
   Hartshorne on, 8–11
   on power, 20n140
   Whitehead on, 5–7
providence, relational model, 125
psychological manipulation, 72

"real" relations, 60–64

Red Sea, parting of, 117, 169–70, 170n195
Reformed Evangelical tradition, 26–28
relational metaphysic, 6, 6n43
relational providence, 125
relational theism, term usage, 4, 4n25
resurrection of Jesus, a non-miraculous event, 117
Rice, Richard, 15
righteousness, love and, 82

1 Samuel 2:25, God's will, 154–55
Sanders, John
   on divine power, 5–6
   Evangelical Theology Society and, 1–2n4
   on open theologies, 21–22
   providence, view of, 23
   on triune nature of God, 17–18
Schelling, F.W.J., 8, 8n52
Scripture
   in doctrinal formulation, 15, 16–19, 28
   impassibility and immutability, 52–53
   metaphysics and (*see* metaphysics)
   ontological nature of, 147–48, 147nn112–13, 148n114
secondary causes, 120n73, 151n130
self-determination, 36–39, 71. *See also* determinism
Setterholm, Vincent M., 164n175
Silva, Moisés, 103–4n187, 103n183
simplicity
   classical definition of, 47–49
   doctrine variations, 47n106
   impassibility/immutability and, 49–52
   inconsistency in, 43–46
   Oord's acceptance of, 73
   pastoral observation, 57
   sustaining, 46–47
   Trinity and, 57–60
sin, Oord on, 132–35
social Trinitarianism, 7, 7n48
socially oriented philosophy, 12
sovereignty dimension of evil, 178–79
special divine action, 116
spiritual formation, term usage, 19

spiritual substance, 122
Spirit/wind analogy, 160, 162
steadfast love, 87, 87n94
Steussy, Marti, 155n145
Strange, Daniel, 88
strategic dimension of evil, 178
substance metaphysics, 6, 31
suffering, 4, 139–40, 143, 180, 180n246
Summa Theologiae (Thomas Aquinas), 61
supernatural act, defined, 119n69
super-relative, aspect of God, 11–12
sympathy, love and, 83
systematic theology, change in, 2

theocentric love, 101
theocosmocentrism, defined, 36n42
theological inquiry, 80
theological mutabilism, 183
theology of love, 95–105
therapeutic dimension of evil, 177–78
Thomas Aquinas
    on miracles, 120n72
    on nature of God, 44n90, 48, 49, 54
    Neoplatonism and, 32n15
    real relationship, meaning of, 59–64
    real relationship, meaning of, 60n165, 62n175
    on simplicity, 47n106
    'substance' and 'being' metaphysics,, 115–16
    Summa Theologiae, 61
    on Trinity, 57n152, 59, 59n164
Thompson, J. A., 87–88
Tillich, Paul, 75, 79
traditional open theism, term usage, 4n25
Trinity
    Aquinas on, 57n152, 59, 59n164
    contemporary philosophy, 7
    divine simplicity and, 43n85
    doctrine of, 17nn119–122
    Kenosis doctrine and, 4
    nature of God, 16–18
    process theology and, 64–71
    simplicity and, 57–60
truth, pursuit of, 183–85

Uncontrolling Love of God: An Open and Relational Account of Providence, The (Oord), 20, 94, 125
unilateral determinism, 22, 33, 36–37, 146–47, 150–52, 150n127, 159. *See also* determinism
unredeemed, 94

Vanhoozer, Kevin J., 3–4, 4n19, 80, 91, 92n120, 140n79
Vicens, Leigh C., 120n75
Vos, Geerhardus, 119n69

Ware, Bruce A., 53–54n137
Webster, John, 49, 50
Weinandy, Thomas, 54, 63, 80, 115n42, 174
well-being
    promoting, 82–83, 93, 93n127, 129–30
    as *shalom*, 90
    understanding of, 129n25
Wenham, Gordon J., 177n229
Wesleyan tradition
    callused heart concept, 153n139
    Oord's background, 29, 31
    prevenient grace, 132–33, 133n48
    process philosophy and, 10–11
Westminster Confession of Faith, 71–72
Westphal, Merold, 61, 63
Whitehead, Alfred North
    on metaphysics, 112, 118n61
    Oord on, 32–33
    panexperientalist hypothesis, 39
    process philosophy, father of, 8–11
    on Trinity doctrine, 18
"Why Open Theism" (Davis), 2n11
Williams, Daniel Day, 37
Williams, Thaddeus, 69
Wilson, Earle L., 161n167
Wolterstorff, Nicholas, 51
world, God's relationship to, 15–16, 16n114, 44, 105–8
worship, love and, 92–93
wrath, of God, 78, 81, 88, 88n100, 89n105
Wright, Christopher, 87n97

Yong, Amos, 75n6

www.ingramcontent.com/pod-product-compliance
Lightning Source LLC
Chambersburg PA
CBHW062025220426
43662CB00010B/1477